The EARLY Intervention Kit™

Nancy B. Swigert

Skill: Language
Ages: Birth–3 years

LinguiSystems, Inc.
3100 4th Avenue
East Moline, IL 61244-9700
1-800 PRO IDEA
1-800-776-4332

FAX: 1-800-577-4555
E-mail: service@linguisystems.com
Web: www.linguisystems.com
TDD: 1-800-933-8331
(for those with hearing impairments)

Copyright © 2004 LinguiSystems, Inc.

All of our products are copyrighted to protect the fine work of our authors. You may only copy the client materials as needed for your own use with clients. Any other reproduction or distribution of the pages in this book is prohibited, including copying the entire book to use as another primary source or "master" copy.

Printed in the U.S.A.

ISBN 0-7606-0597-1

About the Author

Nancy B. Swigert, M.A., CCC-SLP, is the president of Swigert & Associates, Inc., a private practice which has provided services in the Lexington, Kentucky area for over 25 years. The practice provides early intervention services in child care, home and office settings, and through their contractual arrangement with Central Baptist Hospital.

The associates in the practice who contributed to the *Early Intervention Kit* have over 66 years of experience serving young children and their families. **Jennifer Perry Blevins** is a graduate of the University of Kentucky and serves children with developmental delays and a variety of other communication disorders. **Verity Mathews** was educated at the University of Hull, England and at Eastern Kentucky University and has worked extensively with children with communication and feeding/swallowing problems. **Sarah Shoemaker Shields** graduated from the University of Kentucky and has served children with all types of communication disorders. Jennifer wrote Chapter 11: Augmentative and Alternative Communication for the *Therapy Guide* and the Parent Handouts section in the *Activities Book*. She also developed the sign language cards. Verity wrote the majority of the activities for Chapter 9 in the *Activities Book* and consulted with Nancy on Chapter 9: Intervention for Expressive Language in the *Therapy Guide*. Sarah wrote Chapter 4: Medical Disorders and Syndromes Associated with Children Birth to Three in the *Therapy Guide*.

Other associates who contributed significantly to the activities in this *Activities Book* are: **Lissa Wellman Stephens, Michelle Lankster, Sarah Richardson Crain, Kim Gray Helmuth, Julie Bourne**, and **Ashley Kemp Orr**. Their creative ideas for motivating young children are evident throughout the book. They trained at universities in Kentucky (University of Kentucky, University of Louisville, and Eastern Kentucky University) and Ohio (Case Western Reserve University).

(top row – left to right) Kim Gray Helmuth, Michelle Lankster, Nancy Swigert, Sarah Richardson Crain
(middle row – left to right) Julie Bourne, Lissa Wellman Stephens, Ashley Kemp Orr
(front row – left to right) Sarah Shoemaker Shields, Verity Mathews, Jennifer Perry Blevins

Acknowledgments

Two other employees of the practice also made significant contributions:

Geri Cobb, Executive Assistant, provided invaluable direction in the organization and structure of this kit.

Melinda Spurlock compiled and typed many of the activities and found and cross-checked all of our references.

Table of Contents

Introduction 5

Goals and Treatment Objectives for Pre-linguistic Skills (Chapter 7) 7
Activities for Pre-linguistic Skills 10

Goals and Treatment Objectives for Receptive Language Skills (Chapter 8) 43
Activities for Receptive Language Skills 45

Goals and Treatment Objectives for Expressive Language Skills (Chapter 9) 73
Activities for Expressive Language Skills 78

Goals and Treatment Objectives for Sound Production Development (Chapter 10) 121
Activities for Sound Production Development 124

Parent Handouts 151

    Speech and Language Developmental Milestones 152

    Areas of Language Development
    (Information explaining pre-linguistic/play skills, expressive language,
    receptive language, and developmental language delay) 155

    Speech Problems that Affect How Your Child's Speech Sounds
    (Information explaining apraxia, articulation disorders, phonological disorders,
    and fluency disorders) 156

    Strategies to Facilitate Communication 159

    Daily Activities to Target Speech, Language, and Pre-linguistic/Play Skills 162

    Daily Activity to Work on Treatment Objectives 163

    Sample Daily Activity to Work on Treatment Objectives
    (Bath Time, appropriate for all age groups birth to three) 164

    Resources for Parents of Infants and Toddlers 186

Introduction

We hope you will find both the *Therapy Guide* and the *Activities Book* so helpful that you want to keep them handy. However, we suspect that this book, the *Activities Book*, is the one that you will keep in your car, in the therapy room, or wherever you provide services so you can refer to it during your treatment sessions. We've all been told that good therapy doesn't follow a "cookbook" approach but instead is driven by careful analysis of a child's strengths and weaknesses. The information in the *Therapy Guide* should help you perform that analysis (i.e., design the recipe for the child). However, once you have developed the recipe for the child's success, it helps to have a variety of ingredients at your fingertips from which to choose as you put together the recipe. You use these ingredients to vary the recipe to suit your tastes. Consider the treatment objectives and activities in this book to be the ingredients that can help you put together a successful treatment plan for the children you see. Use the activities as we've written them, change them as you see fit given your expertise and what you know about the child, and add others we haven't even thought of!

In this book you will find activities for:

- Pre-linguistic skills
- Receptive language skills
- Expressive language skills
- Sound production development skills

You'll also find:

- Parent handouts
- Completed set of daily living activity forms for birth to 3 years (bath time)

The activities are organized for ease-of-use. Each section starts with the long-term and short-term goals for that area of development (e.g., PG=Pre-linguistic goals). The chart lists the treatment objectives at each expected age of acquisition. The chart also cross references the short-term goal(s) it hopes to accomplish and activities you can use to work on the objective. Most treatment objectives (activities) have only one goal. Additional goals can often be selected for an activity depending on any modifications you make to the activity. Some of our distinctions are arbitrary and you might assign goals differently. The activities are listed with a letter (P = Pre-linguistic, R = Receptive, E = Expressive, S = Sound Production) and a number. When more than one activity is written for a specific treatment objective, lowercase letters (e.g., a, b) follow the number.

Keep in mind that these activities are placed at the ages of expected development in children who are developing normally.* Many children with disabilities show atypical development and don't follow the same sequence in development. A child may be exhibiting skills at age level in one area (e.g., receptive language) but may be nine months behind expected development in expressive language or sound production. There may be skills some children never master. Adjustments in expectations must be made for children so that the treatment objectives are appropriate for that child, considering his or her unique needs and abilities.

*The ages of expected development were drawn from several resources, including *The Rossetti Infant-Toddler Language Scale, Sequenced Inventory of Communication Development, The Receptive-Expressive Emergent Language Scale, Preschool Language Scale-4, The Infant Scale of Communicative Intent, Hawaii Early Learning Profile, The Assessment of Language and Cognitive Abilities Through Play, Screening for Early Cognitive and Communicative Behaviors, Exploring Children's Communicative Intents,* and *Communication Disorders in Infants and Toddlers.*

Introduction, *continued*

- Adaptations may need to be made for infants and children with visual, hearing, and/or motor impairments. Some information is included in Chapter 2 in the *Therapy Guide*, pages 22—23.

- The activities for expressive language (pages 73–120) include information on verbal responses as the primary goal for the communication. However, it also includes a few examples of nonverbal responses (e.g., gestures, signs, pictures) for children who need augmented/alternative expressive communication.

- Treatment objectives are not written for all skills expected to develop at a specific age, but rather those skills that you might work to develop. For example, an expected skill for an 18- to 21- month-old might be to lead an adult to a desired object. However, it would be difficult to target that skill in therapy and therefore a treatment objective is not written for it.

If you have developed a treatment plan using the master list of goals and objectives (See Chapter 12, page 150 in the *Therapy Guide*), you can then use the activities in this book to plan and conduct your treatment sessions. You can even use the numbering system in your progress notes to reference the activities you are working on. The activities suggest toys and materials you might want to take with you for the session. Many of these objects are found in most homes too. The activities are also written in a detailed way so you can copy them and give them to caregivers. Many times children need prompts in order to respond. When appropriate, we included tips on how to prompt the child to respond and noted them in **bold**. It might be a verbal prompt or a physical prompt. Many responses can't be prompted other than by continuing to model. You can't physically prompt a child to say a word. So, in many of the expressive and sound production activities, prompts aren't explicitly stated but are implied.

The parent handouts should be helpful as you strive to serve in a consultant role—helping parents become effective teachers for their child. We've provided information about normal development, specific problems encountered with children birth to three, and strategies to facilitate communication skills.

Many activities of daily living lend themselves to language teaching. We selected "bath time" as an example, and have provided activity sheets for each three-month age span that address each of the four areas of communication (pages 164–185). Space has been provided on those activity sheets for you to add other instructions as needed. We included a list of other daily activities for you to consider developing similar handouts and have provided a blank format of this form for you to use (page 163).

We hope we have included all the ingredients you will need as you provide services to young children and their families. Consider these materials a starting point for your creative approach to early intervention!

Nancy	Kim
Jennifer	Michelle
Sarah S.	Ashley
Verity	Lissa
Sarah C.	Julie

Goals and Treatment Objectives for Pre-linguistic Skills (Chapter 7)

Long-term goal

The child will be able to maintain attention to stimuli and interact with objects and people appropriately.

Short-term goals

PG1 The child will make and maintain eye contact/visual contact with object/picture/person.

PG2 The child will imitate non-vocal actions.

PG3 The child will imitate vocalizations.

PG4 The child will use objects (or imaginary objects) in appropriate play/self-care.

PG5 The child will engage in turn-taking routines.

PG6 The child will demonstrate object permanence.

PG7 The child will respond with appropriate gesture/action to sound, speech, and/or gesture.

PG8 The child will initiate use of appropriate gesture to obtain desired effect.

PG9 The child will demonstrate other problem-solving skills.

An explanation of how these goals were matched to the treatment activities

In addition to selecting goals and treatment objectives based on the child's level of function and when the skill is expected to develop, keep in mind the specific communicative intentions that should be developing at the pre-linguistic stage.

Most treatment objectives (activities) have only one goal, but some have two (e.g., Treatment Objective P55 [matches shapes] is correlated to PG7 [responding appropriately] and PG9 [other problem-solving]). Keep in mind that additional goals can often be selected for an activity (e.g., turn taking can be matched to many activities such as playing games, playing "peek-a-boo," or playing ball). Some of our distinctions are arbitrary and you might assign goals differently.

Receptive Ages of Acquisition/Treatment Objectives

Expected age of development	Short-term goal (PG)	Treatment Objectives	Activities to help achieve treatment objectives
0–3 months	1	Child makes eye contact with adult	P1
	1	Reacts to disappearance of slowly-moving object	P2
	7	Alerts to sound	P3 a, b
	1	Watches speaker's mouth	P4
3–6 months	1	Maintains eye contact	P5
	7	Turns head to voice	P6 a, b
	3	Vocalizes when adult starts vocalization	P7 a, b
	2	Imitates facial expressions with adult	P8
	7	Enjoys repeating newly-learned activity	P9
	8	Reaches for objects	P10
	8	Hits objects when playing	P11 a, b
	6	Finds a partially-hidden object	P12
6–9 months	2	Imitates gestures with adult	P13 a, b
	1	Maintains attention to a speaker	P14
	7	Responds to noisemaker that is not in line of vision	P15
	1	Attends to pictures	P16 a, b
	7	Anticipates what will happen next (e.g., closes eyes, tenses body)	P17 a, b
	5	Cooperates by playing games with adults	P18
	8	Touches toy or adult's hand to restart an activity	P19 a, b
	2	Tries to imitate facial expressions (e.g., puckers, protrudes tongue)	P20
	6	Searches for hidden objects	P21 a, b
	6, 9	Relates sound to object	P22 a, b
9–12 months	5, 6	Plays "Peek-a-boo" by covering and uncovering face with hands or cloth	P23
	7	Waves "Hi" and "Bye"	P24
	8	Points to an object to indicate he knows it is there	P25
	4	Stirs with a spoon	P26
	8	Extends toy to show others but doesn't give it up	P27
	9	Overcomes obstacle to obtain object	P28 a, b
	4	Drops object systematically	P29 a, b
12–15 months	5	Initiates turn-taking routines	P30 a, b
	4	Combs or brushes hair	P31
	4, 7	Hugs dolls, stuffed animals, or people	P32 a, b
	4	Shows functional use of objects	P33 a, b
	1	Maintains attention to pictures	P34
	7	Hands toy back to adult	P35 a, b
15–18 months	4	Uses more than one object in play routine	P36
	4	Pretends action with object	P37 a, b
	8	Requests assistance from adult	P38 a, b, c, d, e
	5	Plays ball with adult	P39
	4, 9	Puts one object inside another	P40 a, b
	7, 9	Identifies self in mirror	P41
	4	Imitates doing housework	P42 a, b, c

continued on next page

Expected age of development	Short-term goal (PG)	Treatment Objectives	Activities to help achieve treatment objectives
18–21 months	4 3 4 7	Pretends to play musical instrument Imitates environmental noises Uses two toys together in pretend play Pretends to dance	P43 P44 P45 a, b P46 a, b
21–24 months	4 4 4, 9 4, 9 7, 9	If mobile, pushes a stroller or shopping cart Flies a toy airplane Stacks and assembles toys and objects (e.g., nesting blocks) Sorts objects Matches sounds to pictures of animals	P47 P48 P49 a, b P50 a, b P51
24–27 months	4 4 7	Pretends to write Pretends to talk on the phone Slaps adult's hand when asked to "Gimme Five"	P52 P53 P54
27–30 months	7, 9 7, 9 4	Matches shapes of toys (e.g., square, circle) Matches colors Dramatizes using doll	P55 a, b, c, d P56 P57 a, b
30–33 months	7, 9 7, 9	Sorts shapes Stacks rings in correct order	P58 P59
33–36 months	4 7, 9	Plays house Sorts colors	P60 a, b, c P61

P1

Treatment Objective: The child will make eye contact with an adult.

Goal: The child will make and maintain eye contact/visual contact with object/picture/person. (PG1)

Activity: Flashlight Fun   **Expected age**: 0–3 months

Materials/Toys: flashlight

Sit on the floor of a dimly lit room. The child should be seated no more than one foot away and should be facing you in some type of infant chair. The closer you sit, the better likelihood the child will look at you. Hold the flashlight in your lap, shining the light up toward your face. Engage in vocalizations that encourage the infant to make eye contact. **Prompt** by saying his name or by moving your face closer. Once eye contact is made, move to another location. Shine light on your face and pleasantly vocalize again, nodding your head and being dramatic.

P2

Treatment Objective: The child will react to the disappearance of a slowly-moving object.

Goal: The child will make and maintain eye contact/visual contact with object/picture/person. (PG1)

Activity: Watch the Rattle   **Expected age**: 0–3 months

Materials/Toys: large rattle or any interesting object that makes noise (e.g., keys on a ring, change purse full of change, empty soft drink can with pennies inside)

While the baby is lying on his back, shake the rattle about 12 inches from his face. Talk to the baby about the object (e.g., "See the pretty toy"). Slowly move the rattle off to one side, periodically shaking it to keep the baby's attention. When the rattle is at the far edge of the baby's peripheral vision, move the rattle out of sight. The baby should turn his head toward the area where the rattle disappeared. If he doesn't, **prompt** by shaking the rattle again while it is out of sight.

P3a

Treatment Objective: The child will alert to sound.

Goal: The child will respond with appropriate gesture/action to sound, speech, and/or gesture. (PG7)

Activity: Radio Play   **Expected age**: 0–3 months

Materials/Toys: toy radio or real radio

Complete this activity when the environment is quiet. The baby should be in his infant seat, lying on the floor, or in his crib. Out of the line of the baby's vision, wind the toy radio so it starts to play or turn the real radio on at a moderate volume. Watch for a response from the baby. Let the sound play for a minute or so and then turn it off. Wait several minutes quietly and then turn the sound on again. **Prompt** by using a slightly louder volume or by using a louder or more unusual sound (e.g., clapping, ringing bell).

P3b

Treatment Objective: The child will alert to sound.

Goal: The child will respond with appropriate gesture/action to sound, speech, and/or gesture. (PG7)

Activity: Foot Stomp   **Expected age**: 0–3 months

Materials/Toys: none

Complete this activity when the environment is quiet. The baby should be in his infant seat, lying on the floor, or in his crib. Out of the line of the baby's vision, stomp your feet loudly. Watch for a response from the baby. Wait a minute or so quietly, and then stomp again. **Prompt** by using a slightly louder stomping.

P4

Treatment Objective: The child will watch the speaker's mouth.

Goal: The child will make and maintain eye contact/visual contact with object/picture/person. (PG1)

Activity: Watch Me Talk   **Expected age**: 0–3 months

Materials/Toys: none

Hold the baby in your lap with his head at your knees. Lean over so your face is about 12-15 inches away from his. Talk to the baby in an interesting voice, using different pitches (i.e., not a monotone). Stimulate language by telling the baby, "Look at me talk." If the baby loses interest in watching your mouth, change the pitch of your voice to regain the baby's attention. You can prompt by taking the child's hand and touching your mouth with his hand. **Prompt** by using exaggerated mouth movements as you talk.

P5

Treatment Objective: The child will maintain eye contact.

Goal: The child will make and maintain eye contact/visual contact with object/picture/person. (PG1)

Activity: Watch Me   **Expected age**: 3–6 months

Materials/Toys: none

Hold the baby in your lap with his head at your knees. Lean over so your face is about 12-15 inches away from the baby's. Talk to the baby in an interesting voice, using different pitches (i.e., not a monotone). Stimulate language by telling the baby, "Look at me." If the baby loses interest in giving eye contact, **prompt** by changing the pitch of your voice to regain his attention.

P6a

Treatment Objective: The child will turn his head toward a voice.

Goal: The child will respond with appropriate gesture/action to sound, speech, and/or gesture. (PG7)

Activity: Can You Hear Me Now?   **Expected age**: 3–6 months

Materials/Toys: paper towel roll or large plastic bottle with bottom cut off

The human voice sounds different when it comes through a megaphone. Make a megaphone out of a paper towel roll or cut off the bottom of a large plastic bottle, taping over any sharp ends. Place the child in his infant seat or have him lie on the floor. Stand to one side of the infant so he is not looking directly at you. Using a pleasant voice, vocalize into the megaphone. **Prompt** the child to turn his head toward the sound by using a different pitch or exaggerated inflection. Change position in the room to encourage the child to look and "find" your voice again.

P6b

Treatment Objective: The child will turn his head toward a voice.

Goal: The child will respond with appropriate gesture/action to sound, speech, and/or gesture. (PG7)

Activity: Where Am I?   **Expected age**: 3–6 months

Materials/Toys: none

Place the child in his infant seat or have him lie on the floor or in his crib. Give the child a toy to play with so the child isn't tempted to follow your movements around the room. When the child becomes interested in the toy, move to one side of the child and begin to talk to him. You can call his name, or say something like "I'm over here. Can you find me?" When the child looks in your direction, praise him. Allow the child to become interested in the toy again as you move to another part of the room. Talk to the child again. If the child does not turn his head to your voice, **prompt** physically by helping the child turn in the direction of your voice.

P7a

Treatment Objective: The child will vocalize when an adult starts vocalization.

Goal: The child will imitate vocalizations. (PG3)

Activity: Where Is Baby?   **Expected age**: 3–6 months

Materials/Toys: none

Hold the child facing you or sit in front of him. Sing the phrase "Where is baby?" to the tune of "Frère Jacques." Pause and give the child a chance to vocalize. If the child doesn't, **prompt** by saying, "Can you sing?" When the child vocalizes and stops, sing another verse ("Here he is, here he is"). Pause and give the child a chance to vocalize if he is not doing this with you. If the child still doesn't vocalize, you can further **prompt** by vocalizing an easy vowel sound like "ahhh."

Activities Book
The Early Intervention Kit

━━━━━━━━━━━━━━━━━━━━━━━━━━━━━ **P7b** ━━━━━━━━━━━━━━━━━━━━━━━━━━━━━

Treatment Objective: The child will vocalize when an adult starts vocalization.

Goal: The child will imitate vocalizations. (PG3)

Activity: Ahh, Pretty Baby   **Expected age:** 3–6 months

Materials/Toys: none

Hold the child facing you or sit in front him. Say to the child, "Ahhh, pretty baby." Then say, "Ahhh" again with a lot of inflection. Pause and give the child a chance to begin vocalizing. **Prompt** by saying, "Ahhh" again to the child. You can also **prompt** by pointing to the child and saying, "You do it."

━━━━━━━━━━━━━━━━━━━━━━━━━━━━━ **P8** ━━━━━━━━━━━━━━━━━━━━━━━━━━━━━

Treatment Objective: The child will imitate facial expressions with an adult.

Goal: The child will imitate non-vocal actions. (PG2)

Activity: Making Funny Faces   **Expected age:** 3–6 months

Materials/Toys: none

Hold the child facing you or sit in front of the child. The easiest way to teach imitation is to follow the child's lead. If the child initiates a facial expression (e.g., raised eyebrows, smile), imitate it and see if the child will take another turn.

If the child does not initiate facial expressions, talk to the child with lots of intonation in your voice. Smile as you talk to the child. This may help to provoke facial expressions. Other expressions you can use include puckering for a kiss, frowning, or opening your mouth. If the child is not imitating any facial expressions, **prompt** by continuing with exaggerated facial expressions.

━━━━━━━━━━━━━━━━━━━━━━━━━━━━━ **P9** ━━━━━━━━━━━━━━━━━━━━━━━━━━━━━

Treatment Objective: The child will enjoy repeating a newly-learned activity.

Goal: The child will respond with appropriate gesture/action to sound, speech, and/or gesture. (PG7)

Activity: Practice, Practice, Practice   **Expected age:** 3–6 months
(Note: This activity should be something the child has just learned how to do. Pulling off the child's socks is provided as an example only. The activity can be non-vocal or vocal.)

Materials/Toys: the child's socks

With the child lying on the floor, pull the child's sock almost off his foot. Leave it dangling on his toes. If the child does not put his leg up so he can see the sock and reach it, you can **prompt** by helping him. When the child pulls the sock off, clap and tell the child, "Good job." Replace the sock on the child's foot and again pull it down so that it is just barely on the child's toes. If the child pulls it off again, reinforce with clapping and stimulate language by saying, "You got the sock." If the child doesn't reach for the sock, **prompt** by wiggling the sock and helping the child lift his leg so he can see the sock. Tell the child to "Get the sock."

P10

Treatment Objective: The child will reach for an object.

Goal: The child will initiate use of appropriate gesture to obtain desired effect. (PG8)

Activity: Shake It Up **Expected age**: 3–6 months

Materials/Toys: rattle or keys

Have the child lie on the floor or sit in an infant seat, or you can hold him. Bring the toy close to the child so he can engage/interact with it. Shake the object. Allow the child to become excited about the toy. Then pull the toy away from the child, out of his reach. When he reaches for it, allow the child to have or play with the toy. If the child doesn't reach for the toy, verbally **prompt**, "Reach for it. Can you get it?" You can also offer a physical **prompt** by gently guiding the child's arm to the object while using the verbal prompt.

P11a

Treatment Objective: The child will hit an object when playing.

Goal: The child will initiate use of appropriate gesture to obtain desired effect. (PG8)

Activity: Making Music **Expected age**: 3–6 months

Materials/Toys: large musical toy that has keys that are easy to hit or wooden spoon and metal bowl/pan

Sit with the child on the floor. Place the child in your lap facing away from you so you can manipulate his hands and arms if needed. Put the musical toy in front of you and the child. Let the child watch as you hit the buttons/keys with your hand or another object to make musical sounds. After the child has watched you several times, place the toy where the child can reach. If the child doesn't attempt to hit the keys, **prompt** by holding the child's hand and hitting the keys with him. Stimulate language by saying, "Let's make music" or "Hit it."

P11b

Treatment Objective: The child will hit an object when playing.

Goal: The child will initiate use of appropriate gesture to obtain desired effect. (PG8)

Activity: Bowl Music **Expected age**: 3–6 months

Materials/Toys: large metal or plastic bowl, wooden spoon

Sit with the child on the floor. Place the child in your lap, facing away from you, so you can manipulate his hands and arms if needed. Put the bowl face down in front of you and the child. Let the child watch as you hit the bowl with the spoon or your hand to make noise. Stimulate language by saying, "Bam" each time you hit the bowl. After the child has watched you several times, place the bowl where the child can reach it. If the child doesn't attempt to hit the bowl, **prompt** by holding the child's hand and hitting the bowl with him. Continue to stimulate language by saying, "Bam" or "Hit it."

P12

Treatment Objective: The child will find a partially-hidden object.

Goal: The child will demonstrate object permanence. (PG6)

Activity: Hide the Baby **Expected age**: 3–6 months

Materials/Toys: doll, blanket

Sit with the child on the floor or have the child sit in his high chair with the tray in place. Let the child watch as you cover the doll with a blanket. Leave part of the doll visible to the child (e.g., leg or arm). Give the child several seconds to pull the blanket off the doll. If the child doesn't attempt to find the doll, **prompt** by saying, "Where's the baby?" If the child still does not attempt to find the baby, give the child a model. You pull the blanket off the baby saying, "There's the baby." You can also offer a physical **prompt** by placing the child's hand on the part of the doll that is visible and pulling the doll out from under the blanket.

P13a

Treatment Objective: The child will imitate gestures with an adult.

Goal: The child will imitate non-vocal actions. (PG2)

Activity: Clap, Clap, Clap **Expected age**: 6–9 months

Materials/Toys: none

When the child completes an activity or action (e.g., finishes his bottle, puts his legs up to have his diaper changed), clap and say, "Good job" or "Yeah." You can elaborate by being specific about what was accomplished, such as "Good job, you drank all your milk" or "Yeah, you got those legs up." Encourage the child to clap. **Prompt** by holding the child's hands and helping him clap. Stimulate language by saying, "Can you clap?"

P13b

Treatment Objective: The child will imitate gestures with an adult.

Goal: The child will imitate non-vocal actions. (PG2)

Activity: Mirror, Mirror **Expected age**: 6–9 months

Materials/Toys: mirror (wall or hand)

Place the child so he can see in the mirror. Sit or stand behind the child so the child can see you and himself in the mirror. Make big smiles and wait for the child to imitate. If the child doesn't smile, **prompt** by slightly touching the corner of the child's mouth and saying, "Big smile."

P14

Treatment Objective: The child will maintain attention to a speaker.

Goal: The child will make and maintain eye contact/visual contact with object/picture/person. (PG1)

Activity: Time to Clean Up **Expected age:** 6–9 months

Materials/Toys: all of the materials you used during the session or the child's toys at home

At the end of the session, with the child sitting in infant seat or being held by the parent (but not where he can reach the toys you are putting away), talk to the child about what you are doing (e.g., "I'll put away our toys. I have to go bye-bye. I'll be back to see you soon"). Look at the child frequently as you are talking. Check to make sure the child is watching you. **Prompt** the child's attention by making noise with the toys as you put them away and using different inflections with your voice (e.g., "Uh-oh, that lid wasn't on tight. There, I fixed it").

P15

Treatment Objective: The child will respond to a noisemaker that is not in line of vision.

Goal: The child will respond with appropriate gesture/action to sound, speech, and/or gesture. (PG7)

Activity: What Was That? **Expected age:** 6–9 months

Materials/Toys: any toy that makes noise (e.g., keys on a ring)

With the child lying in his crib or seated in his infant seat, wait until the child is not looking at you or move out of the child's line of vision. Make noise with the toy and wait to see if the child responds. He might turn in the direction of the sound or stop his activity. If he does, show him what's making the interesting sound. If he doesn't respond, **prompt** by moving the toy into the child's line of vision and making the noise again. Then try it outside the child's line of vision. You can further **prompt** by calling the child's name and showing him the noisy toy. If the child is not turning at all to the sound, gently turn his head in the direction of the sound. If the child is failing to respond to sound, this may indicate hearing loss, and appropriate referrals should be made.

P16a

Treatment Objective: The child will attend to pictures.

Goal: The child will make and maintain eye contact/visual contact with object/picture/person. (PG1)

Activity: Let's Read **Expected age:** 6–9 months

Materials/Toys: books with large pictures (little or no text needed) or family photos

With the child seated in your lap facing away from you, hold a book where the child can see it. Talk about the picture on the page (e.g., "Look at the big doggie"). Let the child help hold the book if he wants to. **Prompt** the child to attend to the picture by tapping the picture on the page and saying, "Look at the _____." Turn the page and repeat with another picture.

═══ **P16b** ═══

Treatment Objective: The child will attend to pictures.

Goal: The child will make and maintain eye contact/visual contact with object/picture/person. (PG1)

Activity: Pretty Pictures   **Expected age**: 6–9 months

Materials/Toys: pictures of interesting things (e.g., animals, toys, people)
(Note: You might want to laminate the pictures for increased durability.)

When the child is seated in his high chair, place a single laminated picture on the tray. Tell the child what the picture is (e.g., "Look at the shoes"). You can also describe the picture. If the child doesn't seem interested in the picture, **prompt** by tapping the picture or picking it up. You can also encourage the child to hold the picture. If the child does not look down at the picture, give a physical **prompt** by picking up the picture and moving it right in front of the child's line of vision.

═══ **P17a** ═══

Treatment Objective: The child will anticipate what will happen next (e.g., closes eyes, tenses body).

Goal: The child will respond with appropriate gesture/action to sound, speech, and/or gesture. (PG7)

Activity: Get Your Nose   **Expected age**: 6–9 months

Materials/Toys: puppet with a mouth that opens or a sock that will fit on an adult's hand

With the child seated in an infant seat or high chair, or lying on the floor, show the child a puppet he is not afraid of. Then show the child how the puppet playfully "gets you" by demonstrating on yourself. Say, "The puppet (or name of the animal represented by the puppet) is gonna get my nose." Slowly move the puppet toward your face and have the puppet gently bite you on the nose. Then try this with the child. Say, "The puppet (animal name) is gonna get your nose." Slowly move the puppet toward the child, making a chomping motion with the puppet's mouth. As you approach the child's nose, anticipation might be indicated by the child closing his eyes or putting hands up to block the puppet. (Note: There are no good prompts for this activity.)

═══ **P17b** ═══

Treatment Objective: The child will anticipate what will happen next (e.g., closes eyes, tenses body).

Goal: The child will respond with appropriate gesture/action to sound, speech, and/or gesture. (PG7)

Activity: Let's Go Flying   **Expected age**: 6–9 months

Materials/Toys: none

Sit on the floor with your knees bent and your feet on the floor with the child facing you. Hold the child under his arms with the child in a standing position. Brace the child against your shins. Slowly roll back and lift the child off the floor. Stimulate language by saying, "Let's fly." Slowly return the child to the supported standing position on the floor. Repeat the activity, again saying, "Let's fly." After returning the child to the supported standing position, say, "Let's fly" but don't start to move. Wait to see if the child moves his body in some way to indicate that he is ready to be lifted up. The child might anticipate the movement by slightly bending his legs or by changing facial expression. **Prompt** by repeating, "Do you want to fly?" and gently moving the child in a slight bouncing motion.

P18

Treatment Objective: The child will cooperate by playing games with an adult.

Goal: The child will engage in turn-taking routines. (PG5)

Activity: Pat-a-Cake   **Expected age**: 6–9 months

Materials/Toys: none

Sit with the child on the floor or have the child sit on your lap facing you. Recite "Pat-a-cake" while doing the hand motions. If the child doesn't begin to move his hands, physically **prompt** the child by taking his hands and helping him do the hand motions.

P19a

Treatment Objective: The child will touch a toy or an adult's hand to restart an activity.

Goal: The child will initiate use of appropriate gesture to obtain desired effect. (PG8)

Activity: Let's Make Music   **Expected age**: 6–9 months

Materials/Toys: toys that make noise or move

Start the toy and let the child become interested in it. When the toy stops, wait for the child to seek help. He will likely do this by touching the toy or your hand. If the child doesn't do anything to get the toy started again, your first **prompt** might be to tap the toy and ask, "Want more?" You can also **prompt** by tapping the toy and then restarting it to show the child that the action results in more movement/sound from the toy. If the child still doesn't do anything, **prompt** by taking the child's hand and touching his hand to your hand. As soon as the child's hand touches yours, activate the toy. The child can also touch or bang the toy to get the action restarted.

P19b

Treatment Objective: The child will touch a toy or an adult's hand to restart an activity.

Goal: The child will initiate use of appropriate gesture to obtain desired effect. (PG8)

Activity: I'm Gonna Get You!   **Expected age**: 6–9 months

Materials/Toys: none

While seated on the floor with the child, or seated in front of the child in his car seat or swing, slowly make your hand crawl across the floor (or across the tray of the swing) saying, "I'm gonna get you." Then lightly tickle the child's tummy. Repeat a few times to ensure that the child understands the game and is enjoying it. Then simply place your hand within reach of the child, but don't move it or say or do anything. Wait for the child to touch your hand to restart the activity. **Prompt** by saying, "You want more?" or "You want me to get you?" and taking the child's hand and helping him tap your hand to restart the game.

P20

Treatment Objective: The child will try to imitate facial expressions.

Goal: The child will imitate non-vocal actions. (PG2)

Activity: Copycat   **Expected age**: 6–9 months

Materials/Toys: none

Lay the child on the floor, hold him up, or place him in an infant seat so he can easily see your face. Model "funny faces" for the child. Stimulate by saying things like, "Give kisses." "Stick your tongue out," and "Big smiles." Wait for the child to imitate you. Offer a physical **prompt** by gently placing your hands on the child's cheeks to manipulate into a pucker or a smile. This will help the child feel the motion made when puckering and smiling. You can help with the lateralization of the lips for the smile by gently stretching the child's lips.

P21a

Treatment Objective: The child will search for hidden objects.

Goal: The child will demonstrate object permanence. (PG6)

Activity: Hungry Puppet   **Expected age**: 6–9 months

Materials/Toys: puppet or sock, small toy
(Note: Make sure the toy is not so small that it will go in the child's mouth.)

Show the child the puppet and a small toy that will fit in the puppet's mouth. Allow the child to become interested in the toy. Then have the puppet act like it's eating the small object by placing the toy inside the puppet's mouth so the toy is hidden. Ask, "Where is the ____?" Encourage the child to look for the toy. Eventually open the puppet's mouth and show the toy to the child. Repeat several times, each time allowing a longer time for the child to look for the toy. (If you don't have a puppet, you can make a puppet with a sock over your hand.)

P21b

Treatment Objective: The child will search for hidden objects.

Goal: The child will demonstrate object permanence. (PG6)

Activity: Hide and Seek   **Expected age**: 6–9 months

Materials/Toys: empty box (e.g., shoebox), an interesting toy that will fit under the box

Let the child become engaged with the interesting toy (e.g., musical toy or action toy that moves). After the child has played with the toy for a few minutes, let the child see you hide it under the box. Wait to see if the child looks for the toy. **Prompt** by saying, "Where's the _____?" If the child still doesn't begin to look for the toy, lift the edge of the box so the child can see part of the toy, but then drop the box down again so the toy is covered. You can also **prompt** by letting an edge of the toy stick out from under the box. You can further **prompt** by taking the child's hand and helping him lift the corner of the box.

P22a

Treatment Objective: The child will relate sound to an object.

Goals: The child will demonstrate object permanence. (PG6)
The child will demonstrate other problem-solving skills. (PG9)

Activity: What Was That Noise 1?   **Expected age:** 6–9 months

Materials/Toys: wooden spoon, sock, small blanket or cloth diaper

Seat the child in his high chair and put the wooden spoon on the tray. Shield his view of the tray with the small blanket/cloth diaper. Bang on the tray with the wooden spoon, making sure the blanket/cloth diaper blocks the child's view. Then put the spoon on the tray and remove the visual barrier. See if the child will pick up the spoon and bang with it. **Prompt** the child by letting him see you bang with the spoon, and then letting him have a turn banging. Repeat using the blanket/cloth diaper as a shield to see if the child begins to associate the sound with the spoon.

P22b

Treatment Objective: The child will relate sound to an object.

Goals: The child will demonstrate object permanence. (PG6)
The child will demonstrate other problem-solving skills. (PG9)

Activity: What Was That Noise 2?   **Expected age:** 6–9 months

Materials/Toys: toy keys or real keys on a key ring, sock or other object that does not make noise

With the child seated in his high chair, shake the keys outside his line of vision. Repeat. Place the keys and the sock (or other quiet object) on the tray of the high chair. See if the child will pick up the keys and shake them. **Prompt** the child by letting him see you shake the keys, and then letting him have a turn shaking the keys. Repeat holding the keys outside the child's line of vision to see if the child begins to associate the sound with the keys.

P23

Treatment Objective: The child will play "peek-a-boo" by covering and uncovering his face with hands or cloth.

Goals: The child will engage in turn-taking routines. (PG5)
The child will demonstrate object permanence. (PG6)

Activity:	Peek-a-Boo	**Expected age**: 9–12 months
Materials/Toys:	a blanket or cloth	

Sit with the child on the floor so he can see your face. You might want to seat the child in an infant seat. Place your hands or the cloth over your face. When you remove your hands or the cloth over your face, say, "Peek-a-boo." Repeat several times so the child may observe the activity. After the child has watched you, pause to give the child time to imitate the activity. If you are using a cloth, give it to the child at this time. **Prompt** with "You do it" or "Your turn." You can also offer a physical **prompt** by placing the child's hands over his face or by placing the cloth over the child's face. When you remove the child's hands or the cloth, say, "Peek-a-boo." Repeat several times, pausing to give the child time to play "Peek-a-boo" on his own.

P24

Treatment Objective: The child will wave "Hi" and "Bye."

Goal: The child will respond with appropriate gesture/action to sound, speech, and/or a gesture. (PG7)
(Note: If you have to keep waving so the child is really imitating your action and not understanding that it necessarily means "Hi" or "Bye," then the goal would be "The child imitates non-vocal actions." [PG2])

Activity:	Howdy!	**Expected age**: 9–12 months
Materials/Toys:	none	

Take advantage of natural situations. When you enter the room or the child's home, be sure to always say, "Hi" as you wave "Hi" to the child. When you leave, say, "Bye" as you wave "Bye." Wait to see if the child waves "Bye." You can also use other family members and people in the environment. For example, if another person enters or leaves the room, have her model the gesture (i.e., saying/waving "Hi"). Respond to the person verbally and with a wave. Physically **prompt** by gently taking the child's arm and helping him make the movement while pairing it with the word.

P25

Treatment Objective: The child will point to an object to indicate he knows it's there.

Goal: The child will initiate use of appropriate gesture to obtain desired effect. (PG8)

Activity:	Look!	**Expected age**: 9–12 months
Materials/Toys:	toy that moves or makes noise	

Turn on the toy and place it away from the child, out of reach. It should be placed so the child may have to move a little to acknowledge interest. Model by pointing to the object and saying, "Look at that." If the child doesn't show interest in the toy, **prompt** by bringing the toy closer so the child can see it, but still keep the toy out of reach. You can also **prompt** with a verbal cue of "Wow, look at this" while pointing to the toy. If the child still is not pointing to indicate knowledge of the toy, leave it in the out-of-reach location during the session. Periodically point to it throughout the session and comment on it. You can make it more interesting to the child by pointing to it and then turning it on to maintain the child's attention to it.

P26

Treatment Objective: The child will stir with a spoon.

Goal: The child will use objects (or imaginary objects) in appropriate play/self-care. (PG4)

Activity: Cooking Soup   **Expected age:** 9–12 months

Materials/Toys: plastic bowl, spoon, toy food, two or three dolls

Sit on the floor with the child sitting facing you. Have the dolls sit nearby. Tell the child that you are going to make soup for the dolls. Put toy food in the bowl and say to the child, "We have to stir it up. Stir, stir, stir." After demonstrating a couple of times, hand the bowl and spoon to the child saying, "Now it's your turn to stir." If the child doesn't imitate, **prompt** by taking his hands and helping him through the motions until he understands and will attempt spontaneously. If the child doesn't stir spontaneously, use a hand-over-hand technique to help him. You can also **prompt** by having one of the dolls or a puppet hold the spoon and stir. Stimulate language by saying, "Look, the baby doll is going to help us stir."

P27

Treatment Objective: The child will extend a toy to show others but not give it up.

Goal: The child will initiate use of appropriate gesture to obtain desired effect. (PG8)

Activity: Look What I Have   **Expected age:** 9–12 months

Materials/Toys: any two objects exactly alike (e.g., stuffed animals, spoons)

Sit in the floor with the child. Hold one of the objects and give the child the other. Extend your arm to show the item and engage in dramatic play (e.g., make the stuffed animal move). Stimulate language by saying, "Look. Look at my ____." Wait to see if the child will extend his arm to show what he is holding. You can even hold your object under a lighted lamp and say, "Look at my ____. I can see it." **Prompt** by saying, "Show me your ____" or take the child's hand that is holding the object and extend it. Say, "Look at your ____."

P28a

Treatment Objective: The child will overcome an obstacle to obtain an object.

Goal: The child will demonstrate other problem-solving skills. (PG9)

Activity: Over the Mountain   **Expected age:** 9–12 months

Materials/Toys: large pillow or cushion, musical toy

Sit on the floor with the child. Play with the musical toy and make sure the child is interested in it. (If the child isn't interested in the toy, use anything else the child is interested in.) Once the child shows interest in the toy, place the large pillow/cushion on the floor between the child and the musical toy (which should still be playing). See if the child will try to crawl over or around the pillow to get the toy. **Prompt** by lifting up the musical toy so the child can see it better, wiggling the toy, and saying, "Get it."

━━━━━━━━━━━━━━━━━━━━━━━━━━━━ **P28b** ━━━━━━━━━━━━━━━━━━━━━━━━━━━━

Treatment Objective: The child will overcome an obstacle to obtain an object.

Goal: The child will demonstrate other problem-solving skills. (PG9)

Activity: Out of the Bag   **Expected age**: 9–12 months

Materials/Toys: mesh bag or large zippered plastic bag (child needs to be able to see in the bag), any toy the child likes

Sit on the floor with the child. Allow the child to play with the interesting toy for a few minutes. Then take the toy and place it in the mesh bag (don't close the top—that's too difficult for this age) or zippered plastic bag (don't zip it). Put the bag with the toy in it in front of the child. See if the child will try to open the bag or reach in the bag to get the toy. The child might also try to turn the bag upside down. **Prompt** by showing the child how to reach in the bag or how to dump the toy out of the bag. You can also wiggle the toy in the bag and say, "Get it."

━━━━━━━━━━━━━━━━━━━━━━━━━━━━ **P29a** ━━━━━━━━━━━━━━━━━━━━━━━━━━━━

Treatment Objective: The child will drop objects systematically.

Goal: The child will use objects (or imaginary objects) in appropriate play/self-care. (PG4)

Activity: A Drop in the Bucket   **Expected age**: 9–12 months

Materials/Toys: bucket or bowl, small toys (e.g., blocks, spoons)

With the child seated in his high chair, place the bucket or bowl on the floor to the side of the high chair. Drop a block into the bucket and say, "Oops! I dropped it." Repeat with another block. Then put a block on the tray of the high chair and encourage the child to drop it in or at least near the bucket. (The object is not to drop the block in the bucket, but just to drop it. The bucket is to make the game more interesting.) **Prompt** by putting the block in the child's hand, moving his hand out over the bucket, and telling him "Let go" or "Make it fall."

━━━━━━━━━━━━━━━━━━━━━━━━━━━━ **P29b** ━━━━━━━━━━━━━━━━━━━━━━━━━━━━

Treatment Objective: The child will drop objects systematically.

Goal: The child will use objects (or imaginary objects) in appropriate play/self-care. (PG4)

Activity: Beanbag Fun   **Expected age**: 9–12 months

Materials/Toys: carpet square, small beanbags or other small items (e.g., spoons)

With the child seated in his high chair, place the carpet square on the floor to the side of the high chair. Drop a beanbag or small item onto the carpet square and say, "Uh-oh! I dropped it." Repeat with another beanbag. Then put a beanbag on the tray of the high chair and encourage the child to drop it on or at least near the carpet square. (The object is not to drop the beanbag on the carpet, but just to drop it. The carpet square is to make the game more interesting.) **Prompt** by putting the beanbag in the child's hand, moving his hand out over the carpet square, and telling him "Let go" or "Make it fall."

P30a

Treatment Objective: The child will initiate a turn-taking routine.

Goal: The child will engage in turn-taking routines. (PG5)

Activity: Go, Go, Go   **Expected age**: 12–15 months

Materials/Toys: toy car or truck that rolls easily or plastic cup to roll

Sit with the child on the floor or have the child sit in his high chair with the tray in place. Have the child watch as you push the car so it rolls toward the child. Make a car noise and stimulate language by saying, "Go" with each push of the toy. After the child watches you a few times, place the car where the child can reach it and see if the child will push it toward you. If the child doesn't do so immediately, **prompt** by saying, "Make it go." You can also offer a physical **prompt**, placing the child's hand on the car and helping him push it. Once the child initiates the routine, take turns. You can give a verbal **prompt** by saying, "My turn now" when you push the car. Continue as long as the child shows interest.

P30b

Treatment Objective: The child will initiate a turn-taking routine.

Goal: The child will engage in turn-taking routines. (PG5)

Activity: Boom, Bing, Beep   **Expected age**: 12–15 months

Materials/Toys: toy drum, keyboard, or bowl turned upside-down

Sit with the child on the floor or have the child sit in his high chair with the tray in place. Let the child watch as you make a sound with the object (e.g., slap your hand on the drum). Stimulate language by saying, "Boom" each time you slap your hand on the drum. If you are using a keyboard, say, "Bing" or "Beep." After the child watches you a few times, place the drum or keyboard where the child can reach it and see if the child will slap it. If the child doesn't do so immediately, **prompt** by saying, "Make it go 'boom' or 'beep.'" You can also offer a physical **prompt**, placing the child's hand on the drum and helping him slap it. Once the child initiates the routine, take turns. Continue as long as the child shows interest.

P31

Treatment Objective: The child will comb or brush his hair.

Goal: The child will use objects (or imaginary objects) in appropriate play/self-care. (PG4)

Activity: Pretty Hair   **Expected age**: 12–15 months

Materials/Toys: doll with hair, hairbrush or comb

Sit with the child on the floor or have the child sit in his high chair with the tray in place. Let the child watch as you brush the doll's hair. Alternate by also brushing the child's hair. Stimulate language by saying, "Brush the baby's hair" and "Brush your hair." After the child has observed this several times, give the child the brush. If the child doesn't attempt to brush the doll's hair or his own hair, **prompt** by saying, "Brush the doll's hair" or "Brush your hair." You can also offer a physical **prompt** by taking the child's hand and brushing the doll's or the child's hair. If the child will brush the doll's hair but not his own, remove the doll and continue to **prompt** the child to brush his own hair.

P32a

Treatment Objective: The child will hug dolls, stuffed animals, and/or people.

Goal: The child will respond with appropriate gesture/action to speech and/or gesture. (PG7)
(Note: PG4 is not included because the child is hugging the clinician, not an object.)

Activity: Hug "Bye-Bye"   **Expected age**: 12–15 months

Materials/Toys: none

When the session is over and you're ready to leave, ask the child for a hug by saying, "Can I have a hug? I'm going bye-bye." Pick up the child or lean down toward the child and put your arms out for a hug. If the child doesn't put his arms out for a hug, **prompt** by initiating the hug.

P32b

Treatment Objective: The child will hug dolls, stuffed animals, and/or people.

Goals: The child will use objects (or imaginary objects) in appropriate play/self-care. (PG4)
The child will respond with appropriate gesture/action to speech and/or gesture. (PG7)

Activity: Hug the Baby   **Expected age**: 12–15 months

Materials/Toys: baby doll, pillow, blanket

Sit on the floor with the child. Put the pillow and blanket on the floor to make a bed. Tell the child you need to put the baby doll to bed. Model how to give the baby doll a hug and then put her on the pillow and cover her up. Stimulate language by saying, "Baby's sleeping." Then hand the baby doll to the child and ask him to give the baby a hug. **Prompt** by modeling again or by putting the baby doll against the child's chest and helping him put his arms around the baby.

P33a

Treatment Objective: The child will show functional use of objects.

Goal: The child will use objects (or imaginary objects) in appropriate play/self-care. (PG4)

Activity: Let's Eat   **Expected age**: 12–15 months

Materials/Toys: spoon, bowl, cup

Seat the child in his high chair with the tray in place, or sit on the floor with the child. Play with the dishes for several minutes. Model stirring and eating with the spoon as well as pretending to drink from the cup. Give either the spoon or cup to the child. **Prompt** by saying, "What do we do with a spoon (cup)?" If the child doesn't demonstrate the function, physically **prompt** by holding the spoon in his hand and either stir with it in the bowl or put the spoon to the child's mouth.

P33b

Treatment Objective: The child will show functional use of objects.

Goal: The child will use objects (or imaginary objects) in appropriate play/self-care. (PG4)

Activity: Make It Go   **Expected age**: 12–15 months

Materials/Toys: toy car or truck

Have the child sit on the floor with you. Show the child how to push the car or truck. Stimulate language by making the noise a car makes. Then put the car in front of the child and see if he pushes it. If he doesn't attempt to push the car, **prompt** by patting the car with your hand and saying, "Can you make it go?" You can also physically **prompt** by helping the child push the car.

P34

Treatment Objective: The child will maintain attention to pictures.

Goal: The child will make and maintain eye contact/visual contact with object/picture/person. (PG1)

Activity: Book Look   **Expected age**: 12–15 months

Materials: books with big colorful pictures (not a lot of words) or family photos (Note: Be sure to select a book that will be interesting to the child or let the child select the book.)

Sit with the child and look at a book (or photos) with him. As you look at the book, point to the pictures. Stimulate language by labeling each picture. To **prompt** the child, tap the picture that you're talking about. Let the child hold the book if he wants to. The goal is for the child to maintain attention to the pictures, not just to glance at them as you would expect at a younger age.

P35a

Treatment Objective: The child will hand a toy back to an adult.

Goal: The child will respond with appropriate gesture/action to sound, speech, and/or gesture. (PG7)

Activity: It's My Turn 1   **Expected age**: 12–15 months

Materials/Toys: doll with hair, hairbrush

Sit with the child and show him the doll and the brush. Model brushing the doll's hair and use simple, short phrases (two to three words) describing what you are doing (e.g., "Brushing hair, pretty hair," or "I'm brushing"). Hand the doll and hairbrush to the child and say, "It's your turn." If the child doesn't brush the doll's hair, **prompt** by assisting the child with hair brushing (hand-over-hand). Model appropriate language (e.g., "brushing hair"). After the child brushes the doll's hair several times say, "It's my turn." If the child doesn't hand the brush back to you, **prompt** by holding out your hand. Continue the exchange several times.

═══ P35b ═══

Treatment Objective: The child will hand a toy back to an adult.

Goal: The child will respond with appropriate gesture/action to sound, speech, and/or gesture. (PG7)

Activity: It's My Turn 2   **Expected age**: 12–15 months

Materials/Toys: stuffed animal or baby doll

Sit with the child and show him the stuffed animal (or doll). Model appropriate language (e.g., "Hug the doggy"). Then pass the stuffed animal to the child and say, "It's your turn. You hug the doggy." If the child doesn't hug the stuffed animal, **prompt** by showing him how to hug the stuffed animal again or by saying, "You hug the doggy." After the child hugs the doggy, request the stuffed animal by saying, "It's my turn." If the child doesn't hand the stuffed animal back, **prompt** by holding out your hand. Continue the exchange several times.

═══ P36 ═══

Treatment Objective: The child will use more than one object in a play routine.

Goal: The child will use objects (or imaginary objects) in appropriate play/self-care. (PG4)

Activity: Mr. Potato Head   **Expected age**: 15–18 months

Materials/Toys: Mr. Potato Head

This activity is good for teaching the child facial features (e.g., eyes, ears, nose). Have Mr. Potato Head and extra parts lying in front of you and the child. Give the child Mr. Potato Head's body and say, "Here is Mr. Potato Head but he's missing his eyes. Let's give him eyes." Pick up the eyes and demonstrate how to put them into the proper holes. Hopefully the child will want to explore the other parts of Mr. Potato Head. After each new Mr. Potato Head piece is introduced, ask the child to point to the corresponding body part on himself (e.g., After you put a nose on Mr. Potato Head, ask the child, "Where is your nose?" Then touch the child's nose and say, "There it is," or "It's on your face").

═══ P37a ═══

Treatment Objective: The child will pretend action with an object.

Goal: The child will use objects (or imaginary objects) in appropriate play/self-care. (PG4)

Activity: Let's Go Night-Night   **Expected age**: 15–18 months

Materials/Toys: pillow, blanket

Sit on the floor with the child. Tell the child you're sleepy. Yawn and stretch and say, "I'm going to sleep." Put your head on the pillow and cover up with the blanket. You can even pretend to snore. Then wake up and put the pillow by the child and hand him the blanket. Ask him, "Can you go to sleep?" **Prompt** by modeling again or even patting the pillow and saying, "Put your head down and go to sleep."

P37b

Treatment Objective: The child will pretend action with an object.

Goal: The child will use objects (or imaginary objects) in appropriate play/self-care. (PG4)

Activity: Tea Party **Expected age**: 15–18 months

Materials/Toys: plastic cups, plastic/play teapot, doll or stuffed animal

Tell the child the doll is thirsty and wants something to drink. Pretend to pour from the teapot to fill up two cups. Model how to take a pretend drink. Then have the doll pretend to take a drink. Each time, stimulate language by saying, "Mmm, good drink." Then pretend to pour something into the child's cup. Wait to see if he will take a drink. **Prompt** by modeling taking another drink and giving the doll another drink. You can also say, "You get a drink" or help the child take the cup to his lips to pretend to get a drink.

P38a

Treatment Objective: The child will request assistance from an adult.

Goal: The child will initiate use of appropriate gesture to obtain desired effect. (PG8)

Activity: I Need Help 1 **Expected age**: 15–18 months

Materials/Toys: board puzzles or pieces for any toy (e.g., animals for a toy farm, rings for a stacking toy), drawstring bag

Before beginning therapy, put the puzzle pieces or toy pieces in the bag. Make sure the bag is securely fastened. Show the puzzle board, farm, or stack ring to the child and give the bag of puzzle/toy pieces to the child. Allow him to try to open the bag. When the child begins to have difficulty, ask him if he needs help. Wait for a response (e.g., The child holds the bag out to you). Verbally **prompt** by modeling "Help me." You can also **prompt** by holding out your hand. If the child becomes frustrated but doesn't hand you the bag, give a verbal model (e.g., "I can help"). Immediately open the bag and give the child the desired object so he begins to associate coming to an adult for help with obtaining a desired object.

P38b

Treatment Objective: The child will request assistance from an adult.

Goal: The child will initiate use of appropriate gesture to obtain desired effect. (PG8)

Activity: I Need Help 2 **Expected age**: 15–18 months

Materials/Toys: tape player or CD player

Set the tape/CD player on floor and turn it on while using the verbal model "on." Allow the child to listen for a short period. When the child becomes engaged, turn the music off. Allow the child to attempt to turn the music on. When he is not able, ask, "What do you want?" or "Do you need help?" Wait for the child to indicate that he needs help (e.g., reaching for your hand, giving tape player to you). **Prompt** by holding out your hand or reaching toward the tape player. If the child becomes frustrated but doesn't gesture for help, turn on the tape player so he begins to associate coming to an adult for help with obtaining a desired object.

Activities Book
The Early Intervention Kit

P38c

Treatment Objective: The child will request assistance from an adult.

Goal: The child will initiate use of appropriate gesture to obtain desired effect. (PG8)

Activity: I Need Help 3   **Expected age**: 15–18 months

Materials: jar of bubbles

Open the bubbles and blow some for the child to pop. Replace the cap on the bubbles and hand the jar to the child. When he can't open it, ask, "Need help?" Wait for the child to indicate that he needs help (e.g., giving you the bottle). **Prompt** by taking the child's hand and placing it on the jar of bubbles. If the child gets frustrated, immediately open the container and let the child blow a bubble so he begins to associate coming to an adult for help with obtaining a desired object.

P38d

Treatment Objective: The child will request assistance from an adult.

Goal: The child will initiate use of appropriate gesture to obtain desired effect. (PG8)

Activity: I Need Help 4   **Expected age**: 15–18 months

Materials/Toys: clear plastic container with a lid you know the child can't open (e.g., screw top), treats to put inside the container (e.g., cereal O's, reinforcement toy)

Put a treat in a clear container with the lid on it in the view of the child. If the child doesn't pick up the container, give it to him. When the child has difficulty opening it, wait to see if the child will hand you the container or put your hand on the container. If not, **prompt** by saying, "Do you need help?" If the child still doesn't respond, **prompt** by holding out your hand and saying, "Want help?" Immediately open the container and give the child the desired object so he begins to associate coming to an adult for help with obtaining a desired object.

P38e

Treatment Objective: The child will request assistance from an adult.

Goal: The child will initiate use of appropriate gesture to obtain desired effect. (PG8)

Activity: I Need Help 5   **Expected age**: 15–18 months

Materials/Toys: child's favorite toy or blanket

Take the child's favorite toy (or blanket) and place it out of reach but still in plain view. Wait to see if the child requests your help. The child may solicit your help by pointing to the object, touching you, and/or requesting to be picked up in order to reach the object. If this doesn't happen, when the child gets frustrated, say to the child, "Do you want help?" If the child doesn't respond, **prompt** by holding out your hands to the child to offer to pick him up so he can reach the item. This will help the child learn that an adult can help him get a desired object.

P39

Treatment Objective: The child will play ball with an adult.

Goal: The child will engage in turn-taking routines. (PG5)

Activity: On a Roll   **Expected age**: 15–18 months

Materials/Toys: ball

Sit with the child on the floor, allowing a short distance between the two of you. Roll the ball toward the child. Stimulate language by saying, "Ball" each time you or the child touches the ball. If the child doesn't roll the ball back to you, **prompt** by saying, "Roll the ball to me" or "Your turn." You can also give a physical **prompt** by placing the child's hand on the ball and rolling it in your direction. (Note: You might have the parent sit next to the child to give the physical prompt.)

You might want to involve a parent or sibling in this activity. Let the child watch as you and the participant roll the ball back and forth to each other. Then give the child an opportunity to participate.

P40a

Treatment Objective: The child will put one object inside another.

Goals: The child will use objects (or imaginary objects) in appropriate play/self-care. (PG4)
The child will demonstrate other problem-solving skills. (PG9)

Activity: One Fish, Two Fish   **Expected age**: 15–18 months

Materials/Toys: plastic fish or bath toys, baby bathtub or plastic container

Sit with the child on the floor. Have him watch you play with the plastic fish or bath toys and a container. Use self-talk to describe your actions (e.g., "That's a big fish, I dropped my fish"). As soon as the child also begins to play with the fish, use parallel talk to describe the child's actions (e.g., "You put this fish on the floor"). Then ask the child to put the fish in the container. If the child doesn't pick up a fish to put in the container, **prompt** by taking his hand, holding a fish, and placing the fish in the container.

P40b

Treatment Objective: The child will put one object inside another.

Goals: The child will use objects (or imaginary objects) in appropriate play/self-care. (PG4)
The child will demonstrate other problem-solving skills. (PG9)

Activity: Scrambled Eggs   **Expected age**: 15–18 months

Materials/Toys: plastic eggs, a basket or any objects that will fit into a container/bowl

Sit with the child on the floor. Have him watch you play with the plastic eggs and basket. Use self-talk to describe your actions (e.g., "That's a big egg, I like this egg"). As soon as the child also begins to play with the eggs, use parallel talk to describe the child's actions (e.g., "You opened your egg"). Then ask the child to put the eggs in the basket. If the child doesn't pick up an egg to put in the basket, **prompt** by taking his hand, holding an egg, and putting the egg in the basket.

P41

Treatment Objective: The child will identify himself in a mirror.

Goals: The child will respond with appropriate gesture/action to sound, speech, and/or gesture. (PG7)
The child will demonstrate other problem-solving skills. (PG9)

Activity: Mirror, Mirror **Expected age:** 15–18 months

Materials/Toys: wall mirror

Take the child into the bathroom, or anywhere else that has a large mirror. Stand behind the child so you are supporting him and can manipulate his hands. Look in the mirror, use your name, and say, "Where is (your name)?" Wait for the child to point to you in the mirror. If he doesn't, **prompt** by pointing to yourself in the mirror and saying, "There's (your name)." Next say, "Where's (child's name)?" Wait for the child to respond. If he doesn't, **prompt** by taking his hand and saying, "There's (child's name)." Try this a few times until the child understands what you want him to do. If the child doesn't understand in the first session, have the parents continue during daily activities such as brushing teeth or getting dressed in the morning. You can also involve siblings and other family members in therapy and/or home practice.

P42a

Treatment Objective: The child will imitate doing housework.

Goal: The child will use objects (or imaginary objects) in appropriate play/self-care. (PG4)

Activity: Swipe and Wipe **Expected age:** 15–18 months

Materials/Toys: paper towels or washcloth

Work with the child to clean a low table that the child can reach. Give the child a sheet of paper towel or washcloth. Stimulate language by describing what you and the child are doing (e.g., "This table is dirty," "Wipe it off," "Let's clean it up"). **Prompt** with hand-over-hand assistance as needed.

P42b

Treatment Objective: The child will imitate doing housework.

Goal: The child will use objects (or imaginary objects) in appropriate play/self-care. (PG4)

Activity: Swept Away **Expected age:** 15–18 months

Materials/Toys: broom, dustpan with brush

Sweep the floor. Give the child the brush that goes with the dustpan so he can help you. Or let him hold the dustpan for you. Stimulate language by describing what you and the child are doing (e.g., "The floor is dirty, "Let's clean it up"). **Prompt** with hand-over-hand assistance as needed.

P42c

Treatment Objective: The child will imitate doing housework.

Goal: The child will use objects (or imaginary objects) in appropriate play/self-care. (PG4)

Activity: Dirty Dishes **Expected age:** 15–18 months

Materials/Toys: dishcloth, toy dishes, dishpan

Sit with the child on the floor. Let the child watch as you pretend to wash the dishes. Use self-talk to teach the child what you are doing (e.g., "The bowl's dirty," "I'm washing the bowl," "It's all clean"). Then give the child the cloth. If the child doesn't pretend to wash the dishes, **prompt** by saying, "You wash the dishes." You can also physically **prompt** the child by taking his hand and helping him wash the dishes.

P43

Treatment Objective: The child will pretend to play a musical instrument.

Goal: The child will use objects (or imaginary objects) in appropriate play/self-care. (PG4)

Activity: Toot, Toot **Expected age:** 18–21 months

Materials/Toys: two empty toilet paper or paper towel rolls

You and the child should each have a cardboard paper tube. Show the child how to make "musical" sounds using the tubes. "Toot" familiar songs or "toot" to a tape or CD of children's music. Move your fingers up and down on the roll like you are playing a clarinet. **Prompt** by saying, "You play too." **Prompt** with hand-over-hand as needed. For more fun, give cardboard tubes to family members so you can all play as a group.

P44

Treatment Objective: The child will imitate environmental noises.

Goal: The child will imitate vocalizations. (PG3)

Activity: Did You Hear That? **Expected age:** 18–21 months

Materials/Toys: none

While you are working with the child, listen for any naturally-occurring environmental noises. When you hear one of the noises, say, "Do you hear the _____?" and then imitate the sound. Then ask the child, "Can you _____ like a _____?" **Prompt** by modeling the sound again.

Possible sounds	What you would say
telephone	Can you ring like the phone?
dog barking	Can you bark like the dog?
birds chirping	Can you chirp like the birds?
doorbell	Can you "ding" like the doorbell?
baby crying	Can you cry like the baby?
car starting	Can you "vroom" like the car?
children laughing	Can you laugh like the kids?

P45a

Treatment Objective: The child will use two toys together in pretend play.

Goal: The child will use objects (or imaginary objects) in appropriate play/self care. (PG4)

Activity: Feed the Baby   **Expected age**: 18–21 months

Materials/Toys: baby doll, baby bottle or spoon, baby blanket

Sit on the floor with the child and have the doll, bottle or spoon, and blanket in front of you. While the child is watching, pick up the doll and say, "The baby is crying. I think she's hungry." Pick up the bottle (or spoon) and say, "I'm going to feed her." Put the bottle in the baby's mouth. Then hand the baby doll to the child saying, "You feed the baby." If the child doesn't respond by feeding the baby doll, **prompt** by taking his hands and helping him put the bottle in the baby's mouth. You can also show the child how to cover the baby when you tell him the baby is cold. **Prompt** by using hand-over-hand assistance to help the child cover the baby doll.

P45b

Treatment Objective: The child will use two toys together in pretend play.

Goal: The child will use objects (or imaginary objects) in appropriate play/self care. (PG4)

Activity: Old MacDonald   **Expected age**: 18–21 months

Materials/Toys: farm set that includes a tractor

Sit on the floor with the child. Put the farm set in front of you. Model using two toys by putting a farm animal (e.g., pig) on the tractor and saying, "The pig needs to go for a ride." Then ask the child to take another animal for a ride. Talk about what you are doing with the animals and demonstrate animal sounds to encourage language use. **Prompt** the use of two toys by handing the child two farm objects that can be used together (e.g., animal and tractor, food and animal).

P46a

Treatment Objective: The child will pretend to dance.

Goal: The child will respond with appropriate gesture/action to sound, speech, and/or gesture. (PG7)

Activity: Dancing Feet 1   **Expected age**: 18–21 months

Materials/Toys: music, wooden spoon, pan or tabletop

Play a slow, steady beat with the spoon on the pan or tabletop. Ask the child to participate by moving slowly up and down to the rhythm. Demonstrate as needed. Singing as you beat the spoon on the pan provides another fun addition to the game. You can sing real words, made-up words, or just hum along. **Prompt** by taking the child's hand and bouncing up and down together.

P46b

Treatment Objective: The child will pretend to dance.

Goal: The child will respond with appropriate gesture/action to sound, speech, and/or gesture. (PG7)

Activity: Dancing Feet 2   **Expected age**: 18–21 months

Materials/Toys: a toy that makes music or a radio/stereo

Turn on the music and tell the child, "Let's dance." Pick the child up. Hold the child in your arms, dancing together to music. Stimulate language by saying, "We're dancing" while moving. Stop suddenly and then start dancing again. Do this several times. Eventually you will feel the child jump in your arms to make you start dancing again. If the child doesn't move, **prompt** by saying, "Want to dance some more?"

P47

Treatment Objective: The child will push a stroller or shopping cart.

Goal: The child will use objects (or imaginary objects) in appropriate play/self-care. (PG4)

Activity: Time for a Stroll   **Expected age**: 21–24 months
(Note: The child must be mobile for this activity.)

Materials/Toys: child's own stroller or toy shopping cart, baby doll

Ask the child if he wants to go for a walk. Get the child's stroller or shopping cart and put a baby doll in it. Stimulate language by saying, "Let's take the baby for a walk." Put the stroller in front of the child and wait to see if he will start pushing. **Prompt** by saying, "Push the baby." You can also help the child put his hands on the stroller and push.

P48

Treatment Objective: The child will fly a toy airplane.

Goal: The child will use objects (or imaginary objects) in appropriate play/self-care. (PG4)

Activity: Let's Fly   **Expected age**: 21–24 months

Materials/Toys: toy airplane or paper airplane

Demonstrate to the child how to make the airplane take off and "fly" in the air. Stimulate language by saying, "Go up, up, up . . . fly." Hold onto the plane and move around the room (or actually let go of the plane/throw it). Then give the plane to the child, and ask, "Can you make it fly?" Model the action again or help the child move his hand with the plane as you say, "Fly."

P49a

Treatment Objective: The child will stack and assemble toys and objects.

Goals: The child will use objects (or imaginary objects) in appropriate play/self-care. (PG4)
The child will demonstrate other problem-solving skills. (PG9)

Activity: Box Builder **Expected age:** 21–24 months

Materials/Toys: blocks of graduated sizes or empty boxes of all shapes and sizes (e.g., cereal boxes, shoe boxes, gift boxes)

Sit on the floor with the child. Put the blocks or boxes in the middle of the floor. Build towers with larger blocks on the floor, stacking smaller blocks on top. Then knock the tower over. Stimulate language by saying, "Uh-oh, they fell down!" Put the largest block on the floor again and hand the child the block next in size. If the child doesn't start to stack the blocks, **prompt** by taking the child's hand with the block and helping him place it on the stack.

P49b

Treatment Objective: The child will stack and assemble toys and objects.

Goals: The child will use objects (or imaginary objects) in appropriate play/self-care. (PG4)
The child will demonstrate other problem-solving skills. (PG9)

Activity: In, In, In **Expected age:** 21–24 months

Materials/Toys: nesting cups or empty boxes of all shapes and sizes (e.g., cereal boxes, shoe boxes, gift boxes)

Sit on the floor with the child. Put the cups or boxes in the middle of the floor. Demonstrate how to put the cups together by choosing the correct size. You can even make mistakes on purpose. Try putting a big cup inside a smaller cup and saying, "Uh-oh! That doesn't fit!" Then take the cups apart and hand the child the largest cup and the cup of the next size. Stimulate language by saying, "Put it in" or "Put them together." If the child doesn't start to put the cups together, **prompt** by taking the child's hand with the smaller cup and helping him place it in the larger cup.

P50a

Treatment Objective: The child will sort objects.

Goals: The child will use objects (or imaginary objects) in appropriate play/self-care. (PG4)
The child will demonstrate other problem-solving skills. (PG9)

Activity: Piece-by-Piece **Expected age:** 21–24 months

Materials/Toys: two wooden board puzzles (e.g., animals, cars), bag, or forks and spoons

Mix up the puzzle pieces in the bag. Place the two puzzle boards on the floor in front of the child. Have the child take one puzzle piece out of the bag. Ask him if it goes with the animal or car puzzle and have him show you the correct board. If he doesn't show you, **prompt** by modeling the procedure, "This is a cow. It goes with the animal puzzle." Then place the piece on the correct board. Continue with the rest of the puzzle pieces. If using forks and spoons, start the activity by mixing the forks and spoons together in a pile. Pull out two spoons and put them in a separate pile. Pull out two forks and start a fork pile. Use self-talk to describe your actions (e.g., "These are both spoons. They go here"). Ask the child to reach in the large pile of utensils and get one. Then ask the child if the utensil he chose goes in the spoon or fork pile. If he doesn't show you, **prompt** by modeling the procedure.

P50b

Treatment Objective: The child will sort objects.

Goals: The child will use objects (or imaginary objects) in appropriate play/self-care. (PG4)
The child will demonstrate other problem-solving skills. (PG9)

Activity: That's Not a Car   **Expected age**: 21–24 months

Materials/Toys: toy cars, toy people, non-see-through bag, two small boxes (one with a car drawn in the bottom and one with a person drawn in the bottom); or several pairs of shoes from the child and another family member

Put the cars and toy people in the bag. Model the activity by taking an object out of the bag and saying, "It's a car. I'll put it in the box with the car." Have the child reach into the bag and take out one object. Tell the child "It's a car" or "It's a person," depending on what he has chosen. Then show him the two boxes, and ask him to put the object in the correct box. Continue to model this when you take a turn reaching into the bag. As you pull out an object, name it and say, "It's a car, so I'll put it with the cars." **Prompt** by putting the correct box a little closer as he decides which box to put the object he has chosen in.

If using shoes, start the activity by putting them all in one big pile. Pull out two of the child's shoes and put them in a separate pile. Say, "These are your shoes." Then pull out two adult shoes and start another pile. Use self-talk to describe your actions (e.g., "I'll put Mom's shoes over here"). Ask the child to reach into the pile of shoes and get one. Then ask the child if the shoe he chose goes in his pile of shoes or Mom's pile of shoes. If he doesn't show you, **prompt** by modeling the procedure.

P51

Treatment Objective: The child will match sounds to pictures of animals.

Goals: The child will respond with appropriate gesture/action to sound, speech and/or gesture. (PG7)
The child will demonstrate other problem-solving skills. (PG9)

Activity: Moo, Oink   **Expected age**: 21–24 months

Materials/Toys: pictures of animals (e.g., cow, duck, pig) or a See 'n Say with animals

Sit with the child on the floor or have the child seated in his high chair with the tray in place. For this activity, it is best to start with two or three pictures of animals. Show the child a picture and make the corresponding animal sound. Stimulate language by saying, "Look at the cow. The cow says, 'Moo.' " Repeat with all of the pictures. Then place two pictures in front of the child and make an animal sound. If the child doesn't point to or pick up the correct matching picture, **prompt** by saying, "Who says 'moo'?"

You can also physically **prompt** the child by taking his hand and touching the picture of the cow. Continue with the other animal pictures. (Note: A See 'n Say will make animal sounds. Ask the child to point to the matching animal.)

P52

Treatment Objective: The child will pretend to write.

Goal: The child will use objects (or imaginary objects) in appropriate play/self-care. (PG4)

Activity: Baby Shakespeare   **Expected age**: 24–27 months

Materials/Toys: paper, crayons or markers

While sitting at the table, tell the child that you need help writing a letter to someone in the child's family (e.g., Dad, Grandma). As you start to write, ask the child to write something so the person you are writing to will know the child helped. If the child has difficulty holding the crayon, assist by putting your hand over the child's hand as he holds the crayon. If the child doesn't pretend to write, **prompt** by saying, "Can you write?" or by taking his hand and helping him write/scribble.

P53

Treatment Objective: The child will pretend to talk on the phone.

Goal: The child will use objects (or imaginary objects) in appropriate play/self-care. (PG4)

Activity: Grandma's Calling   **Expected age**: 24–27 months

Materials/Toys: toy phone, baby doll

Tell the child his grandma (or someone else he likes to talk to on the phone) is calling. Pretend to talk to the child's grandmother. Hold the phone to your ear and say, "Hello, how are you?" Carry on a conversation with "Grandma," pausing as if you are listening part of the time. Then give the phone to the child and wait to see if he pretends to talk to Grandma. If the child doesn't talk into the phone, **prompt** by cueing him what to say (e.g., "Tell Grandma 'Hi'" or "Tell Grandma you love her"). Reinforce him when he does pretend to talk into the phone. You can also **prompt** by putting the phone to the doll's ear and using a doll's voice to talk to Grandma.

P54

Treatment Objective: The child will slap an adult's hand when asked to "Gimme Five."

Goal: The child will respond with appropriate gesture/action to sound, speech, and/or gesture. (PG7)

Activity: Good Job!   **Expected age**: 24–27 months

Materials/Toys: any toys/tasks

This activity needs to occur naturally during other activities. This might be any problem-solving activity (e.g., stacking rings, putting together puzzles) or any activity of daily living (e.g., finishing the targeted amount of food on his plate). When the child has completed the activity, stimulate language by saying, "That was a great job! Gimme five." Hold your hand out, palm up for the child to slap. If the child doesn't slap your hand, **prompt** by repeating, "Gimme five" and "Can you slap my hand?" If the child still doesn't slap your palm, further **prompt** by taking the child's hand and helping him slap your palm. This is a fun activity to involve other children (e.g., siblings, classmates) as they can model how to "give five."

P55a

Treatment Objective: The child will match shapes of toys.

Goals: The child will respond with appropriate gesture/action to sound, speech, and/or gesture. (PG7)
The child will demonstrate other problem-solving skills. (PG9)

Activity: Star, Circle, Square 1 **Expected age**: 27–30 months

Materials/Toys: shape sorter toy or items of different shapes (e.g., two of each shape: paper plate and jar lid for circle, block and CD case for square, envelope and sheet of paper for rectangle)

Sit on the floor with the child. Dump the shapes from the shape sorter onto the floor. Work with the child to put shapes into the sorter. If the child has trouble finding the right spot in the sorter, help him. Talk about how many sides the piece has and what it looks like. Have him find the correct side on the sorter. Stimulate language by saying, "Look, they are the same. They're the same shape." **Prompt** by helping the child move his hand and manipulate the block so it fits in the right hole. After helping the child with three or four shapes, he should begin to understand that he should look to find the appropriate hole to put the shape in.

If using items of different shapes, put them all in front of the child. Have him find the shapes that are the same. Model the procedure by matching two items of the same shape. Use self-talk to describe your actions (e.g., "This paper plate and this jar lid are the same shape. They are both circles"). Then ask the child to match two other shapes. If he doesn't, prompt by modeling the procedure again or by using hand-over-hand assistance to find matching shapes.

P55b

Treatment Objective: The child will match shapes of toys.

Goals: The child will respond with appropriate gesture/action to sound, speech, and/or gesture. (PG7)
The child will demonstrate other problem-solving skills. (PG9)

Activity: Star, Circle, Square 2 **Expected age**: 27–30 months

Materials/Toys: wooden puzzle with basic shapes

Sit on the floor with the child. Spread the puzzle pieces in front of you. Pick up a puzzle piece and ask, "Where does this circle go?" Let the child try to put it in the correct spot. If he has trouble, **prompt** by pointing to the right hole or by taking his hand and helping him put it in the correct spot. Stimulate language by saying, "The round one goes in the round hole" or "The square piece goes in the square hole." Show him how each puzzle piece fits in its spot on the board.

P55c

Treatment Objective: The child will match shapes of toys.

Goals: The child will respond with appropriate gesture/action to sound, speech, and/or gesture. (PG7)
The child will demonstrate other problem-solving skills. (PG9)

Activity: King's Castle   **Expected age**: 27–30 months

Materials/Toys: assorted shapes of wooden blocks

Sit with the child on the floor with the blocks spread out around you. As you build the castle, pick up a square block and ask the child to find another "square block." Stimulate language and **prompt** by saying, "Find one that is the same as this." If the child has trouble, **prompt** by finding one for him and holding the two together to explain how they are the same. You can also **prompt** by helping him pick up one that is the same shape. Do the same with other shapes. Switch roles and have the child choose a block for you to find the match.

P55d

Treatment Objective: The child will match shapes of toys.

Goals: The child will respond with appropriate gesture/action to sound, speech, and/or gesture. (PG7)
The child will demonstrate other problem-solving skills. (PG9)

Activity: Play Dough Fun   **Expected age**: 27–30 months

Materials/Toys: play dough, cookie cutters (e.g., circle, square), rolling pin

Sit at the kitchen table with the child and roll out the play dough so it's flat. Take a round cookie cutter and make a circle in the play dough. Then make a square, and then another shape. To simulate language, name the shapes as you go along. Point to a shape made of play dough and ask the child to make one just like it. Stimulate language by saying, "Make a square one like this one." If the child doesn't pick up the correct cookie cutter, **prompt** by handing him the correct cookie cutter and saying, "This one is the same. They are both square." Continue with other shapes.

P56

Treatment Objective: The child will match colors.

Goals: The child will respond with appropriate gesture/action to sound, speech, and/or gesture. (PG7)
The child will demonstrate other problem-solving skills. (PG9)

Activity: This One, That One   **Expected age**: 27–30 months

Materials/Toys: black and white blocks

Sit with the child on the floor or have him sit in his high chair with the tray in place. Spread several black and white blocks between you and the child. Let the child watch as you divide the blocks into a black group and a white group. Use language to describe what you are doing (e.g., "The white ones go in this pile"). Repeat a few times. Then remove all of the blocks. Place one black block and one white block in front of the child. Give the child another block and wait several seconds to see if the child will put the block in his hand with the matching color, as you have modeled. **Prompt** by saying, "Where is the black (or white) block?" If a verbal prompt is not effective, physically **prompt** the child by moving the child's hand with the block and placing it with its match. Give the child another block and repeat the activity until all blocks are in their respective piles.

P57a

Treatment Objective: The child will dramatize with a doll.

Goal: The child will use objects (or imaginary objects) in appropriate play/self-care. (PG4)

Activity: Bedtime for Baby   **Expected age**: 27–30 months

Materials/Toys: doll, blanket or towel

Sit with the child on the floor with the doll and the blanket or towel. Use self-talk as you pretend to put the doll down to sleep by saying, "The baby's tired. Night-night baby." Lay the doll on the floor and place the blanket over the baby. Then give the doll and the blanket to the child. **Prompt** by saying, "The baby's sleepy." If the child doesn't pretend to put the doll down to sleep, help the child lay the doll down. Repeat the routine.

P57b

Treatment Objective: The child will dramatize with a doll.

Goal: The child will use objects (or imaginary objects) in appropriate play/self-care. (PG4)

Activity: Baby's Hungry   **Expected age**: 27–30 months

Materials/Toys: plastic bowl, spoon, doll

Sit on the floor with the child and the doll, spoon, and bowl. Let the child watch you pretend to feed the doll. Then give the spoon to the child and see if he will pretend to feed the doll. **Prompt** by saying, "You feed the baby." Offer a physical **prompt** by taking the child's hand with the spoon and moving it toward the doll's mouth.

P58

Treatment Objective: The child will sort shapes.

Goals: The child will respond with appropriate gesture/action to sound, speech, and/or gesture. (PG7)
The child will demonstrate other problem-solving skills. (PG9)

Activity: Circle, Circle Everywhere   **Expected age**: 30–33 months

Materials/Toys: shapes from a shape sorter toy or a variety of plastic shapes (e.g., circles, squares, triangles)

Sit on the floor with the child and the shapes from the shape sorter toy. Mix up the shapes together. Model for the child that you want him to sort the shapes. Look through the pile and find a circle. Stimulate language by saying, "This one is round. I need to find the other round ones." As you look through the other shapes in the pile, stimulate language by saying, "Not a round one, not a round one . . . Here's another round one." Continue until you have sorted out all of the circles. Then pick out a square and ask the child to find the others like it. As the child looks through the pile, stimulate language by saying, "That's not a square, that one is a square." **Prompt** by touching the shape the child is looking for. After the child has sorted all of the squares, continue with different shapes.

P59

Treatment Objective: The child will stack rings in the correct order.

Goals: The child will respond with appropriate gesture/action to sound, speech, and/or gesture. (PG7)
The child will demonstrate other problem-solving skills. (PG9)

Activity: Big, Bigger, Biggest   **Expected age:** 30–33 months

Materials/Toys: stacking toy in which the things to stack are graduated in size (e.g., stacking rings)

Take apart the stacking toy one piece at a time. Stimulate language by saying, "I'll take off this little one. Next I'll take off this one; it's a little bit bigger. Then I'll take off this one; it's bigger. And here's the last one. It's the biggest." Then hand the child all of the stacking pieces to see if he can put it back together. **Prompt** by putting the biggest item closest to the child, then the next size, etc. You can **prompt** even further by handing the items to the child one at a time in the correct order. Model the activity for the child by placing the pieces back together yourself, using language to describe what you are doing. Or, you can purposely choose the wrong size and comment on how it doesn't fit.

P60a

Treatment Objective: The child will play house.

Goal: The child will use objects (or imaginary objects) in appropriate play/self-care. (PG4)

Activity: Dollhouse Time   **Expected age:** 33–36 months

Materials/Toys: dollhouse with male and female adult and children dolls

Sit with the child in front of the dollhouse. Tell the child that he is going to be the daddy and you will be the mommy (or let the child choose his role). Create role-playing situations such as dinnertime, bath time, or naptime during which the child has to pretend to be the mommy or daddy to the doll. If he has difficulty, provide a model using one of the adult dolls.

P60b

Treatment Objective: The child will play house.

Goal: The child will use objects (or imaginary objects) in appropriate play/self-care. (PG4)

Activity:	Let's Have a Tea Party	**Expected age**: 33–36 months

Materials/Toys: dress-up clothes (e.g., Mom's old dress, Dad's shirt, a tie), toy tea set, toy dishes, favorite dolls or stuffed animals

Help the child dress up in the adult clothes. Tell him that you and he are going to have some friends over for a tea party. Talk about who you want to invite over to the tea and let him set the table using toy dishes. Sit one or two of his favorite dolls or stuffed animals at the table. Explain to the child that he needs to serve the guests their tea and cookies. Model language by saying things like, "Does Mr. Bunny want some tea?" or "Let's let Mr. Monkey have another cookie."

P60c

Treatment Objective: The child will play house.

Goal: The child will use objects (or imaginary objects) in appropriate play/self-care. (PG4)

Activity:	Let's Play House	**Expected age**: 33–36 months

Materials/Toys: child-sized toy stove, pots, pans, broom, table, and dishes or real items from around the house

Tell the child you are going to play house. (Note: The children often enjoy being able to decide if they will be the mommy or the daddy, though these traditional roles are often blurred in many families.) Set the scene by telling the child what aspect of "playing house" you'll engage in. Some choices include cooking, setting the table, washing dishes, sweeping the floor, cleaning up the toys, and giving the baby a bath. It might also include outside activities like raking leaves or mowing the grass. If the child doesn't readily engage in play with the objects, **prompt** using language such as, "I wonder if we should put the bowls on the table? Should we put the bread in the oven?" or "If we could find the broom, we could sweep this dirty floor." Try to avoid giving specific directions. You can even **prompt** by using very general comments such as, "The kids are hungry. What should we do?" to see if the child will begin to cook, or "How did this house get to be such a mess?" If the child needs a further **prompt**, begin the activity using language to describe what you are doing (e.g., "The kids are hungry. I guess I'll cook some soup for lunch").

P61

Treatment Objective: The child will sort colors.

Goals: The child will respond with appropriate gesture/action to sound, speech, and/or gesture. (PG7)
The child will demonstrate other problem-solving skills. (PG9)

Activity:	Pretty Colors	**Expected age**: 33–36 months

Materials/Toys: three of each color crayon or anything with colors (e.g., plastic cups)

Show the child a crayon or plastic cup and name the color. Then ask him if he can put all the red items together. Stimulate language by describing the child's actions (e.g., "No, that one isn't the same color," or "Yes, that's red, just like this one." Go through all of the colors. Continue this activity until the skill is mastered. **Prompt** by pushing items of the target color closer to the child or by tapping each item of the target color.

Goals and Treatment Objectives for Receptive Language Skills (Chapter 8)

Long-term goal

The child will exhibit optimal receptive language skills.

Short-term goals

RG1 The child will respond to speech.

RG2 The child will understand single words from a variety of word classes.

RG3 The child will follow simple one-step commands accompanied by gestures/context clues.

RG4 The child will follow simple one-step commands without gesture/context support.

RG5 The child will follow two-step (and three-step) commands.

RG6 The child will understand simple questions.

Receptive Ages of Acquisition/Treatment Objectives

Expected age of development	Short-term goal (RG)	Treatment Objectives	Activities to help achieve treatment objectives
3–6 months	1 2 1	Recognizes own name Responds to "no" about half the time Smiles in response to pleasant speech	R1 R2 R3
6–9 months	2 2 3	Responds to "no" most of the time Moves toward or searches for named family member Responds to request to "Come here"	R4 R5 R6
9–12 months	2 4 4 4 3 2, 4 2	Gives object in response to verbal request Performs a routine activity in response to verbal request Gestures in response to verbal request (e.g., "Wanna come up?") Verbalizes or vocalizes in response to verbal request Participates in speech routine games (e.g., "So big") Identifies two body parts on self or doll Understands some action words	R7 R8 R9 a, b R10 a, b R11 R12 R13 a, b
12–15 months	4 2, 4 2, 4 2, 6 2, 4 2, 4	Follows one-step commands during play May give kiss on request Responds to "Give me" while holding object Points to two action words in pictures Understands some prepositions Identifies three body parts on self or doll	R14 a, b R15 R16 R17 R18 R19

continued on next page

Expected age of development	Short-term goal (RG)	Treatment Objectives	Activities to help achieve treatment objectives
15–18 months	2, 4	Identifies six body parts or clothing items on doll	R20
	2, 4	Shows or points to an object on request	R21
	2, 4	Finds familiar objects not in sight	R22
	2, 4	Completes two separate one-step requests with one object	R23
	2, 4	Chooses two familiar objects upon request	R24
	2, 4	Identifies object by category	R25
	2, 6	Finds "baby" in picture	R26
	2	Understands 50 words	R27
18–21 months	2, 4	Identifies four body parts and clothing items on self	R28
	3	Follows commands to "Sit down," "Come here," or "Give me" with gesture	R29
	2, 6	Chooses five familiar objects on request	R30
	2	Understands meaning of action words	R31
	2, 4	Understands words for absent objects by locating them	R32
	2, 4	Identifies pictures when named	R33
	2, 4	Demonstrates some understanding of personal pronouns (e.g., "Give it to her.")	R34 a, b
21–24 months	4	Puts away toy on request	R35
	2, 4	Chooses one object from a group of five upon verbal request	R36
	2, 4	Identifies body parts on caregiver or doll	R37
	5	Follows two-step related command	R38
24–27 months	2, 4	Points to four action words in pictures	R39
	2, 4	Understands concept of *one*	R40
	2, 4	Understands size concepts	R41
	2, 4	Points to three or more small body parts on self or caregiver	R42
27–30 months	6	Responds to simple questions	R43
	2, 6	Identifies clothing on self or caregiver	R44
	2, 4	Understands prepositions *on*, *in*, *under*, *out of*	R45
30–33 months	2, 4	Understands five common action words	R46
	5	Follows two-step unrelated commands	R47 a, b
	2, 4	Understands concepts of *one* and *all*	R48
	6	Answers *yes/no* questions correctly	R49 a, b
	6	Understands function of objects	R50
	2, 4	Understands *big* and *little*	R51 a, b
33–36 months	5	Follows three-step unrelated command	R52
	6	Responds to *wh-* questions	R53 a, b, c
	4	Identifies parts of an object	R54 a, b

R1

Treatment Objective: The child will recognize her own name.

Goal: The child will respond to speech. (RG1)

Activity: Name Game **Expected age**: 3–6 months

Materials/Toys: flashlight or musical toy

Place the child on the floor. Hold a flashlight or musical toy and call out different names (e.g., Mom's name, dog's name). Then call the child's name. If she looks at you, clap and say, "That's a good girl, (child's name)." If the child needs a prompt when you say her name, be overdramatic (e.g., clap, interact with her, turn on light/toy).

R2

Treatment Objective: The child will respond to "No" about half the time.

Goal: The child will understand single words from a variety of word classes. (RG2)

Activity: No-No **Expected age**: 3–6 months
(Note: This activity can be used again at 6-9 months. See R4, page 46.)

Materials/Toys: none

Teaching a child to respond to "No" becomes important once she is able to move around and can reach and hold objects. When the child is doing something she's not supposed to do or that is dangerous (e.g., putting something small in her mouth), tell the child "No" with a firm voice and slightly louder volume than normal. If you don't want to raise your voice, use the same intonation every time you tell the child "No." For example, you could always use a strong, falling inflection to gain the child's attention. If the child doesn't stop, **prompt** understanding of the word by physically assisting the child (e.g., moving her hand with the small object in it away from her mouth and saying "No mouth"). Whichever technique you choose, it's best to take advantage of naturally-occurring events in the child's day rather than setting up artificial circumstances.

Additional Suggestion for Parents

When the child reaches for forbidden objects (e.g., vase, TV remote), say, "No-no, that's not a toy," or "No-no, the vase is Mommy's." Or when the child is in her high chair with food on the tray, stimulate language by saying, "(Child's name) eat (name of food item)." When the child tires of eating and begins to throw the food or play with the food, say, "No-no. Eat lunch," "No-no. All done," or "No-no. Are you all done?"

R3

Treatment Objective: The child will smile in response to pleasant speech.

Goal: The child will respond to speech. (RG1)

Activity: Listen and Smile **Expected age**: 3–6 months

Materials/Toys: none

Place the child in an infant seat or on your lap facing you so you can get close to her face. Use lots of intonation as you talk to her about pleasant things (e.g., "What a sweet baby," "You are so quiet today," or "(Child's name) is a pretty girl"). Pause after each utterance and wait for the child to smile. **Prompt** by smiling broadly as you talk to the child.

R4

Treatment Objective: The child will respond to "No" most of the time.

Goal: The child will understand single words from a variety of word classes. (RG2)

Activity: No-No   **Expected age**: 6–9 months

Materials/Toys: none

See R2, page 45, for the activity. In this activity, however, the child should respond to "No" the majority of the time.

R5

Treatment Objective: The child will move toward or search for a named family member.

Goal: The child will understand single words from a variety of word classes. (RG2)

Activity: Where's Mommy (Daddy)?   **Expected age**: 6–9 months

Materials/Toys: any toy that will engage the child's attention

If the child is mobile, let her sit or lie on the floor so she's able to move freely. If she's not mobile, have her sit in an infant seat or high chair. Instruct a family member to be in the vicinity, just not seated directly in front of the child. Begin to engage the child in play with the toy. When the child is engaged, ask, "Where's Mommy (or Daddy)?" If the child doesn't look or move toward the named family member, **prompt** by repeating the question and adding, "Let's show Mommy (or Daddy) what we're playing with. Find Mommy (or Daddy)." You can further **prompt** by pointing to the named family member or having the family member wave and say, "Here I am."

R6

Treatment Objective: The child will respond to the request to "Come here."

Goal: The child will follow simple one-step commands accompanied by gestures/context clues. (RG3)

Activity: Follow the Ribbon   **Expected age**: 6–9 months
(Note: The child must be mobile for this activity.)

Materials/Toys: yarn or colored string, music, child's favorite toys

Seat yourself and the child on the floor on opposite sides of the room. Place a long piece of yarn or string on the floor that goes from you to the child. Then say, "Come here" to the child. If the child doesn't begin to crawl, **prompt** by repeating the command and gesturing with your hand while slowly pulling the yarn toward you to encourage the infant to follow it. It can also help to have children's music playing behind you or to put some of the child's favorite toys in front of you at your end of the string. You can further **prompt** the child by tying one of her favorite toys to the end of the yarn and pulling it slowly in front of her as she crawls.

R7

Treatment Objective: The child will give a familiar object in response to a verbal request.

Goal: The child will understand single words from a variety of word classes. (RG2)

Activity: Gimme!   **Expected age**: 9–12 months

Materials/Toys: three or four toys or objects the child is very familiar with

Seat yourself across from the child on the floor with the toys/objects between you. Allow the child to play with the items for a few minutes. Then ask the child to give you one of the items by naming it (e.g., "Give me the car"). If the child doesn't respond to your verbal request, ask her again. Give a physical **prompt** by taking the child's hand and helping her pick up the car and place it in your hand. Continue to ask the child to give you different objects by naming them. Use the physical prompt until the child completes the verbal request independently. Keep in mind that some children don't like to give up an item they're holding. In these instances, it will help to immediately return the item to the child after she has given it to you.

R8

Treatment Objective: The child will perform a routine activity in response to a verbal request.

Goal: The child will follow simple one-step commands without gesture/context support. (RG4)

Activity: Putting Away Toys   **Expected age**: 9–12 months

Materials/Toys: toys

Sit on the floor with the child near several toys. Ask the child to pick up the toys. If the child doesn't begin picking up the toys, start picking them up yourself. Use self-talk to stimulate language (e.g., "Time to clean up. I'm putting away the toys"). If the child doesn't begin to help, give a verbal **prompt** (e.g., "It's your turn to clean up" or "You help pick up the toys"). You can also physically **prompt** by taking her hand and placing it on a toy. You can even help the child pick up the toy. Offer praise when the child performs the routine to provide reinforcement.

================ R9a ================

Treatment Objective: The child will gesture in response to a verbal request.

Goal: The child will follow simple one-step commands without gesture/context support. (RG4)

Activity: Want One? **Expected age**: 9–12 months

Materials/Toys: snack or drink

Put a snack or drink where the child can see it, but can't reach it. Ask, "Do you want a cookie?" or "Does (child's name) want a cookie?" If the child doesn't reach toward the cookie, **prompt** by modeling the reaching gesture and encouraging the child to imitate it.

================ R9b ================

Treatment Objective: The child will gesture in response to a verbal request.

Goal: The child will follow simple one-step commands without gesture/context support. (RG4)

Activity: Come Up **Expected age**: 9–12 months

Materials/Toys: none

Stand facing the child, who can also be standing on the floor, or who can be in a playpen, crib, or swing. Ask the child, "Want to come up?" If the child doesn't respond by holding her hands in the air, **prompt** by holding out your hands to the child. You can also **prompt** by raising the child's arms for her and then picking her up. Continue practicing this activity when you have the opportunity until the child begins raising her arms spontaneously.

(Note: If the child has an older sibling, demonstrate this activity with the older child while the younger child watches. You shouldn't have to lift the older child's arms.)

================ R10a ================

Treatment Objective: The child will vocalize or verbalize in response to a verbal request.

Goal: The child will follow simple one-step commands without gesture/context support. (RG4)

Activity: Moo, Oink **Expected age**: 9–12 months

Materials/Toys: toy tractor, toy farm animals (e.g., cow, pig)

Sit on the floor with the child or have her sit in a high chair with the tray in place. Engage the child in playing with the animals and the tractor. While playing, make each animal sound and the tractor sound several times. Then ask the child to make one of the animal sounds (e.g., "What does the cow say?"). If the child doesn't respond, verbally **prompt** the child (e.g., "The cow says 'moo.' You say 'moo' "). Offer praise when the child makes the animal sound to reinforce the child's vocalization. The child's production may not be an exact replica of what you have modeled, but an approximation of the vowel in the word (e.g., "ooo" for "moo").

R10b

Treatment Objective: The child will vocalize or verbalize in response to a verbal request.

Goal: The child will follow simple one-step commands without gesture/context support. (RG4)

Activity: Vrroom, Vrroom	**Expected age**: 9–12 months

Materials/Toys: toy cars

Sit on the floor with the child or have her sit in a high chair with the tray in place. Engage the child in playing with the cars. As the child is pushing a car, make car sounds (e.g., "vroom-vroom, beep-beep"). Then ask the child to say "vroom." If the child makes some attempt to verbalize or vocalize, offer praise and then **prompt** for more sounds. If the child doesn't attempt to vocalize, verbally **prompt** her again (e.g., "You say 'vroom.'" or "How does the car go?"). You may also physically **prompt** the child by lightly tapping her lips or chin as you say one of the car sounds.

R11

Treatment Objective: The child will participate in speech routine games.

Goal: The child will follow simple one-step commands accompanied by gestures/context clues. (RG3)

Activity: Peek-a-Boo/Pat-a-Cake	**Expected age**: 9–12 months

Materials/Toys: none

Seat the child in your lap facing you or in her high chair with the tray in place. Begin to demonstrate peek-a-boo to the child. If the child doesn't attempt to cover her face or vocalize, give her a verbal **prompt** (e.g., "You play peek-a-boo" or "Your turn"). You may also physically **prompt** the child by using her hands to help her cover and uncover her eyes. To encourage verbalization, pause after you uncover your eyes to give the child an opportunity to provide the verbalization.

Model pat-a-cake for the child and encourage her to participate. You can physically **prompt** the child by taking her hands and doing the motions. Pause intermittently to allow the child to provide the verbalization. Praise the child when she participates in the game.

R12

(Note: This activity is used again in R19, 20, 28, 37, and 42. The difference is in the number of body parts and/or clothing items the child is expected to identify and whether the child is to identify the body parts and clothing items on a doll, herself, someone else, etc.)

Treatment Objective: The child will identify two body parts on herself or on a doll.

Goals: The child will understand single words from a variety of word classes. (RG2)
The child will follow simple one-step commands without gesture/context support. (RG4)

Activity: Body Parts	**Expected age**: 9–12 months

Materials/Toys: doll

Sit on the floor with the doll and the child and say, "The baby is dirty. Let's get her ready for her bath." Begin to take the doll's clothes off. As you expose a body part (e.g., feet when the shoes come off) say, "Here are the baby's feet. Show me your feet." If the child doesn't point to her feet, **prompt** by taking her hands and helping her touch her feet. Repeat this sequence with several other body parts. At this age, the child will probably only know "big" body parts like feet, hands, tummy, and head rather than small body parts like eyes and fingers. As the child gets older, you can introduce these smaller body parts as well as elbow and knee.

R13a

Treatment Objective: The child will understand some action words. (Note: See pages 93 and 94 in the *Therapy Guide* for suggestions of early verbs and protoverbs to teach.)

Goal: The child will understand single words from a variety of word classes. (RG2)

Activity: Wanna Eat?   **Expected age:** 9–12 months
(Note: This activity describes "Wanna Eat?," but can also be done with "Wanna Go?" when getting ready to go for a walk or a ride (e.g., in stroller, on swing), and for "Wanna Sleep?" when the child is going to take a nap or when putting a baby doll to bed.)

Materials/Toys: food/bottle

Teaching vocabulary is best done in natural contexts. For example, when it's time to eat a meal or a snack, ask the child, "Do you want to eat?" The child may respond by moving toward the high chair, putting out her arms to be picked up, or showing increased movement. If the child doesn't do one of these things, **prompt** comprehension of the word by using a manual sign for *eat* and pointing to the food/bottle. You can also use the word *eat* during play, when feeding a doll, stuffed animal, or puppet. Stimulate language by saying, "I think the cow wants to eat. He's hungry."

R13b

Treatment Objective: The child will understand some action words. (Note: See pages 93 and 94 in the *Therapy Guide* for suggestions of early verbs and protoverbs to teach.)

Goal: The child will understand single words from a variety of word classes (RG2).

Activity: Come Here   **Expected age:** 9–12 months
(Note: The child must be mobile for this activity.)

Materials/Toys: yarn or colored string, music, child's favorite toys

Seat yourself and the child on the floor on opposite sides of the room. Place a long piece of yarn or string on the floor that goes from you to the child. Then say, "Come here" to the child. If the child doesn't begin to crawl, **prompt** by repeating the command and gesturing with your hand while slowly pulling the yarn toward you to encourage the child to follow it. It can also help to have children's music playing behind you or to put some of the child's favorite toys in front of you at your end of the string. You can further **prompt** by tying one of the child's favorite toys to the end of the yarn and pulling it slowly in front of her as she crawls.

R14a

Treatment Objective: The child will follow one-step commands during play.

Goal: The child will follow simple one-step commands without gesture/context support. (RG4)

Activity: Wash the Baby   **Expected age**: 12–15 months
(Note: Although this activity is similar to R12, the treatment objectives differ.)

Materials/Toys: doll, real or toy shampoo, soap, baby bathtub or large bowl, baby hairbrush, rubber duck, small towel, washcloth

You can either give the doll a pretend or real bath for this activity. Sit on the kitchen or bathroom floor with the child and say, "The baby is dirty. Let's give her a bath." Have all of the materials on the floor around you and say, "Put the baby in the bathtub, please." If the child doesn't respond, physically **prompt** by repeating the command and taking the child's hands to help her put the baby in the bathtub. Give the child the washcloth and say, "We need soap. Get the soap, please." Then say, "Let's wash the baby's feet." If the child has trouble, take her hands to assist her. Give several one-step commands during this activity (e.g., "Get the shampoo," "Wash the baby's hair," "Dry off the baby," "Give me the baby").

Begin to take the doll's clothes off. As you expose a body part (e.g., feet when the shoes come off) say, "Here are the baby's feet. Show me your feet." If the child doesn't point to her feet, you can physically **prompt** by taking her hands and helping her touch her feet. Repeat this sequence with several other body parts. At this age, the child will probably only know "big" body parts like feet, hands, tummy, and head, rather than small body parts like eyes and fingers. As the child gets older, you can introduce these smaller body parts as well as parts like elbow and knee.

R14b

Treatment Objective: The child will follow one-step commands during play.

Goal: The child will follow simple one-step commands without gesture/context support. (RG4)

Activity: Picnic Time   **Expected age**: 12–15 months

Materials/Toys: dolls and/or stuffed animals, toy dishes, play food

Tell the child that you are going to have a picnic with the dolls and/or stuffed animals. Sit on the floor with the dolls/animals in a circle around you and the child. Ask the child to give each "person" at the picnic a bowl, then a cup, and then a spoon. If the child has difficulty completing these one-step commands, repeat each command and physically **prompt** by taking her hands and manipulating the objects according to the command. Here are some other one-step commands you can give the child during this activity:

Give the baby a drink.	Give one to the bear/doll.
Stir the soup.	Take a bite.
Give me a cup (or some other object).	Give the bear/baby a bite.

R15

Treatment Objective: The child may give a kiss on request.

Goals: The child will understand single words from a variety of word classes. (RG2)
The child will follow simple one-step commands without gesture/context support. (RG4)

Activity: Give Me a Kiss   **Expected age:** 12–15 months

Materials/Toys: dolls or stuffed animals

Sit on the floor with the child as she is playing with dolls/stuffed animals. Begin role-playing with the dolls, taking two of them and saying, "Give her a kiss" while you manipulate the two dolls kissing. Do this a couple of times and then say, "Now you give the doll a kiss." If the child does not respond, **prompt** by putting the doll up to her cheek and making a kissing noise. Next say, "Give me a kiss." If the child doesn't kiss you, **prompt** by repeating the command and leaning over so your cheek is close to her mouth.

R16

Treatment Objective: The child will respond to "Give me" while holding the object.

Goals: The child will understand single words from a variety of word classes. (RG2)
The child will follow simple one-step commands without gesture/context support. (RG4)

Activity: Sharing Time   **Expected age:** 12–15 months

Materials/Toys: blocks or other small items, a box/container to hold the items

Sit on the floor with the child with the box/container between you. Arrange the blocks or other small items close to the child, but not within your reach. This makes asking the child for a block more natural than if the blocks are within your reach.

As the child is playing with the blocks, say, "Give me a block." (It's okay if the child is putting the blocks in the box as she is playing with them.) **Prompt** by pointing at one of the blocks. You can also **prompt** by using your other hand to tap the palm of your outstretched hand as you say, "Give me a block." Physically **prompt** by taking the child's hand (with the block) and placing it in your outstretched hand. When the child releases the block, praise her and thank her. Immediately give the block back to the child so she does not become upset. If you don't think the child minds you having the block, drop it in the box and clap for this accomplishment. Continue playing with the child, dropping some blocks in the box and periodically saying to the child, "Give me a block" so you can drop one in too.

To make this activity a little more demanding, try it when the child is holding a single toy (i.e., not one of many blocks). After the child gives you the toy she was holding, replace it with another toy. It's important that the other toys be out of the child's sight and that you don't offer one toy in exchange for what she was holding. If you do that, the child may not be responding to your command to "Give me," but rather just trading one toy for another that looks more interesting.

(Note: This activity works best when the child is playing with multiple items and doesn't have to give up the only one she has when you ask her to "give me.")

R17

Treatment Objective: The child will point to two action words in pictures.

Goals: The child will understand single words from a variety of word classes. (RG2)
The child will understand simple questions. (RG6)

Activity: Library Time   **Expected age:** 12–15 months

Materials/Toys: books that have examples of different action words

While looking at books with the child, ask her to show you the person/animal that is doing the action (e.g., "Who is kicking?" "Who is sleeping?"). If the child is able to do so, move on to another action word. If she cannot do this, **prompt** by pointing to the picture and labeling the action. You could also physically **prompt** by helping the child point to the target action.

Books that are good for this activity have clear pictures of at least two actions on the same page. If there is only one action occurring on the page, there is no way to determine if the child understands the action word you have used. Here are some suggested books:

Babies by Gyo Fujikawa
Carl's Birthday by Alexandra Day
Cat's Play by Lisa Campbell Ernst
Chester's Way by Kevin Henkes
D. W.'s Guide to Preschool by Marc Brown
I Love You Because You Are You by Liza Baker
I Used to Be the Baby by Robin Ballard
Jesse Bear, What Will You Wear? by Nancy White Carlstrom
Jessica by Kevin Henkes
Only You by Rosemary Wells
There is a Big, Beautiful World Out There by Nancy Carlson
What Mommies Do Best by Laura Numeroff

If the child is having difficulty with this activity, you may need to first use easier books that feature only one action per page. **Prompt** the child by pointing to the picture and labeling the action. You could also physically **prompt** by helping the child point to the target action. When the child has mastered this task, then move on to books that feature more than one action per page. Some easier books you might consider reading are:

Max Drives Away by Rosemary Wells
Sam Loves Kisses by Yves Got
Show Me! by Tom Tracey
Wibbly Pig Likes Bananas by Mick Inkpen

R18

Treatment Objective: The child will understand some prepositions.

Goals: The child will understand single words from a variety of word classes. (RG2)
The child will follow simple one-step commands without gesture/context support. (RG4)

Activity: Up, Down, In, and Out   **Expected age:** 12–15 months

Materials/Toys: doll or stuffed animal, furniture the item will fit under/on; or toy cars, blocks, and boxes for pretend garages that the cars can fit in

Give the doll or stuffed animal to the child to play with. Then give the child directions that include simple prepositions (e.g., "Put the doll under the chair," "Put the doll on the floor"). If the child is unable to perform the activities, **prompt** by modeling the requests/prepositions. You can also **prompt** by touching where you want the object to go.

If you use cars, give the child directions that include simple prepositions (e.g., "Put the car in the garage," "Put the car on the garage," "Put the car under a block").

R19

Treatment Objective: The child will identify three body parts on herself or on a doll.

Goals: The child will understand single words from a variety of word classes. (RG2)
The child will follow simple one-step commands without gesture/context support. (RG4)

Activity: Body Parts **Expected age:** 12–15 months

Materials/Toys: doll

See R12, pages 49–50 for the activity. At this age, the child will probably only know big body parts like feet, hands, tummy, and head rather than smaller body parts like eyes and fingers. As the child gets older, introduce these smaller body parts, as well as elbow and knee.

R20

Treatment Objective: The child will identify six body parts or clothing on a doll.

Goals: The child will understand single words from a variety of word classes. (RG2).
The child will follow simple one-step commands without gesture/context support. (RG4)

Activity: Body Parts/Clothing **Expected age:** 15–18 months

Materials/Toys: doll with removable clothing

See R12, pages 49–50, for the activity. At this age the child will know big body parts like feet, hands, tummy, and head, but she may also be able to identify some smaller body parts like eyes, nose, and fingers. Use this activity to introduce additional body parts, as well as clothing items (e.g., shirt, socks, shoes, hat).

R21

Treatment Objective: The child will show or point to an object on request.

Goals: The child will understand single words from a variety of word classes. (RG2)
The child will follow simple one-step commands without gesture/context support. (RG4)

Activity: Label This, Label That **Expected age:** 15–18 months

Materials/Toys: toys

While playing, ask the child to show you or point to a familiar toy (e.g., "Show me the _____"). If the child does not do so, provide a model by pointing or handing the desired object to the child and saying, "Here's the _____." Label the object as you give it or point it out to the child. **Prompt** by moving the target object closer to the child so that it is the logical choice. For example, if there are three toys on the floor (e.g., ball, baby, book), move the book slightly closer to the child and then say, "Show me the book" or "Point to the book."

A slightly more difficult command for some children is "Give me the _____." This is harder because the child may not want to release the object. While playing, hold out *your* hand and say, "Give me the _____." If the child chooses the right object but doesn't give it to you, put your hands on the object and take it briefly, saying, "You give me the _____." Then quickly return the object to the child.

R22

Treatment Objective: The child will find familiar objects not in sight.

Goals: The child will understand single words from a variety of word classes. (RG2)
The child will follow simple one-step commands without gesture/context support. (RG4)

Activity: Hide and Seek Toys   **Expected age**: 15–18 months

Materials/Toys: toys or objects the child is familiar with (e.g., book, ball, car, cup, bottle, shoe, blanket)

Sit on the floor with the child and play with a familiar toy or object that the child seems to know the name of (e.g., a ball). Then switch and play with a different toy. When the child is not looking, put the ball somewhere out of her sight (e.g., under a blanket, in a box, behind your back). Then ask the child, "Where's the ball? Get the ball." You may need to remove the toy the child is currently playing with in order for her to be interested enough to look for the ball.

If the child is mobile, you can also ask her to find toys or objects that you have not been playing with. Perhaps the child has something that you routinely play with together, such as books. Begin the session playing with something else. Then say, "Get the books. Let's read some books."

R23

Treatment Objective: The child will complete two separate requests with one object.

Goals: The child will understand single words from a variety of word classes. (RG2)
The child will follow simple one-step commands without gesture/context support. (RG4)

Activity: Can You Do Two?   **Expected age**: 15–18 months

Materials/Toys: socks, shoes

Lay out an article of clothing that the child can put on herself or can put on with your help. For example, place a pair of the child's socks where she can see them. Ask the child to bring you her socks or say, "Go get your socks." When she brings them to you say, "Now put on the socks." (Note: The child has completed two requests with one object and is learning a routine, so the next time you say, "Go get your socks," she will know that the next step is to put them on.) If the child is unable to put on her socks by herself, you might ask, "Do you want me to help you put on your socks?"

You could also practice commands by asking the child to throw something in the trash (e.g., "Pick up the paper. Now put it in the trash can.") or to use the TV remote (e.g., "Please get the remote. Now give it to Mommy/put it on the table/turn on the TV").

R24

Treatment Objective: The child will choose two familiar objects upon request.

Goals: The child will understand single words from a variety of word classes. (RG2)
The child will follow simple one-step commands without gesture/context support (RG4)

Activity: This and That   **Expected age:** 15–18 months

Materials/Toys: various toys or items that are familiar to the child, a bag to hold the toys

Present a variety of toys/items to the child. During play, ask the child to give you two toys. If the child does not choose the items you've requested, **prompt** by reaching for the two named toys yourself. As you do, say, "Here are the ____ and the ____." Physically **prompt** by helping the child pick up the two named items.

To make this a more difficult activity, place three or four toys in the bag, labeling the toys as you go. Shake the bag to mix the toys and to cause excitement for the child. Open the bag and tell the child to find two of the toys (e.g., "Find the ____ and the ____"). If the child does not choose the named items, **prompt** by reaching into the bag and pulling them out. Then say, "Here's the ____ and here's the ____." Put the items back in the bag and repeat the direction.

R25

Treatment Objective: The child will identify an object by its category.

Goals: The child will understand single words from a variety of word classes. (RG2)
The child will follow simple one-step commands without gesture/context support. (RG4)

Activity: Toy, Toy, Not a Toy   **Expected age:** 15–18 months

Materials/Toys: a bag, several toys, other types of items (e.g., clothes, cups)

Put all of the materials in the bag and sit on the floor with the child. Tell the child that your bag has some toys in it, but it also has things in it that are not toys. Tell the child that you are going to find the toys. Take some toys out of the bag one at a time. As you take each one out, say, "Here's a toy. It's a ____." Let the child examine/play with each one. After a while, take one of the other items out of the bag. Use exaggerated expression and shake your head while saying, "That's not a toy." Continue taking objects out of the bag and identifying whether each one is a toy.

After the child has played with the toys and other objects for a while, tell her that you want to put only the toys back in the bag. Take two toys and put them in the bag. Then ask, "Can you give me another toy?" or "Where's one like this?" If the child gives you a toy, praise her and let her put it in the bag. If the child gives you something that is not a toy, say, "That's not a toy," and put that object behind your back.

Prompt the child by pointing to a toy and saying, "That's a toy. Give me that one for the bag." You can physically **prompt** by taking the child's hand and helping her pick up a toy to put in the bag.

You can also do this activity with food and clothing items.

Activity: Food, Food, Not Food

Materials/Toys: a bag, food items (e.g., food boxes, jars of baby food, toy food), other non-food items (e.g., clothes, utensils), a doll, doll blanket

Place the doll on the floor on her blanket and put all of the materials in the bag. Sit on the floor with the child and tell her that the doll is hungry and wants to eat. Explain to the child that your bag has some food in it, but it also has things in it that are not food. Tell the child that you are going to find the food. Reach into the bag and pull out two food items, each time saying, "This is food. The baby can eat this," and placing the food on the blanket with the doll. On the next trial, take an item out of the bag that is not food and say, "This is not food. Let's put it over there." Place the item away from the baby. Take a food item out of the bag and say, "Put it with the other food." **Prompt** by pointing to the food on the doll blanket. Continue taking items out of the bag and letting the child decide whether to put the items on the doll blanket or away from the doll. On subsequent visits, complete the activity without modeling.

Activity: Clothes, Clothes, Not Clothes

Materials/Toys: clothing, other non-clothing items, a laundry basket or large box

Spread the clothes and other items on the floor where you and the child are sitting. Tell the child that you need to pick up all the clothes so you can wash them. Hold up an item of clothing and say, "This is a _____. A _____ is clothes. Let's put it in the laundry basket." Then pick up an item that is not clothing and say, "This is not clothes. It can't go in the laundry basket." Place the item away from the basket. Then ask the child to find some more clothes. **Prompt** the child by pointing to an item of clothing and saying, "There, that ____ is clothes. Let's put it in the laundry basket."

R26

Treatment Objective: The child will find "baby" in a picture.

Goals: The child will understand single words from a variety of word classes. (RG2)
The child will understand simple questions. (RG6)

Activity: Cute Baby **Expected age**: 15–18 months

Materials/Toys: a book with a baby on several pages

As you sit down with the child to read the book, talk about the baby you see on the first few pages. Say, "Look at the baby" as you point to it and talk about what the baby is doing. After a couple of pages of talking about the baby and pointing to it, turn to a new page and ask the child, "Where is the baby?" If the child does not point to the baby, **prompt** by taking her hand and pointing to it saying, "There's the baby." Try this several times until the child begins to understand the concept.

Try this same activity with the child's family photo album that has several pictures of the child in it. Using books with real photos teaches the child that she is a baby and that there are other babies who are different from her. Books with photos of babies are listed on the next page.

Babies by Gyo Fujikawa
Babies 1, 2, 3 by Neil Ricklen
Baby's Friends by Neil Ricklen
Baby's Home by Neil Ricklen
Baby's Good Night by Neil Ricklen
The Big Book of Beautiful Babies by David Ellwand

R27

(Note: See pages 93-94 in the *Therapy Guide* for early vocabulary words.)

Treatment Objective: The child will understand 50 words.

Goal: The child will understand single words from a variety of word classes. (RG2)

Materials/Toys: none   **Expected age**: 15–18 months

Note: Ensuring comprehension of words can take place in almost any of the activities described or in other day-to-day situations.

The activities so far have addressed improving the child's comprehension of words and phrases. In order to determine if the child really understands the meaning of the target word, you have to be sure any command or direction you are giving does not provide information about the word. For example, imagine the child is playing with a book and a car, and you give the direction to "push the car." If she does, this does not necessarily mean that she has understood the word *push*. This is a logical action to use with a car. You also have to be sure the child is responding to the word and not to the context. For example, imagine the child is getting dressed and all that is left to put on are her shoes. Giving the child credit for responding to "get your shoe" probably does not assure her comprehension of the word *shoe*, but rather her understanding of what happens next in this context or routine. (Note: At this age, children will be likely to understand names of toys, family members, items of clothing, and common verbs.)

R28

Treatment Objective: The child will identify four body parts and clothing items on herself.

Goals: The child will understand single words from a variety of word classes. (RG2)
The child will follow simple one-step commands without gesture/context support (RG4)

Activity: Body Parts/Clothing   **Expected age**: 18–21 months

Materials/Toys: none

See R12, pages 49–50, for the activity. At this age, the child should be able to point to body parts and clothing items on herself. (At earlier levels, the child was expected to identify body parts and clothing items on a doll.)

R29

Treatment Objective: The child will follow commands to "Sit down," "Come here," or "Give me" with gestures.

Goal: The child will follow simple one-step commands accompanied by gestures/context clues. (RG3)

Activity: Come, Sit, and Give **Expected age**: 18–21 months

Materials/Toys: any toys or objects

At the beginning of the session, gesture to the child to come to the area of the room where you are as you say, "Come here." If the child comes, sit down on the floor, pat the floor and say, "Sit down with me." During the course of the session, as the child is playing with toys, extend your hand and say, "Give me the ____." **Prompt** on any of these directions by physically assisting the child to comply.

R30

Treatment Objective: The child will choose five familiar objects on request.

Goals: The child will understand single words from a variety of word classes. (RG2)
The child will understand simple questions. (RG6)

Activity: Farmer Brown **Expected age**: 18–21 months

Materials/Toys: toy farm animals, tractor, some items not associated with a farm

Sit on the floor with the child with the farm set and other items. While playing with the child, be sure to label all objects. Ask the child to show you the tractor (e.g., "Where's the tractor?"). If the child does not correctly identify the tractor, pick up the tractor and say, "Here's the tractor." Physically **prompt** by taking her hand and touching the tractor. Repeat for a total of five objects. When you ask the child to identify the farm animals, keep in mind that some children associate all animals as being one specific animal (e.g., all animals with four legs are dogs).

R31

Treatment Objective: The child will understand the meaning of action words. (Note: See pages 93 and 94 in the *Therapy Guide* for suggestions of early verbs and protoverbs to teach.)

Goal: The child will understand single words from a variety of word classes. (RG2)

Activity: Now You Do It **Expected age**: 18–21 months

Materials/Toys: none

Tell the child that you want her to do what you do. Then say an action verb (e.g., *throw, dance, sit, walk*) and perform the action. Give the child a verbal cue to start by saying, "Now you do it." Wait for the child to do the action. If she does it correctly, move on to another verb. If not, say the word and model the verb again while physically **prompting** by helping the child perform the action. Later, drop the visual model of the verb and see if child will perform the action on her own. You could also try having the child become the leader and giving you actions to model.

R32

Treatment Objective: The child will understand words for absent objects by locating them.

Goals: The child will understand single words from a variety of word classes. (RG2)
The child will follow simple one-step commands without gesture/context support. (RG4)

Activity: Let's Find the _____ **Expected age**: 18–21 months

Materials/Toys: any toys that the child knows the name of, bag or box

Before beginning the session, get out two or three toys that you often play with and that you are sure the child knows the names of. Put them in a bag or box, or hide them somewhere in the room without the child seeing you. As you get other items out to play, remark, "Uh-oh, where's the _____?" Then ask the child, "Can you find the _____?" If the child does not start looking around, **prompt** by asking questions like, "Do you think the _____ might be in the box?" or "I wonder if the _____ is under the chair."

=== R33 ===

Treatment Objective: The child will identify items or people in pictures when they are named.

Goals: The child will understand single words from a variety of word classes. (RG2)
The child will follow simple one-step commands without gesture/context support. (RG4)

Activity: Book Time **Expected age**: 18–21 months

Materials/Toys: books containing pictures of a variety of items

While looking at books with the child say, "Where is the (name of item)?" Then point to the item and say, "There it is. There's the ____." Repeat a couple of times. **Prompt** by asking, "Where is the ____? Can you show me?" If the child does not begin to point to the target picture, physically **prompt** by taking her hand and helping her point. Continue this pattern with other pictured items in books or with people in the child's family photographs until she is able to spontaneously identify the item or person when you ask.

=== R34a ===

Treatment Objective: The child will demonstrate some understanding of personal pronouns.

Goals: The child will understand single words from a variety of word classes. (RG2)
The child will follow simple one-step commands without gesture/context support. (RG4)

Activity: To Her, To Him **Expected age**: 18–21 months

Materials/Toys: doll with an obvious gender (so the child will understand when you call it *him* or *her*)

Sit on the floor with the child. Put the boy doll (or the girl doll) on the floor with you. Give the child a direction using the pronoun *him* (or *her*). Directions can be things you do to the doll (e.g., kiss, rock, hug, pat) or things you make the doll do (e.g., dance, go to sleep, jump, roll over). Intersperse these with directions in which you are the object (e.g., "Give me a hug" or "Touch my nose"). If the child does not follow the direction, **prompt** by moving the doll a little closer to her. You can also **prompt** by demonstrating the action for the child. Use the same carrier phrase to describe your actions. For example, say, "I'm going to give him a hug" (hug the doll) and "I'm going to give you a hug" (hug the child). Then tell the child, "Now you give him a hug" and "Now you give me a hug." Be sure to vary the order you give the directions (i.e., don't always do the doll first).

R34b

Treatment Objective: The child will demonstrate some understanding of personal pronouns.

Goals: The child will understand single words from a variety of word classes. (RG2)
The child will follow simple one-step commands without gesture/context support. (RG4)

Activity: Silly Soup   **Expected age:** 18–21 months

Materials/Toys: doll with an obvious gender (boy or girl), sets of three identical objects (e.g., three socks, three spoons, three blocks, three crayons, three balls), a bag or box, three small bowls

Put the girl doll (or boy doll) on the floor with you and the child. Put a bowl in front of each of you. Tell the child you are going to make silly soup. Tell the child you have three of everything. Say, "I have one for you, one for her (girl doll), and one for me. Can you pass them out for me?" Take three identical objects from the bag or box and place them on the floor by the child. Give the child one of the objects and say, "This one is for me." The child should put that object in your bowl. Then give the child the next item and say, "This one is for her." The child should put that object in the doll's bowl. Then say, "This one is for you," and the child should put that item in her bowl. Be sure to alternate who gets the first object on subsequent turns. **Prompt** by pointing to the "person" who is to receive the object or by scooting that individual's bowl a little closer to the child. You can also physically **prompt** by helping the child put the item in the correct bowl. Repeat the pronoun, "That's right. That one is for her" or "That one is for you."

R35

Treatment Objective: The child will put away a toy on request.

Goal: The child will follow simple one-step commands without gesture/context support. (RG4)

Activity: Clean Up   **Expected age:** 21–24 months

Materials/Toys: toys, something to keep the toys in (e.g., toy box, large bag, shelf, plastic tub)

This activity is a natural at the end of each session. Tell the child it's time to put away the toys. Wait for the child to start putting away the toys on her own. If she doesn't, repeat the direction to "Put away the toys." **Prompt** by opening the container for the toys and placing it close to the child. You can also model by putting away a toy yourself. Further physically **prompt** by giving the child a toy and helping her drop it into the container.

R36

Treatment Objective: The child will choose one object from a field of five upon verbal request.

Goals: The child will understand single words from a variety of word classes. (RG2)
The child will follow simple one-step commands without gesture/context support. (RG4)

Activity: Baby's Bath   **Expected age:** 21–24 months

Materials/Toys: doll, plastic tub, washcloth, toothbrush, soap, shampoo, comb

Put five objects on the floor in front of the child. Tell the child, "Find the ____." The child does not have to give you the object, but simply indicate that she has found the one that you named. If the child is having a hard time doing this, **prompt** by rearranging the objects and placing the one you are going to name closer to the child. You can also offer a physical **prompt** by placing the child's hand on the named object. If the child doesn't seem to know the names of the objects, talk about what each one is called. Allow the child to examine each object and play with it. Then try giving your directions. The child may be more willing to find the one you name after she has had time to explore each item.

R37

Treatment Objective: The child will identify body parts on her caregiver or on a doll.

Goals: The child will understand single words from a variety of word classes. (RG2)
The child will follow simple one-step commands without gesture/context support. (RG4)

Activity: Body Parts   **Expected age:** 21–24 months

Materials/Toys: doll

See R12, pages 49–50, for the activity. At this level, the child should be able to point to the body parts on her caregiver or on a doll. (At earlier levels, the child was expected to identify body parts on a doll and on herself.)

R38

Treatment Objective: The child will follow two-step related commands.

Goal: The child will follow two-step (and three-step) commands. (RG5)

Activity: What's in the Bag?   **Expected age:** 21–24 months

Materials/Toys: toys, a bag

Allow the child to help unpack the toy bag. As she helps, give her two-step directions (e.g., "Get the bag of puzzle pieces and pour them out over here," "Find the cards and take them to Mommy," "Get out the bear and give him a hug"). If the child is not able to follow the two-step command, give one verb at a time. Tell the child to "Get the bag of puzzle pieces." After she has completed that action, tell the child to "Pour them out over here." Later in the session, you can try the command with the verbs in a two-step command. You can also **prompt** by performing the two actions at the same time as the child. Take the child's hand and say each verb as you perform it and help the child to perform it with you. Then remove the **prompt** and see it the child can repeat the two-step command with just a verbal direction.

R39

Treatment Objective: The child will point to four action words in pictures.

Goals: The child will understand single words from a variety of word classes. (RG2)
The child will follow simple one-step commands without gesture/context support. (RG4)

Activity:	Busy People	**Expected age**: 24–27 months
Materials/Toys:	four pictures with each showing a single verb/action	

Seat the child in her high chair with the tray in place or sit on the floor with the child. Show each picture to the child, explaining the action (e.g., "See this boy? He's eating"). After showing the child each picture several times, place the four pictures in front of the child. Say, "Show me who's eating." If the child does not pick up or point to the correct picture, verbally **prompt** by saying, "Look. He's eating," while pointing to the corresponding picture. You can also physically **prompt** by taking the child's hand and touching the correct picture.

R40

Treatment Objective: The child will understand the concept of *one*.

Goals: The child will understand single words from a variety of word classes. (RG2)
The child will follow simple one-step commands without gesture/context support. (RG4)

Activity:	Color Time	**Expected age**: 24–27 months
Materials/Toys:	several crayons, coloring books/paper; or blocks	

Seat your child in her high chair with the tray in place. Place the crayons on the tray. Allow the child to start coloring a picture while you color your own picture. Periodically ask the child to hand you one crayon. This needs to be alternated with "Hand me a bunch of crayons" or "Hand me lots of crayons" so you can be sure the child actually understands the concept of *one*. You may use visual and verbal **prompts** if the child does not demonstrate the skill correctly. Show the child the number of crayons you want as you tell her how many crayons you want. You can also **prompt** comprehension of *one* by holding up one finger when you ask for one. If the child continues to give you one when you ask for a bunch, try saying, "No, not just one crayon. Give me more."

This activity could also be done with blocks. Place the blocks on the floor in a pile. Allow the child to start playing with the blocks while you build your own building. Periodically ask the child to hand you "one block." To make sure the child understands the concept of *one*, alternate this command with requests to "Hand me a bunch of blocks" or "Hand me lots of blocks."

R41

Treatment Objective: The child will understand size concepts.

Goals: The child will understand single words from a variety of word classes. (RG2)
The child will follow simple one-step commands without gesture/context support. (RG4)

Activity:	Big Ones	**Expected age**: 24–27 months
Materials/Toys:	a large ball, a small ball, measuring cups	

Note: When introducing size concepts, it is better to focus on only one concept at a time and to work on it until the child has mastered it. For example, if the child is learning *big*, work on this concept until the child consistently understands it. Then begin introducing the concept of *small* or *little*.

Sit on the floor with the child, and let the child begin playing with the two balls. Say to the child, "Get the big ball." If the child grabs the wrong ball, **prompt** by saying, "no, the *big* ball" and grab the big one. While rolling the big ball with the child, repeatedly say "the big ball" so that she associates the concept of *big* with the larger size. You can use this method with any toy or object (e.g., cars, measuring cups, blocks) that come in different sizes.

R42

Treatment Objective: The child will point to three or more small body parts on herself or on her caregiver.

Goals: The child will understand single words from a variety of word classes. (RG2)
The child will follow simple one-step commands without gesture/context support. (RG4)

Activity: Body Parts   **Expected age**: 24–27 months

Materials/Toys: none

See R12, pages 49–50, for the activity. In this activity, the child should be able to point to/identify several small body parts on you and on herself.

R43

Treatment Objective: The child will respond to simple questions.

Goal: The child will understand simple questions. (RG6)

Activity: Where's the _____?   **Expected age**: 27–30 months

Materials/Toys: some of the child's favorite toys, a bag for the toys

Begin with only one of the child's favorite toys, such as a stuffed animal. Hide the toy from the child. Then ask, "Where's the _____?" The child can answer with words or she can look for the toy. Either response indicates that the child has understood the question. **Prompt** by asking specific questions like, "Is it on the chair?" Go with the child to the place you asked about and look for the toy. If the toy is not there, ask, "Is it under the table?" Go with the child to that place and look for the toy. Continue until the child finds the toy.

For more of a challenge, sit on the floor with the child with several toys near you. Talk about each toy. Then say, "Let's play a game. I'll put all of these toys in the bag. Then I'll ask you questions to see which one you want to play with." Put all of the toys in the bag. Reach in and pretend to mix them up. With your hand still in the bag, hold one of the toys in your hand (e.g., car). You can ask questions like, "Do you want a toy with wheels?" If the child answers, "Yes," hand the child a car. If the child says, "No," ask, "What would you like?" You can also ask questions requiring an answer other than "yes" or "no" (e.g., "What is in my bag that is soft and says 'Meow'? ").

R44

Treatment Objective: The child will identify clothing on herself or on her caregiver.

Goals: The child will understand single words from a variety of word classes. (RG2)
The child will understand simple questions. (RG6)

Activity:	Where's Your Shirt?	**Expected age**: 27–30 months

Materials/Toys: clothes you are wearing

Ask, "Where is your _____?" If the child correctly points to the item of clothing, praise her and say, "You found your _____." **Prompt** by pointing to the same item of clothing on you and saying, "Here's my _____. Where's your _____?" You can also physically **prompt** by taking the child's hand and touching the item of clothing on the child as you say, "Here's your _____." If the child is really having difficulty identifying the items of clothing, get extra clothing items (the child's or doll-size) and put two different items in front of the child. Label each and then ask the child to point to the one you name.

R45

Treatment Objective: The child will understand the prepositions *on*, *in*, *under*, and *out of*.

Goals: The child will understand single words from a variety of word classes. (RG2)
The child will follow simple one-step commands without gesture/context support. (RG4)

Activity:	Animals Up, Animals On	**Expected age**: 27–30 months

Materials/Toys: farm set (e.g., barn, tractor, wagon, toy farm animals)

Sit on the floor with the child and the farm set and animals. As you and the child are playing, use self-talk and parallel talk to teach the prepositions (e.g., "I put the cow *in* the wagon," "You put the tractor *in* the barn," "The chicken is *on* the roof"). After you have used each preposition several times, give the child a command (e.g., "Take the cow *out of* the wagon"). You can give a physical **prompt** by placing the child's hand on the cow when you give the command. Continue the activity using all of the prepositions. Praise the child as reinforcement when she shows understanding of a preposition.

You can also do this activity with a doll, baby bathtub, and a blanket. Have the child follow your commands using a variety of prepositions (e.g., Place the doll *in* the bathtub," "Take the doll *out of* the tub," "Put the doll *under* the blanket").

R46

Treatment Objective: The child will understand five common action words. (See pages 93 and 94 in the *Therapy Guide* for suggestions of early verbs and protoverbs to teach.)

Goals: The child will understand single words from a variety of word classes. (RG2)
The child will follow simple one-step commands without gesture/context support. (RG4)

Activity:	Let's Play Ball	**Expected age**: 30–33 months

Materials/Toys: ball or play dishes

Playing ball with the child is an activity that you can do to reinforce many action words (e.g., *throw*, *roll*, *kick*, *catch*, *stop*). As you play, model the action word as you demonstrate the action. After you have demonstrated the action, ask the child to do it to assess her knowledge of the word (e.g., Say, "Kick the ball!"). If the child does not respond with the appropriate action, **prompt** by continuing to demonstrate the action and helping her do it. You can also do this activity with play dishes. Pretend to cook with the child. As you do, emphasize and demonstrate activities such as *eat*, *drink*, *wash*, *spill*, and *pour*.

R47a

Treatment Objective: The child will follow a two-step unrelated command.

Goal: The child will follow two-step (and three-step) commands. (RG5)

Activity: Can You Do What I Say? **Expected age:** 30–33 months

Materials/Toys: a variety of small toys or objects

Have the child sit on the floor or at a small table. Place five objects in front of the child, and give her a two-step direction (e.g., "Ring the bell. Push the car"). Some of the directions might include the objects, but others might not. Praise the child after she follows each direction. **Prompt** by providing a model for the child. You can also modify this activity to make it easier by keeping the second part of the directions the same (e.g., "Pick up the pen. Stomp your feet" and then "Open the box. Stomp your feet"). This way the child will not have such a hard time remembering both parts of the direction.

R47b

Treatment Objective: The child will follow a two-step unrelated command.

Goal: The child will follow two-step (and three-step) commands. (RG5).

Activity: Follow the Leader **Expected age:** 30–33 months

Materials/Toys: none

Tell the child you are going to play "Follow the Leader." Then give her a two-step direction (e.g., "Walk and then clap your hands," "Wave your hand and then scratch your head," "Stomp your feet and then jump"). To expose the child to past tense verbs, label each action after she performs it (e.g., "You jumped and you sat down").

If the child is unable to follow the two-step command, give her one action at a time. First tell the child to "jump." After she has completed that action, tell the child to "sit." Then ask the child to perform the same two actions again using a two-step command (e.g., "Now, can you jump and then sit?"). You can also **prompt** by performing the two actions at the same time as the child. Take the child's hand and say each verb as you perform it, and help the child to perform the action with you. Then remove the **prompt** to see if the child can repeat the two-step command with only a verbal direction.

R48

Treatment Objective: The child will understand the concepts *one* and *all*.

Goals: The child will understand single words from a variety of word classes. (RG2)
The child will follow simple one-step commands without gesture/context support. (RG4)

Activity: One Block, Two Blocks **Expected age:** 30–33 months

Materials/Toys: Legos/blocks or snack food

Frequently model the concepts *one* and *all* while playing. If the child is playing with blocks, as you hand her one say, "Here is *one* block" or "Here are *all* of the blocks." In turn, build with the child and give her control of the blocks. Ask the child for one of the blocks. If she hands you more than one block, give the extras back to her and say, "I have one. Thank you." Do the same with "all." If the child only gives you one block when you ask for all of them, encourage her to give you more by saying, "I want them all." **Prompt** by taking them yourself to demonstrate the concept.

You can also do this activity with snack foods the child enjoys (e.g., Goldfish, raisins). Reinforce the concepts *one* and *all* while the child is enjoying a favorite snack.

R49a

Treatment Objective: The child will answer *yes* and *no* questions correctly.

Goal: The child will understand simple questions. (RG6)

Activity: Is This a _____?   **Expected age**: 30–33 months

Materials/Toys: toys the child can name, a bag or book

Before the session, put the toys in the bag. When the child arrives, tell her that you have forgotten the names of all the toys in your bag. Ask if she will help you remember the names. Pull a toy out of the bag and ask, "Is this a _____?" If the child does not answer or answers incorrectly, **prompt** by saying, "Yes, this is a _____" or "No, this is not a _____." You can further **prompt** by nodding or shaking your head in addition to saying "yes" or "no."

You can also do this activity with books. Sit on the floor with the child or let her sit in a chair at a table. Place a book in front of the child and say, "Let's read a book." Begin reading, pausing after each page to ask the child simple *yes/no* questions.

R49b

(Note: This can also be R50, page 68, as this will demonstrate if the child understands function of objects.)

Treatment Objective: The child will answer *yes* and *no* questions correctly.

Goal: The child will understand simple questions. (RG6)

Activity: Do You Eat a Chair?   **Expected age**: 30–33 months

Materials/Toys: toys the child knows the function of, a bag to hold the toys

Before the session, gather toys or objects that the child knows and understands the function of (e.g., ball—kick/throw; spoon—eat with; shoe—wear; car—push; cookie—eat; cup—drink out of; book—read). Put the toys in the bag. When the child arrives, tell her that you need help remembering what to do with the items in your bag. Pull a toy out of the bag and ask a *yes/no* question about the item (e.g., "Do you read a book?" "Do you eat a car?"). If the child does not answer or answers incorrectly, **prompt** by saying, "Yes, we read a book" or "No, we don't eat a car!" You can further **prompt** by nodding or shaking your head in addition to saying "yes" or "no."

R50

Treatment Objective: The child will understand the functions of objects.

Goal: The child will understand simple questions. (RG6)

Activity: What's That For? **Expected age:** 30–33 months

Materials/Toys: items that are familiar to the child (e.g., book, cup, spoon, car, toothbrush, towel)

Seat the child in her high chair with the tray in place or on the floor with you. As you and the child play with the objects, talk about the function of each item (e.g., "We eat with a spoon," "We read a book," "We use a cup to get a drink"). After the child has heard each object's function several times, ask her to identify an object by its function (e.g., "Show me what we use to eat"). If the child does not point to or pick up the spoon, give a verbal **prompt** by saying, "We eat with the spoon." You can also give a physical **prompt** by placing the child's hand on the spoon while giving the verbal prompt. To give the child reinforcement, offer her praise when she correctly identifies an object by its function.

R51a

Treatment Objective: The child will understand the concepts *big* and *little*.

Goals: The child will understand single words from a variety of word classes. (RG2)
The child will follow simple one-step commands without gesture/context support. (RG4)

Activity: Big Bounce, Little Bounce **Expected age:** 30–33 months

Materials/Toys: one big ball, one little ball

Sit on the floor a few feet away from the child, with the child facing you. Use gestures to illustrate the difference between *big* and *little*. Then throw or roll the big ball to the child. Next throw or roll the little ball to the child. When the child has both balls, tell her you will ask for either the big ball or the little ball. Then tell the child, "Roll me the big (or little) ball." If the child does not use the right ball, you can **prompt** by using gestures to indicate *big* or *little* or by pointing to the ball you want. Return that ball to the child so she has both and give the direction again. Be sure you don't simply alternate between *big* and *little* (i.e., Ask for the big ball several times in a row).

If the child is not catching on, concentrate on one concept at a time. (See R41, pages 63–64.) Play with the little ball for a while and emphasize *little* throughout the day with any object that may be little. Slowly add the concept *big* and then use both to assess the child's understanding.

R51b

Treatment Objective: The child will understand the concepts *big* and *little*.

Goals: The child will understand single words from a variety of word classes. (RG2)
The child will follow simple one-step commands without gesture/context support. (RG4)

Activity: Big Bag **Expected age:** 30–33 months

Materials/Toys: a big paper sack (like a grocery sack), a little paper sack (like a lunch sack), toys that will fit in either sack

Get out the two paper sacks. With a flourish, open the big sack and tell the child, "Wow! This sack is really big." Then open the other sack and say, "This is just a little sack." Then get out the objects and hold one up. Tell the child, "Put this in the little (or big) sack." Continue with the other objects. Be careful not to simply alternate between the big and little sacks. Mix things up by giving the command for *big* several times in a row or *little* several times in a row. **Prompt** by moving the correct sack closer to the child or touching the correct sack as you give the command.

R52

Treatment Objective: The child will follow a three-step unrelated command.

Goal: The child will follow two-step (and three-step) commands. (RG5)

Activity: Follow Me **Expected age**: 33–36 months

Materials/Toys: toys or objects that the child can name

Tell the child you're going to play "Follow Me." Begin by giving the child some easy, one-step commands with models. For example, say, "I'm going to hop." (Begin hopping.) "Now you hop." Next give the child some one-step commands without modeling. If the child is following the one-step commands, try giving her a two-step command with a model. If the child is successful with these commands, tell her you're going to give her some more directions. Say, "Listen carefully as I tell you three things to do." Then give the three-step unrelated command. If the child cannot do all three actions, **prompt** by modeling the three actions, by modeling one action at a time, by repeating the entire command, or by repeating the command one action at a time. When the child has successfully completed the command with whatever prompts were needed, give the same three-step command again without prompts.

Examples of actions that can be combined into three-step commands:

sit down	blink your eyes	touch your tummy
stand up	touch your head	touch your toes
lie down	touch your nose	turn around
run slowly	scratch your head	blow a kiss
walk	stand on one foot	close your eyes
clap	jump up and down	say your name
wiggle your fingers	stick out your tongue	smile

You can also do this activity with a toy farm and animals or a doll that the child can move.

Examples of actions the animals can do:

stand up	run
lie down	hide
moo (whinny, bark, etc.)	jump
go in the barn	get a drink
smell the floor	knock on the barn door

======= R53a =======

Treatment Objective: The child will respond to *wh-* questions.

Goal: The child will understand simple questions. (RG6)

Activity: What Do You Do With It?   **Expected age**: 33–36 months

Materials/Toys: toys/items that the child knows the function of, a bag the items fit in, a puppet

Let the child look at, manipulate, and name all of the toys/items as she puts them in the bag. Then put the puppet on one hand and reach into the bag with the other. Hold one of the items in your hand, but do not take it out of the bag. Have the puppet ask, "What is it?" Take the item out of the bag and say, "It is a ____." Repeat with another item. Once the items are out of the bag, have the puppet point to one and ask, "What do you do with a ____?" Help the child formulate a response (e.g., "You eat a cookie," "You throw a ball").

Then give the child a turn putting her hand into the bag while you have the puppet ask her a question. If the child needs help, **prompt** by repeating the question that the puppet asked and helping a little bit. For example, say, "The puppet asked what you are holding. Can you tell the puppet what you have?"

If the child needs extra help answering questions, here are some books you might read:

Where
Where Are You Going? To See My Friend! by Eric Carle & Kazuo Iwamura

Who
Everyone Hide From Wibbly Pig by Mick Inkpen
The Grouchy Ladybug by Eric Carle
Who Hoots? by Katie Davis
Who Hops? by Katie Davis

What
The Very Hungry Caterpillar by Eric Carle
Brown Bear, Brown Bear, What Do You See? by Bill Martin Jr & Eric Carle
Polar Bear, Polar Bear, What Do You Hear? by Bill Martin Jr & Eric Carle
Panda Bear, Panda Bear, What Do You See? by Bill Martin Jr & Eric Carle

======= R53b =======

Treatment Objective: The child will respond to *wh-* questions.

Goal: The child will understand simple questions. (RG6)

Activity: Which One?   **Expected age**: 33–36 months

Materials/Toys: pairs of objects that differ by one attribute that the child understands (e.g., big and little spoon, yellow and green ball, wet and dry cloth, Daddy's and child's shoe), a bag

Tell the child that you have some things in your bag, but you are all mixed up. You need her to help you figure out which one is the one you need. Reach into the bag and pull out a pair of objects. Say, "See, I have two _____, but I don't know which one is _____" (e.g., "I have two shoes, but I don't know which one is Daddy's shoe" or "I have two pencils, but I don't know which one is the little pencil"). If the child needs help, **prompt** by moving the correct choice a little closer to the child.

R53c

Treatment Objective: The child will respond to *wh-* questions.

Goal: The child will understand simple questions. (RG6)

Activity: When Do We _____?   **Expected age**: 33–36 months

Materials/Toys: pictures of day and night and summer and winter
(Note: If you live in an area without seasons, eliminate the summer and winter pictures and questions.)

Tell the child you're going to play the "When" game. Look at each picture and describe it (e.g., "This picture shows the daytime. It is sunny and light. We wake up in the daytime. We eat our breakfast. We go to school"). Then put all four pictures in front of the child and ask her some *when* questions. **Prompt** by moving the correct picture closer to the child or by giving additional semantic cues (e.g., If you ask the child, "When do we build a snowman" and she points to the summer day, you could say, "That picture has kids swimming and it looks very hot. Could we build a snowman when it is very hot, or do we need to find the picture that shows when it is cold and there is some snow?").

Day Questions
When do we wake up?
When do we go to school?
When does Mommy go to work?
When do we get dressed?

Night Questions
When do we take a bath?
When do we hear a bedtime story?
When do we put on our pajamas?
When do we go to sleep?

Winter Questions
When is it very cold?
When can we build a snowman?
When do we wear hats and mittens?
When can we ride on a sled?

Summer Questions
When is it very hot?
When can we go swimming?
When can we go barefoot?
When can we play with the hose?

R54a

Treatment Objective: The child will identify parts of an object.

Goal: The child will follow simple one-step commands without gesture/context support. (RG4)

Activity: Playhouse   **Expected age**: 33–36 months

Materials/Toys: toy house with doors and windows that open

As you play house with the child, reinforce the parts of the house like the doors, windows, and doorknobs. Show the child how the doors and windows open and close. Then give the child some simple one-step directions (e.g., "Open the door so the people can go in" or "Make the dog jump through the window").

To assess understanding, ask the child where the window is or ask her to do an action like knock on the door or window. **Prompt** as needed by touching the part of the object you are asking about.

R54b

Treatment Objective: The child will identify parts of an object.

Goal: The child will follow simple one-step commands without gesture/context support. (RG4)

Activity: Wheels, Doors, and Handles **Expected age**: 33–36 months

Materials/Toys: toy car/vehicle with a door that opens

Having a car with doors that open will give additional cueing for "parts of an object." While playing with the car, direct the child's attention to the parts of the car. For example, pretend that people are getting into the vehicle or, if you have a Fisher Price Little People Bus, open the doors and put the people in it. Emphasize "door" while opening the doors. Then move to asking the child to open the door. You can also turn the vehicle over and demonstrate how the wheels turn. You can sing "The Wheels on the Bus/Car" while you direct the child's attention to the wheels and other parts.

Goals and Treatment Objectives for Expressive Language Skills (Chapter 9) *by Verity Mathews*

Long-term goal: The child will exhibit optimal expressive language skills.

This chart summarizes which aspects of language may be related to the goals you address.

Short-term Goals	Communicative Intent	Communicative Function	Semantic-syntactic relations	Morphemes	Sentence Structures
(EG1) The child will increase imitation of vocalizations of non-speech sounds, speech sounds, and sound sequences.					
(EG2) The child will increase imitation of words.	X	X			
(EG3) The child will increase spontaneous use of vocalizations of non-speech sounds, speech sounds, and sound sequences.	X				
(EG4) The child will increase spontaneous use of single words.	X	X			
(EG5) The child will increase spontaneous use of word combinations.	X		X	X	X

This chart gives more specific information about each aspect of expressive language.

Communicative Intent types	Communicative Function types	Semantic-syntactic relations types	Morpheme types	Sentence Structure types

Repeating/practicing
Calling attention
Requesting
  Object
  Action
  Information
Protesting
Commenting
  On object
  On action
Greeting
Answering
Acknowledging
	Negation
	  Nonexistence–
	    disappearance
	  Rejection
	  Denial
	Recurrence
	Existence
	Action on object
	Locative action
	Attribution
	Naming
	Possession
	Commenting
	Social Interaction
		Attribute-entity
		Possessor-possession
		Agent-action
		Action-object
		Agent-object
		Demonstrative-entity
		Entity-locative
		Action-locative
		Recurrence
		Nonexistence-
		  disappearance
		Rejection
		Denial
			Present progressive *-ing*
			In
			On
			Regular plural *-s*
			Irregular past tense
			Possessives
			Uncontractible copula
			Articles
			Regular past tense
			Regular third
			Irregular third
			Contractible copula
			Contractible auxiliary
				Declarative
				Negative
				Interrogative
				Embedded
				Conjoined

The activities include the goals listed on pages 76 and 77. The specific communicative intents, communicative functions, semantic-syntactic relations, morphemes, and/or sentence types are included in the activities. With slight modifications, you can easily address other intents, functions, relations, or morphemes.

Some activities have tips about additional words/word combinations that could be stimulated. This was done to provide many activities that relate to the development of a core lexicon. (See Appendix 9B in the *Therapy Guide*, pages 107–108.) However, because those are not the objectives of that particular activity, they have been added in italics. The intents, functions, relations, morphemes, and/or sentence types are also marked in italics. (See Activity E20b below and E26a on the next page for examples.)

> A special note regarding the two imitation goals:
>
> - EG1 The child will increase imitation of vocalizations of non-speech sounds, speech sounds, and sound sequences.
>
> - EG2 The child will increase imitation of words.
>
> These goals were matched to treatment objectives when the actual objective is imitation (e.g., Activity E27 echoes prominent or last word spoken) or if imitation is inherent in the treatment objective (e.g., child will vocalize in response to singing). In this example, the child is not expected to initiate the vocalization, so it seems inherently imitative in nature. Most treatment objectives intend for the child to produce the utterance, word, or phrase spontaneously. Therefore, even though imitation is used during the related activity, the applicable spontaneous goal is selected and the communicative intent(s), communicative function(s), semantic-syntactic relations, morphemes, and/or sentence types were selected to describe how the goal is used in that activity if the child were doing it spontaneously.

E20b

Treatment Objective: The child will use early-developing modifiers.

Goal: The child will increase spontaneous use of single words. (EG4)

Communicative Intent (pragmatics)	Communicative Function
Commenting	Attribution
On object	Negation
Requesting	*non-existence or disappearance*
Action	*Action on object*

Activity: Icky **Expected age**: 12–15 months

Materials/Toys: construction paper, brightly colored small pieces of paper to glue on the construction paper, glue stick

Have the child sit at a small table or in his high chair with the tray in place. Put some glue on the back of one of the small pieces of paper and then stick it on the construction paper. Encourage the child to watch. Wait and see if the child asks for a turn. *Stimulate the use of "do" (e.g., "You wanna do it?" or "Wanna?").* Then put lots of glue on another small piece of paper, hand it to the child, and say, "Your turn. Stick it on." The child will inevitably get glue on himself. When he does, say, "Icky! It feels icky." If necessary, gently take the child's finger and touch some glue. **Prompt** by saying, "Ick." When you put the glue away, stimulate use of *"all gone"* or *"all done."*

Note: Children with sensory deficits may find this activity upsetting because they may not like the feel of the glue. If you note such sensory issues, an occupational therapy consult may be indicated.

This is *requesting an action* (communicative intent). The communicative function is *action on object*, so those two are italicized.

Using the words "all gone" or "all done" achieves the same intent (commenting on an object) as the main word you are stimulating ("ick"). Therefore, the words "commenting on object" are not italicized. The function is different, however, so *negation/non-existence* is italicized. (The function for "ick" is attribution.)

Activity E26a stimulates the use of the word "more." If the child uses "more," the communicative intent is **requesting** and the communicative function is **recurrence**. The activity also states: *"If the child wants a turn blowing, this is a good opportunity to stimulate 'Gimme bubbles,' 'Wanna blow?' or 'me.'"* Those additional targets address *requesting an action* as the communicative intent and *action on object* as the communicative function, and are also marked in italics.

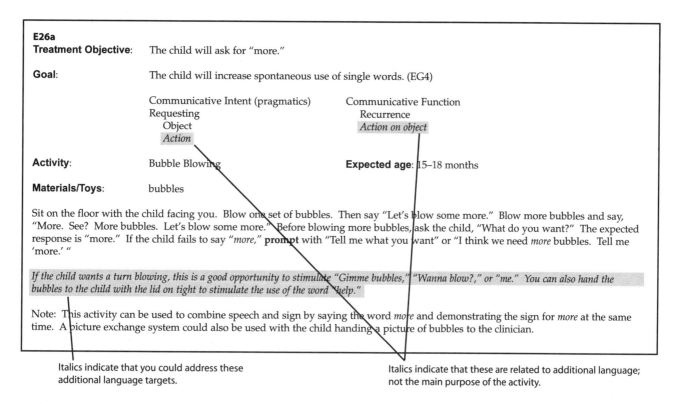

Italics indicate that you could address these additional language targets.

Italics indicate that these are related to additional language; not the main purpose of the activity.

Sometimes the objective of an activity addresses more than one communicative intent, function, semantic-syntactic relation, morpheme, and/or sentence type. In that case, you will find more than one listed. It should be clear from the activity which one is being developed by which part of the activity.

Activity E28 has the child naming objects. If the child names the object spontaneously when you pull it out of the bag, the communicative intent is "commenting on an object." If, however, you have to ask the child what it is and he responds, the intent is "answering." Thus, both of those types of communicative intents are listed. If the activity is modified (as is often the case when following the child's lead), remember that all possibilities are not listed. Use your judgment to determine what you have addressed. For example, if the child doesn't like doing this activity and starts saying "No," then you have addressed "protesting" as an intent.

Note: Some activities are so open-ended that any of the communicative intent(s), communicative function(s), semantic-syntactic relations, morphemes, and/or sentence types might be targeted. If that is the case, the area heading remains listed but not the specific targets. For example, the treatment objective in Activity E41 (pages 105–106) is "sings phrases of songs." Depending on the song selected, any of the communicative intent(s), communicative function(s), semantic-syntactic relations, morphemes, and/or sentence types might be demonstrated by the words in the song.

Expressive Ages of Acquisition/Treatment Objectives

Expected age of development	Short-term goal (EG)	Treatment Objectives	Activities to help achieve treatment objectives
3–6 months	1	Vocalizes in response to singing	E1
	1	Takes turns vocalizing	E2 a, b
	3	Produces "raspberries"	E3
	3	Stops babbling when another person vocalizes	E4
6–9 months	3	Vocalizes four different syllables	E5
	1	Vocalizes two-syllable combination	E6
	3	Vocalizes in response to objects that move	E7 a, b, c
	1	Imitates duplicated syllables	E8 a, b
9–12 months	4	Says "Mama" or "Dada" meaningfully	E9 a, b
	1	Imitates consonant and vowel combinations	E10 a, b, c, d
	1	Imitates non-speech sounds	E11 a, b, c
	1	Imitates correct number of syllables/sounds heard	E12 a, b
	4	Says one or two words spontaneously	E13
	2	Imitates names of familiar objects	E14 a, b
12–15 months	3	Varies pitch when vocalizing	E15 a, b
	2	Tries to sing with familiar song	E16
	2	Imitates new words	E17 a, b
	4	Uses exclamatory expressions (e.g., "Uh-oh," "No-no")	E18
	1	Imitates three animal sounds	E19
	4	Uses early-developing modifiers	E20 a, b, c
15–18 months	4	Answers questions with one word	E21
	4	Uses word to call attention to something	E22
	4	Uses word to comment on action or object	E23
	4	Uses word to request action	E24
	5	Asks, "What's that?"	E25
	4	Asks for "more"	E26 a, b
	2	Echoes prominent or last word spoken	E27
	4	Names five to seven familiar objects on request	E28
18–21 months	5	Uses attribute-entity	E29
	5	Uses possessor-possession	E30
	5	Uses agent-action	E31
	5	Uses action-object	E32
	5	Uses agent-object	E33
	4	Uses vocalizations and gestures to request toys or food	E34
	4, 5	Names a few pictures	E35
21–24 months	5	Uses entity-locative	E36
	5	Uses action-locative	E37
	4	Uses own name to refer to self	E38 a, b
	4, 5	Uses early pronouns occasionally	E39

continued on next page

Expected age of development	Short-term goal (EG)	Treatment Objectives	Activities to help achieve treatment objectives
24–27 months	2 5 4, 5 4, 5	Imitates two numbers or unrelated words on request Sings phrases of songs Names objects in photographs Uses action words	E40 a, b E41 E42 E43
27–30 months	4, 5 4, 5 5 4 5 5 4, 5 5	Names one color Consistently refers to self by pronouns Uses two sentence types Responds to greetings consistently Uses past tense Requests actions or objects Names five pictures Uses negation	E44 E45 E46 E47 E48 E49 E50 E51
30–33 months	4 2 4, 5 5 4, 5 4	Answers questions with "yes" or "no" Imitates series of three numbers or unrelated words Uses plurals Uses prepositions States gender States first and last name	E52 E53 E54 E55 E56 E57
33–36 months	5 5 4 5	Uses verb forms Asks "what," "who," and "where" questions Counts to three Recites a few nursery rhymes	E58 E59 a, b, c E60 a, b, c, d E61

E1

Treatment Objective: The child will vocalize in response to singing.

Goal: The child will increase imitation of vocalizations of non-speech sounds, speech sounds, and sound sequences. (EG1)

Activity: Twinkle, Twinkle **Expected age:** 3–6 months

Materials/Toys: none

When the child is awake and happy, hold him so he can see your face and sing "Twinkle, Twinkle Little Star." The desired response is for the child to make some vocalization in response to your singing. When the child vocalizes, smile at him and continue to sing. If he continues to vocalize, stay quiet for a few seconds so he can hear the sound of his own voice. When he stops, start singing again to see if he will copy.

Note: A child closer to 6 months may enjoy some hand motions (e.g., lift your hand above your head and open and close your fingers to represent a twinkling star). He will not be able to copy but will enjoy watching. Other good songs to try are "Pat-a-Cake" and "Itsy Bitsy Spider" as both have good hand movements to go along with them.

E2a

Treatment Objective: The child will take turns vocalizing.

Goal: The child will increase imitation of vocalizations of non-speech sounds, speech sounds, and sound sequences. (EG1)

Activity: La-La-La **Expected age:** 3–6 months

Materials/Toys: none

Place the child in a bouncy seat or have him sit on your lap facing you. As you interact with the child, begin to sing, either a song with words or a tune (e.g., "la-la-la," nonsense syllables). Then pause and smile at the child. Stimulate language by saying, "Can you sing too?" Continue singing and giving eye contact to the child. If the child "sings," give lots of smiles and clap.

Note: Some babies are more likely to continue the activity without a lot of clapping and "in your face" activity.

E2b

Treatment Objective: The child will take turns vocalizing.

Goal: The child will increase imitation of vocalizations of non-speech sounds, speech sounds, and sound sequences. (EG1)

Activity: Ah, Baby **Expected age:** 3–6 months

Materials/Toys: none

With the child seated or lying in front of you, establish eye contact with him. Wait to see if the child will begin vocalizing. If he does, wait for him to pause. Then imitate the sound he has been making. Pause again to give the child a chance to vocalize again. This works best if the child has been the first to vocalize, but if he doesn't, **prompt** by vocalizing an easy vowel sound like "ah, ah" with an interesting inflection. Then wait for the child to imitate. When he does, smile and vocalize again.

E3

Treatment Objective: The child will produce "raspberries."

Goal: The child will increase spontaneous use of vocalizations of non-speech sounds, speech sounds, and sound sequences. (EG3)

Communicative Intent (pragmatics)
 Calling attention

Activity: Making Raspberries **Expected age**: 3–6 months

Materials/Toys: none

With the child seated or lying so that your face is close to his, gain the child's eye contact. Demonstrate how to make raspberries. Pause and wait for the child to imitate. If the child does not respond, model the sound again. **Prompt** by touching your lips, making the sound, and then touching the child's lips. Stimulate language by saying, "Can you do it? Can you make the sound?"

E4

Treatment Objective: The child will stop babbling when another person vocalizes.

Goal: The child will increase spontaneous use of vocalizations of non-speech sounds, speech sounds, and sound sequences. (EG3)

Communicative Intent (pragmatics)
 Answering

Activity: Attention, Please! **Expected age**: 3–6 months

Materials/Toys: may need a rattle or other toy that makes a pleasant sound

This is best worked on incidentally, as you need to have the child babbling before doing this activity. Find out from the caregiver things that elicit babbling from the child (e.g., being changed, being placed under a baby gym activity set, sitting in his car seat or bouncy seat where he can see trees outside).

Then, once the child is babbling, simply call his name and make sure that you are in his visual field so he can switch his attention to you. If initially he doesn't stop babbling, pair his name with another attractive sound such as a rattle. When the child has stopped babbling, make the sound he was making when he babbled. Then stop and let the child start to babble again. Repeat the activity.

E5

Treatment Objective: The child will vocalize four different syllables.

Goal: The child will increase spontaneous use of vocalizations of non-speech sounds, speech sounds, and sound sequences. (EG3)

    Communicative Intent (pragmatics)
        Requesting
            Action

Activity: Fun Sounds   **Expected age**: 6–9 months

Materials/Toys: none

Boo!
With the child seated or lying in front of you, establish eye contact with him. When the child is looking at you, say, "Boo." Do it again and tickle the child at the same time. When he stops laughing, say it again and tickle him some more.

If you still have his interest, he may imitate the sound you made. When he imitates, clap to acknowledge that he has done something special. Then tickle him some more. If the child doesn't imitate, **prompt** by pausing as you approach to tickle him and wait for a response.

Down (Da)
Hold the child facing you while you are standing up. Get the child's attention and stimulate language by saying, "Let's go down." Then as you bend at the knees and lower the child, say, "Da, da, da, da" each time you bend your knees and go a little lower.

If you still have his interest, he may imitate the sound you made. When he imitates, go down a little further. If the child doesn't imitate, **prompt** by pausing as you bend your knees and wait for a response. Acknowledge that he has done something special by saying, "Good talking."

Goo Goo
With the child seated or lying in front of you, establish eye contact with him. Once the child is looking at you, say "goo" and tickle the child under his chin. Say, "Goo" again and tickle the child under the chin at the same time. When he stops laughing, say it once again and tickle him some more.

If you still have his interest, he may imitate the sound you made. When he imitates, clap to acknowledge that he has done something special. Then tickle him some more. If the child doesn't imitate, **prompt** by pausing as you approach to tickle him and wait for a response.

Kiss, Kiss
With the child seated or lying in front of you, establish eye contact with him. Once the child is looking at you, give kisses on the belly, arms, hands. Say "muh" with each kiss. The child will feel your lips on his skin as you say, "Muh." When he stops laughing, kiss him again and say, "Muh" with each kiss.

If you still have his interest, he may imitate the sound you made. When he imitates, clap to acknowledge that he has done something special. Then tickle him some more. If the child doesn't imitate, **prompt** by pausing as you approach to tickle him and wait for a response.

E6

Treatment Objective: The child will vocalize a two-syllable combination.

Goal: The child will increase imitation of vocalizations of non-speech sounds, speech sounds, and sound sequences. (EG1)

Activity: Peek-a-Boo   **Expected age:** 6–9 months

Materials/Toys: towel, blanket, or small cloth

With the child positioned in front of you, cover your head for a couple of seconds with the cloth and then remove it and say, "Peek-a-boo." It is unlikely that a child this age will attempt to imitate this word combination but he may come up with something of his own (e.g., "Pee boo"). When and if he does, repeat back to him what he says to encourage further repetition.

Note: A child is more likely to produce a two-syllable combination when he is actively involved in something of interest. You may need to let the child take the lead and simply repeat back to him what he says to encourage him to do it again.

E7a

Treatment Objective: The child will vocalize in response to objects that move.

Goal: The child will increase spontaneous use of vocalizations of non-speech sounds, speech sounds, and sound sequences. (EG3)

>Communicative Intent (pragmatics)
>>Commenting
>>>On action

Activity: Brrrmmm   **Expected age:** 6–9 months

Materials/Toys: toy car

Sit on the floor with the child. If the child can sit unassisted, have him sit a couple of feet away facing you. If he can't sit by himself, have a parent give him support or have him sit on your knee so he can still see your face. If he is sitting away from you, gently push the car toward him and say, "Brrrrrrrrm brrrrrrrm." If he is on your lap, push the car in a semi-circle around you when making the sound.

Push the car while making the noise several times. Then push the car without making a sound to see if the child will vocalize. If the child is just watching and not vocalizing, **prompt** by getting more animated and making the car crash into you or him.

E7b

Treatment Objective: The child will vocalize in response to objects that move.

Goal: The child will increase spontaneous use of vocalizations of non-speech sounds, speech sounds, and sound sequences. (EG3)

Communicative Intent (pragmatics)
   Commenting
      On action

Activity: Bumble Ball   **Expected age**: 6–9 months

Materials/Toys: bumble ball or any ball that will bounce a few times

Position the child so he is close enough to you that he can hear you speak. Turn on the bumble ball and act animated as the ball bounces around. Say two-syllable phrases such as, "Buh, buh" or "Do, do" as the ball bounces. Catch the ball and turn it off. Then tell the child, "Let's do it again!" Turn on the ball again, but this time, don't vocalize. Wait to see if the child will use the two-syllable combination you have been using. **Prompt** by getting your face a little closer to the child as you make the sound.

(Note: Some children are frightened by these balls simply because of the noise so be prepared to turn it off quickly if the child reacts negatively.)

E7c

Treatment Objective: The child will vocalize in response to objects that move.

Goal: The child will increase spontaneous use of vocalizations of non-speech sounds, speech sounds, and sound sequences. (EG3)

Communicative Intent (pragmatics)
   Commenting
      On action

Activity: Block Crash   **Expected age**: 6–9 months

Materials/Toys: stacking blocks (large soft ones are ideal but smaller ones will work) or boxes

Sit on the floor by or in front of the child. Stack the blocks or boxes. When the stack is tall, knock it over. As it falls, be animated and say, "Oooo" and "Oops." Do it again and be sure to vocalize as it falls. The child may grab blocks as you stack them which may make the stack fall. If this happens, just react to it. Anticipate that the child will vocalize as this happens. The child may also grab and throw the blocks so be prepared! **Prompt** by building the tower out of the child's reach and then pausing before you knock it over. This pause may trigger the child to vocalize in order to get you to knock over the stack.

E8a

Treatment Objective: The child will imitate duplicated syllables.

Goal: The child will increase imitation of vocalizations of non-speech sounds, speech sounds, and sound sequences. (EG1)

Activity: Wooo-Wooo   **Expected age**: 6–9 months

Materials/Toys: toy train

With the child seated in an infant seat, gain his attention. Show the child the train and stimulate language by saying, "Let's make the train go. Wooo-wooo." Push the train and say, "Wooo-wooo" as it moves. Wait to see if the child will vocalize in response. The child is not expected to imitate "Wooo-wooo," but to vocalize in any way, perhaps with the "ooo" sound. If the child does not vocalize, **prompt** by saying "Wooo-wooo" again and pushing the train.

E8b

Treatment Objective: The child will imitate duplicated syllables.

Goal: The child will increase imitation of vocalizations of non-speech sounds, speech sounds, and sound sequences. (EG1)

Activity: Mama/Dada Peek-a-Boo   **Expected age**: 6–9 months

Materials/Toys: blanket

Have the child sit on his caregiver's lap. Put a small blanket or small towel over the caregiver's head. As you pull the cover away, say "Mama" (or "Dada"). Encourage the child to pull the blanket away as you model the production of "Mama" (or "Dada"). **Prompt** for "Mama" by touching the child's lips or even helping to close the child's lips if he will tolerate the touch.

E9a

Treatment Objective: The child will say "Mama" or "Dada" meaningfully.

Goal: The child will increase spontaneous use of single words. (EG4)

Communicative Intent (pragmatics)	Communicative Function
Calling attention	Negation
Greeting	Non-existence or disappearance
	Naming
	Social interaction

Activity: Where's Mama/Dada?   **Expected age**: 9–12 months

Materials/Toys: none

Tell the child that you are going to play "Hide and Seek." Have the caregiver hide somewhere in the room (e.g., behind the couch, behind the door). Tell the child, "We're going to find Mama (Dada)." Pick up the child and start looking as you call out "Mama, Mama, Mama!" **Prompt** by calling out "Mama," and then waiting to see if the child will imitate the duplicated syllable.

Look in a few places first and then find the child's caregiver. Make a big show of how clever the child is because he found his caregiver. In this activity, you are anticipating that by calling for "Mama (Dada)" the child will use that word. When you find Mama, **prompt** the child to say "Mama" again. *You can also stimulate the use of "Hi!" when you find the caregiver.*

E9b

Treatment Objective: The child will say "Mama" or "Dada" meaningfully.

Goal: The child will increase spontaneous use of single words. (EG4)

Communicative Intent (pragmatics)
 Calling attention
 Greeting

Communicative Function
 Naming
 Social interaction

Activity: There's Mama/Dada!   **Expected age**: 9–12 months

Materials/Toys: none

This activity must be done in a situation in which it would be natural for the child to use the words *Mama* or *Dada*. If the caregiver does not participate in the session, then a logical time is at the end of the session. As the session is concluding, say to the child, "Let's go find Mama (Dada)." When you go to the area where Mama (Dada) is waiting, say "There's Mama (Dada)." with excited inflection. After several sessions of doing this, the next time you go to the area where the caregiver is waiting, pause and see if the child will say "Mama (Dada)" to acknowledge the caregiver is waiting. **Prompt** by asking, "Who's that?" when you see the child's parent. *When the child leaves the treatment setting, it's the perfect time to stimulate use of "Bye-bye."*

If the parent participates in the session, simulate the above situation by having the caregiver leave the treatment area and hide. The child will probably notice the parent's absence and call for her/him. If not, **prompt** by asking, "Where's Mama (Dada)?" *When you find Mama (Dada), stimulate the use of "Hi!"*

E10a

Treatment Objective: The child will imitate consonant and vowel combinations.

Goal: The child will increase imitation of vocalizations of non-speech sounds, speech sounds, and sound sequences. (EG1)

Activity: Ha, Ha!   **Expected age**: 9–12 months

Materials/Toys: any stuffed animal that is a little unfamiliar (i.e., not a dog or bear)

With the child seated in an infant seat or seated on the floor with you, show the child the stuffed animal (e.g., a frog). Tell the child, "This frog is funny. Ha, ha, ha." Hide the frog behind your back. Have the frog jump out, say, "Ha ha ha," and then hide again. The next time the frog jumps out say, "Ha, ha, ha." Wait for the child to imitate. **Prompt** by telling the child, "You say Ha, ha."

E10b

Treatment Objective: The child will imitate consonant and vowel combinations.

Goal: The child will increase imitation of vocalizations of non-speech sounds, speech sounds, and sound sequences. (EG1)

Activity: No, No!   **Expected age**: 9–12 months

| **Materials/Toys**: | puppet whose mouth opens or a sock that can be put over your hand as a puppet, a toy/object that is illogical to eat (e.g., shoe, car) |

Have the child sit on the floor with you or sit in an infant seat. Show the child the puppet (e.g., dog) and the non-edible toy (e.g., shoe). Tell the child, "This doggie wants to eat this shoe. He shouldn't eat the shoe. No-no doggie." Have the doggie pretend to eat the shoe. Shake your finger at the dog puppet and say, "No-no!" Put the puppet behind your back and the shoe in front of you. Have the dog puppet approach the shoe again. Shake your finger and say, "No no!" **Prompt** by saying, "Help me stop the doggie. Say, 'No-no.' "

E10c

Treatment Objective: The child will imitate consonant and vowel combinations.

Goal: The child will increase imitation of vocalizations of non-speech sounds, speech sounds, and sound sequences. (EG1)

Activity: Ding-Dong **Expected age**: 9–12 months

Materials/Toys: a toy that makes a ringing noise, a bell, or a doorbell

With the child seated in an infant seat or seated on the floor with you, show the child the toy or bell. As you ring it, say, "Dee-doh" (to approximate "ding dong"). Let the child ring the bell and say, "Dee-doh" each time he rings it. If the child can't hold the bell and ring it, he may be able to hit it to make it ring as you hold it. If the child doesn't imitate "dee" or "doh," **prompt** by telling the child, "Say 'dee-doh.' " You can also wait after you ring the bell to see if the child will say the sound.

E10d

Treatment Objective: The child will imitate consonant and vowel combinations.

Goal: The child will increase imitation of vocalizations of non-speech sounds, speech sounds, and sound sequences. (EG1)

Activity: Whee! Up We Go! **Expected age**: 9–12 months

Materials/Toys: infant swing (optional)

When pushing the child in his swing (or swinging him in your arms), say, "Wheee." Stimulate language by saying, "Wanna swing? Here we go. Wheee." Continue to push (swing) the child, but wait to see if the child will imitate the sound. **Prompt** by stopping and asking, "Wanna swing? Wheee" to see if the child will imitate the consonant + vowel sound.

E11a

Treatment Objective: The child will imitate non-speech sounds.

Goal: The child will increase imitation of vocalizations of non-speech sounds, speech sounds, and sound sequences. (EG1)

Activity:	Copycat	**Expected age**: 9–12 months
Materials/Toys:	blanket or towel	

When you have the child's attention, cover your head with the blanket. Then take it off quickly and make a non-speech sound (e.g., an animal sound, the sound of a car engine). Do this several times. Then take the blanket off your head and pause to see if the child copies by making the sound. If he doesn't, **prompt** by putting the blanket over the child's head and helping him take it off. As it falls from his face, make the non-speech sound.

This is a great activity for siblings to participate in. Watching his sibling(s) do this may be more of an enticement for the child to do it himself.

E11b

Treatment Objective: The child will imitate non-speech sounds.

Goal: The child will increase imitation of vocalizations of non-speech sounds, speech sounds, and sound sequences. (EG1)

Activity:	Sirens	**Expected age**: 9–12 months
Materials/Toys:	toy fire truck or police car	

Sit with the child on the floor. Push the toy fire truck or police car and make a siren sound. Do this several times. Then let the child push the truck/car as you make the siren sound. The next time the child pushes the truck/car, don't make the sound to see if the child will produce it. **Prompt** by modeling the siren sound again and saying, "You do it."

E11c

Treatment Objective: The child will imitate non-speech sounds.

Goal: The child will increase imitation of vocalizations of non-speech sounds, speech sounds, and sound sequences. (EG1)

Activity:	Moo Cow	**Expected age**: 9–12 months
Materials/Toys:	toy farm with animals or a picture book with farm animals	

Sit with the child on the floor and put the farm animals on the floor. Let the child play with the animals. Stimulate language by telling the child the names of the animals as he examines them. Choose one of the animals and, whenever the child plays with that animal, tell the child, "The cow says 'moo.'"
(Note: Do not make the sounds of all the animals because it might confuse the child.)

Then take a turn holding the cow and making it walk around, saying, "Moo." Hand the cow back to the child and say, "Moo" to see if the child will imitate the sound. **Prompt** by saying, "You say 'moo.'" Provide a physical **prompt** by touching the child's lips. In other sessions, choose a different animal and its sound. You can also do this activity with a picture book of animals. Point to an animal and make its sound (e.g., "The cow says 'moo'"). Point to the animal again to see if the child will imitate the sound. **Prompt** as needed.

═══ E12a ═══

Treatment Objective: The child will imitate the correct number of syllables/sounds heard.

Goal: The child will increase imitation of vocalizations of non-speech sounds, speech sounds, and sound sequences. (EG1)

Activity: Bouncy Ball   **Expected age**: 9–12 months

Materials/Toys: ball

Sit a few feet away from the child on the floor. Bounce the ball to the child and say, "Bouncy, bouncy ball." Say it repeatedly so the child hears it. He may simply say "ball" or may attempt to repeat the number of syllables.

You may need to take the child's lead during this activity. While playing with the ball, the child may produce a series of syllables (true words or simple babbling). For example, he may say, "bububu." If this happens, simply repeat syllable for syllable what the child says. This may cause him to repeat it. Then change what he said (e.g., "Bububu" to "Bubububu") to see if he will repeat it. **Prompt** by clapping for each syllable or tapping the child's hand for each syllable. Throughout the activity, you and the child can play with the ball. He probably won't be able to throw the ball back to you, but you can make a game out of retrieving the ball when he tries to throw it to you.

═══ E12b ═══

Treatment Objective: The child will imitate the correct number of syllables/sounds heard.

Goal: The child will increase imitation of vocalizations of non-speech sounds, speech sounds, and sound sequences. (EG1)

Activity: Night-Night Baby   **Expected age**: 9–12 months

Materials/Toys: baby doll or stuffed animal, blanket

Tell the child that the "baby" is going to go to sleep. Kiss the baby, lay it down, cover it with a blanket, and say, "Shhhh" with your index finger in front of your mouth. Wait a few seconds and then say, "Night-night" with good intonation and a definite beat for each syllable. Wait a few more seconds and repeat "Night-night." Then "wake" the baby up and give her a hug. Let the child hug the baby. Put the baby to sleep again and say, "Night-night." The desired response is for the child to say two syllables. The syllables do not have to sound like "Night-night," but they should have the two beats. **Prompt** by patting the baby's tummy once for each syllable as you say, "Night-night" or taking the child's hand and patting the baby's tummy as you say each syllable.

═══ E13 ═══

Treatment Objective: The child will say one or two words spontaneously.

Goal: The child will increase spontaneous use of single words. (EG4)

Communicative Intent (pragmatics)   Communicative Function
   Commenting   Attribution
      On action

Activity:	Uh-Oh!	**Expected age**: 9–12 months
Materials/Toys:	high chair (or whatever a child sits in to eat), familiar food, utensils, cup	

Ask the caregiver to place a few food items, some utensils, and a cup in front of the child. When food, a utensil, or the cup falls off the high chair tray (as they inevitably will if they are given to the child) say, "Uh-oh." Model this routine several times and ask the parent to repeat at subsequent mealtimes. If the child doesn't drop something, push something off the tray and **prompt** by saying, "Uh-oh." It would be anticipated that the child would spontaneously produce "Uh-oh" at subsequent meals.

Note: It is most likely that a child will spontaneously say a word when he is placed in a routine activity with which he is most familiar (e.g., getting dressed or changed, mealtimes, reading a book that has been read many times before, picking up a sibling at preschool). Spontaneous use of words may not occur until an activity such as the one outlined above has happened numerous times. You may not be present. Having a parent keep a journal of utterances is very useful for documentation.

E14a

Treatment Objective: The child will imitate the names of familiar objects.

Goal: The child will increase imitation of words. (EG2)

Communicative Intent (pragmatics)   Communicative Function
   Acknowledging   Naming

Activity: What's in the Bag?   **Expected age**: 9–12 months

Materials/Toys: small pillowcase or grab bag (drawstring, cloth 12" by 12" is ideal), a variety of objects that the child is familiar with and might be able to name (e.g., spoon, ball, car, baby doll, shoe, book, block)

Sit the child on your lap with the bag on the child's lap so he can feel that there are things inside. Put your hand into the bag and in a surprised voice say, "I found something! I found something!" Pull it out and label it. "A car! I found a car! Look! I found a car! See? The car goes 'brum.'" Give the object to the child and simply say, "car." The child may imitate. **Prompt** the child to label the item by saying the word *car* several more times. Repeat with the other items in the bag.

E14b

Treatment Objective: The child will imitate the names of familiar objects.

Goal: The child will increase imitation of words. (EG2)

Communicative Intent (pragmatics)   Communicative Function
   Acknowledging   Naming

Activity: Hide and Find   **Expected age**: 9–12 months

Materials/Toys: box with lid large enough to hide the objects in, common objects that are familiar to the child and that will be easy to name (e.g., ball, book, doggie, shoe, car)

Sit with the child on the floor. Show him the objects and let him play with each one. Label each object as he examines it, then drop it in the box and put the lid in place. Continue with each of the other objects. When all of the objects are in the box, tell the child, "We need to get them out of the box. Let's see what we can find." Lift the lid just a little bit, reach in, and grab an object. When you take it out, say the name of the object several times, "Ball. I found a ball. Ball." Wait to see if the child will imitate the name of the object. **Prompt** by telling the child, "You say it. 'Ball.' " Repeat with the other objects in the box.

E15a

Treatment Objective: The child will vary pitch when vocalizing.

Goal: The child will increase spontaneous use of vocalizations of non-speech sounds, speech sounds, and sound sequences. (EG3)

Communicative Intent (pragmatics)
    Requesting
        Object

Activity: Where Are You? **Expected age:** 12–15 months

Materials/Toys: large things to hide behind/under (e.g., table, chair)

The target is for the child to use varied pitch when asking the question "Where are you?" Have another person hide somewhere where she isn't immediately obvious (given the age of the child, she doesn't have to be too creative). Then start calling, "Where are you?" being sure to use different intonations for each word you say. Call several times. **Prompt** by waiting after you call to allow time for the child to imitate. When you find the person, make a big deal of finding her. Trade places and have the person (and the child) call using the same "Where are you?" utterance.

(Note: A child this age will probably limit his production to "Are you?" or "You" or may even just use a rising inflection vocalization of vowel sounds.)

E15b

Treatment Objective: The child will vary pitch when vocalizing.

Goal: The child will increase spontaneous use of vocalizations of non-speech sounds, speech sounds, and sound sequences. (EG3)

Communicative Intent (pragmatics)
    Requesting
        Action

Activity: Up and Down **Expected age:** 12–15 months

Materials/Toys: none

Pick up the child and tell him you're going to fly like an airplane. Lift the child above your head as you say, "Up" with a higher pitch and rising inflection. Lower the child as you say, "Down" with a lower pitch and falling inflection. Repeat several times, then pause to see if the child will use a change in inflection to get the activity to start again. **Prompt** by making the expression easier. Instead of using words, just use the syllable "uh." Produce "uh" with a high pitch and then a low pitch as you move the child up and down.

E16

Treatment Objective: The child will try to sing with a familiar song.

Goal: The child will increase imitation of words. (EG2)

Communicative Intent (pragmatics) Communicative Function
   Repeating/practicing
   Acknowledging

Activity: Singing "Old MacDonald" **Expected age:** 12–15 months

Materials/Toys: toy farm animals (optional)

Position the child so he is comfortable and can see your face. Sing "Old MacDonald," stressing the variety of animal sounds as you go and keeping eye contact with the child as much as you can. When the child attempts to imitate an animal sound, smile, tickle him, or clap to let him know that he did something special.

Note: Once a child realizes he can join in, he may use the same animal sound repeatedly, irrespective of the context. This is simply overgeneralization and not something that needs to be corrected at this point. If you are singing about sheep and the child "moos" like a cow, your laughter will no doubt make him do it again and again. This is fine at this stage.

E17a

Treatment Objective: The child will imitate new words.

Goal: The child will increase imitation of words. (EG2)

Communicative Intent (pragmatics) Communicative Function
   Requesting   Negation
      Object   Non-existence or disappearance
      Action   Recurrence
   Commenting   Attribution
      On object   Naming
      On action   Commenting

Activity: Bubble Talk **Expected age:** 12–15 months

Materials/Toys: bubbles

Sit on the floor with the child or let him stand while you kneel so you are closer to eye level. Blow some bubbles and say, "Bubbles." Say it several times without saying anything else while you continue to blow bubbles. Hearing the word several times may simply be sufficient for the child to say "Bubbles." If he doesn't say "Bubbles" the first time you do this activity, he may say it if you repeat the activity at another time. **Prompt** the child to say the word by asking between blows, "What do you want?" or "You want bubbles?"

This activity can also be used to stimulate the following words for a child to imitate: *off*, *pop*, *more*, *all gone*, *blow*, *yuck* (if he gets bubble mixture on himself), *big* (big bubbles), *little* (little bubbles), *see* or *there* (to point out bubbles), *shake* (as you shake the container), *out* (as you take the wand out of the container), and *all done* (when you finish the activity).

═══ E17b ═══

Treatment Objective: The child will imitate new words.

Goal: The child will increase imitation of words. (EG2)

Communicative Intent (pragmatics)   Communicative Function
  Requesting   Locative action
  Commenting
    On action

Activity: Doggie, Sit!   **Expected age:** 12–15 months

Materials/Toys: stuffed dog (or any animal the child likes to play with), a box the stuffed animal will fit in

While sitting on the floor with the child, put the stuffed animal out of reach. Use the word "Come" as you make the stuffed animal come to you. Stimulate the child to imitate the word "Come." Then tell the stuffed animal to "Go" and have him start running fast. Tell the stuffed animal to "Stop" as you make him stop quickly. Continue this activity, asking the child to imitate "Go" and "Stop." You can also have the stuffed animal get "Up" on the box and make him come "Down" when you tell him to. The stuffed animal can also hide "In" the box until you tell him to come "Out."

═══ E18 ═══

Treatment Objective: The child will use exclamatory expressions (e.g., "Uh-oh," "No-no").

Goal: The child will increase spontaneous use of single words. (EG4)

Communicative Intent (pragmatics)   Communicative Function
  Commenting   *Attribution*
    On object   *Existence*
                                                           Locative action
                                                           Naming

Activity: Knock It Down   **Expected age:** 12–15 months

Materials/Toys: blocks, cereal boxes, or other empty containers that can be stacked

Have the child sit by you on the floor. Stack the blocks or containers and then knock them down. *As you are building, you can stimulate the child to use the words "block, on," and "here."* As you knock over the blocks, say "Uh-oh." Perform the activity several times and overreact each time the blocks fall with a theatrical "Uh-oh!" If the child is unable to stack the blocks, do it for him. Elicit "Uh-oh" by stacking the blocks or having the child stack them and not saying "Uh-oh" to see if the child initiates the utterance.

═══ E19 ═══

Treatment Objective: The child will imitate three animal sounds.

Goal: The child will increase imitation of vocalizations of non-speech sounds, speech sounds, and sound sequences. (EG1)

Activity: Sing Along   **Expected age**: 12–15 months

Materials/Toys: none

Sit the child on your lap and say, "Let's sing a song." Tell the child that you are going to be a cow and that a cow says "moo."

Old MacDonald had a farm, E-I-E-I-O.
And on that farm there was a cow, E-I-E-I-O.
With a moo, moo here and a moo, moo there,
Here a moo, there a moo, everywhere a moo moo,
Old MacDonald had a farm, E-I-E-I-O.

Stop and say, "Let's do it again." Repeat the song. Then say, "Now we're going to be horses. Horses say 'neigh.' " Repeat the song twice, replacing "moo" with "neigh."

The important thing here is the repetition and simply telling the child what to expect. When the child becomes more savvy with this activity, you can let him pick what he wants to be.

E20a

Treatment Objective: The child will use early-developing modifiers.

Goal: The child will increase spontaneous use of single words. (EG4)

Communicative Intent (pragmatics)	Communicative Function
Action	Attribution
Commenting	Action on object
On object	Negation
On action	Non-existence or disappearance
Requesting	

Activity: Yucky Bubbles   **Expected age**: 12–15 months

Materials/Toys: no-spill bubble container, non-toxic bubble mixture

Blow a few bubbles for the child and then allow him to try to blow. He will inevitably get bubble mixture on his hands (and maybe around his mouth). As he notices the bubble mixture on him say, "Yuck!" If the child won't take the bubble wand or is oblivious to what it is, gently put some bubble mixture on his hand and **prompt** by saying, "Yuck! This is yucky!" Use intonation to show that it is slimy and wet. *When you put the bubbles away, stimulate use of "All gone." You can also use this activity to stimulate "Blow" and "Shake" (as you shake the mixture). If the child is reaching for the bubbles or vocalizing to request the bubbles, stimulate "Want" or "Mine."*

E20b

Treatment Objective: The child will use early-developing modifiers.

Goal: The child will increase spontaneous use of single words. (EG4)

Communicative Intent (pragmatics)	Communicative Function
Commenting	Attribution
On object	Negation
Requesting	Non-existence or disappearance
Action	Action on object

Activity: Icky   **Expected age:** 12–15 months

Materials/Toys: construction paper, brightly-colored small pieces of paper to glue on the construction paper, glue stick

Have the child sit at a small table or in his high chair with the tray in place. Put some glue on the back of one of the small pieces of paper and then stick it on the construction paper. Encourage the child to watch. Wait and see if the child asks for a turn. *Stimulate the use of "Do" (e.g., "You wanna do it?" or "Wanna?").* Then put lots of glue on another small piece of paper, hand it to the child, and say, "Your turn. Stick it on." The child will inevitably get glue on himself. When he does, say, "Icky! It feels icky." If necessary, gently take the child's finger and touch some glue. **Prompt** by saying, "Ick." When you put the glue away, stimulate use of *"All gone"* or *"All done."*

(Note: Children with sensory deficits may find this activity upsetting because they may not like the feel of the glue. If you note such sensory issues, an occupational therapy consult may be indicated.)

E20c

Treatment Objective: The child will use early-developing modifiers.

Goal: The child will increase spontaneous use of single words. (EG4)

Communicative Intent (pragmatics)	Communicative Function
Commenting	Attribution
On object	

Activity: It's Cold!   **Expected age:** 12–15 months

Materials/Toys: ice block (the reusable kind like Blue Ice), strong zippered plastic bag

Before the activity, put the ice block in the plastic bag. Hand the plastic bag with the ice block to the child. Say, "Cold. Brrrrr. It's cold." Encourage the child to take it to family members so they can feel it. Each time, model the word "Cold" and say, "Brrrrrr." Encourage the child to say "Cold." **Prompt** by asking, "Can you say 'cold'?"

E21

Treatment Objective: The child will answer questions with one word.

Goal: The child will increase spontaneous use of single words. (EG4)

Communicative Intent (pragmatics)	Communicative Function
Answering	Action on object
Commenting	Negation
On action	Non-existence or disappearance

Activity:	Snack Time	**Expected age**: 15–18 months

Materials/Toys:	high chair, typical snacks or meal foods

This activity works best during a routine with which the child is quite familiar. When it is time for a snack or a meal, ask the child, "What do you want to do?" Wait for the child to give you a response. If the child doesn't use a single word, such as "eat" to answer the question, **prompt** by modeling the word or by giving a choice (e.g., "Do you want to eat or take a nap?"). When the child is seated in the high chair, ask again "What do you want?" and await a response. If the child doesn't use a single word response, **prompt** by offering a choice of words (e.g., "Do you want a cracker or juice?").

This is also a good activity to stimulate other words that might occur naturally in this situation, including "Drink," "Throw" (if the child throws food or a spoon), and the name of the child's least favorite food. At the end of the activity, it's a good time to stimulate the word "Wash" as the child's hands and face are washed off, as well as "Get down" as the child is taken out of the high chair. You can also stimulate "All gone" or "No more" when the snack is all gone.

E22

Treatment Objective: The child will use a word to call attention to something.

Goal: The child will increase spontaneous use of single words. (EG4)

Communicative Intent (pragmatics)	Communicative Function
Commenting	Existence
On object	

Activity:	Do You See That?	**Expected age**: 15–18 months

Materials/Toys:	any new, interesting toy (especially one that makes noise or moves)

Without commenting on what you are doing, turn on/wind up the new toy and place it out of the child's reach. Don't engage in any other activities, but wait and see what the child does. If he doesn't use a word to call your attention to the toy, **prompt** by modeling a word (e.g., "that," "gimme," "see") while you point to the toy. Other opportunities will present themselves during treatment for the child to use a word to call attention. Whenever the child picks out a toy, act like you aren't paying attention to see if he will use a word to get your attention.

E23

Treatment Objective: The child will use a word to comment on an action or object.

Goal: The child will increase spontaneous use of single words. (EG4)

Communicative Intent (pragmatics)	Communicative Function
Commenting	Naming
On object	Commenting
On action	

Activity:	Outside Adventure	**Expected age**: 15–18 months

Materials/Toys:	none

Take the child outside and start looking, feeling, and listening. Wait to see what the child comments on. This is a good activity to stimulate the words "Inside" and "Outside" (or "Out") as well as "Open" and "Close" when you go in and out of the door. Point to and label everything that you see, feel, and hear (e.g., When you hear a plane, look up, point, and say, "Plane. I see a plane. I hear a plane"). **Prompt** by saying, "You say ____."

E24

Treatment Objective: The child will use a word to request an action.

Goal: The child will increase spontaneous use of single words. (EG4)

Communicative Intent (pragmatics)　　　Communicative Function
　Requesting　　　　　　　　　　　　　　Action on object
　　Action

Activity: Let's Go　　　　　**Expected age**: 15–18 months

Materials/Toys: child's swing, riding horse, or wagon (or anything that needs an adult to make it go)

Put the child in his swing, on the horse, or in the wagon. Wait to see if the child will use a word (e.g., "go," "push," "ride") to request that the adult start pushing or pulling. If the child doesn't say anything, **prompt** by asking, "What do you want?" You can further **prompt** by modeling the word to make the request.

E25

Treatment Objective: The child will ask, "What's that?"

Goal: The child will increase spontaneous use of word combinations. (EG5)

Communicative Intent (pragmatics)　　　Sentence Structure
　Requesting　　　　　　　　　　　　　　Interrogative
　　Information　　　　　　　　　　　　　　What/Where
　Commenting
　　On action

Activity: What's Under There?　　　　**Expected age**: 15–18 months

Materials/Toys: familiar items to the child (e.g., spoon, bib, keys, ball, sock, shoe, baby doll, phone, hat), kitchen towel or pillowcase, hand puppet

Take one of the items and hide it under the towel or in the pillowcase. Either put the hand puppet on or ask the parent to participate in the next step. With the hand puppet, feel the item through the towel and ask repeatedly, "What's that?" in an animated fashion. If the parent is participating, simply ask her to feel the item, act puzzled, and say lots of times, "What's that?" Then allow the child to pull the towel away to discover what the item is. *Stimulate the use of "pull" when you pull off the cover.* Try this first step a few times. Then encourage the child to put the puppet on himself and ask the question, "What's that?" as he feels the item. If he doesn't want the puppet (and some children won't), let him feel the item and **prompt** by modeling the question as he is doing so. The child may approximate the phrase by saying, "Whazzat?" or even just, "That?" with rising inflection.

E26a

Treatment Objective: The child will ask for "more."

Goal: The child will increase spontaneous use of single words. (EG4)

    Communicative Intent (pragmatics)   Communicative Function
        Requesting   Recurrence
            Object   *Action on object*
            Action

Activity: Bubble Blowing   **Expected age**: 15–18 months

Materials/Toys: bubbles

Sit on the floor with the child facing you. Blow one set of bubbles. Then say, "Let's blow some more." Blow more bubbles and say, "More. See? More bubbles. Let's blow some more." Before blowing more bubbles, ask the child, "What do you want?" The expected response is "More." If the child fails to say "More," **prompt** with, "Tell me what you want" or "I think we need more bubbles. Tell me 'More.' "

If the child wants a turn blowing, this is a good opportunity to stimulate "Gimme bubbles," "Wanna blow?," or "Me." You can also hand the bubbles to the child with the lid on tight to stimulate "Help."

(Note: This activity can be used to combine speech and sign by saying the word "more" and demonstrating the sign for "more" at the same time. A picture exchange system could also be used with the child handing a picture of bubbles to the clinician.)

E26b

Treatment Objective: The child will ask for "more."

Goal: The child will increase spontaneous use of single words. (EG4)

    Communicative Intent (pragmatics)   Communicative Function
        Requesting   Recurrence
            Object   *Action on object*
            Action

Activity: More For Me   **Expected age**: 15–18 months

Materials/Toys: cereal, Goldfish crackers, or other small snacks that the child especially likes

Give the child one or two pieces of snack and let him eat them. (Note: If you start with too many pieces, the child will spend too long eating them and won't want more.) Say, "I want more. Let's get more." Get out one more piece. When the child has eaten it, ask him what he wants. If he fails to say (or sign) "more," **prompt** by saying, "I bet you want more. I do!" Take a piece and eat it and watch for the child's reaction. **Prompt** him to say "more" by reminding him "Use your 'more' word to tell me what you want." If the child never makes an attempt to say the word, terminate the activity. *You can also stimulate use of "eat" during this activity.*

E27

Treatment Objective: The child will echo the prominent or last word spoken.

Goal: The child will increase imitation of words. (EG2)

Communicative Intent (pragmatics)
   Acknowledging

Communicative Function
   Action on object

Activity: Time to Eat   **Expected age:** 15–18 months

Materials/Toys: plastic spoons, cups, plates and bowls, pretend food, a small doll or character toy (e.g., Barney)

Set out the objects above with a place setting for the child, the doll/toy, and yourself. Say to the child, "I wanna eat!" Then, in reference to the doll/toy, say, "____ wants to eat!" In reference to the child, say, "(Child's name) wants to eat!" Keep using the word "eat" so the child hears it several times. Each time you say the word, be sure to be quiet for a few seconds so that the child has the nonverbal cue that he can say it too. If he does say the word, say "Yes! That's right! We are hungry and we want something to eat. I wanna eat. ____ wants to eat and (child's name) wants to eat." **Prompt** by asking, "Can you say 'eat'? "

(Note: This activity can be used to combine speech and sign by saying the word *hungry* and demonstrating the sign for *hungry* at the same time.)

E28

Treatment Objective: The child will name five to seven familiar objects on request.

Goal: The child will increase spontaneous use of single words. (EG4)

Communicative Intent (pragmatics)
   Commenting
      On object
   Answering

Communicative Function
   Naming

Activity: Name That Thing   **Expected age:** 15–18 months

Materials/Toys: cloth bag (preferably with drawstring) or box, items that are very familiar to the child (e.g., ball, plastic car, spoon, sock, block, baby doll, bib, plastic keys)

Fill the bag or box with the items. Make a big deal out of the container and say, "What's in here?" Put your hand in and pull out something. Tell the child what it is and let him touch it and feel it. If he labels it, tell him, "That's right. It's a ____." On the next try, encourage the child to put his own hand in and pull out something (some children may be reluctant to do this). Wait to **prompt** until the child has had sufficient time to do it on his own (up to 10 seconds). Then **prompt** by asking, "What's that?" or by labeling the object for the child to imitate.

E29

Treatment Objective: The child will use attribute-entity.

Goal: The child will increase spontaneous use of word combinations. (EG5)

Communicative Intent (pragmatics)
    Commenting
        On object
        On action

Semantic-Syntactic Relations
    Attribute-entity
    Action-object

Activity: Cars, Cars, Cars?

Expected age: 18–21 months

Materials/Toys: several toy cars (one that is noticeably bigger than the others and one that is broken in some way) that can be hidden

Engage the child in play with the cars. Label the cars with an attribute as you play. For example, "Big car, Broken car," or "Dirty car." See if the child will use the attribute and the word "car" to tell about one of the cars. Hold up two cars and ask the child, "Which one do you want?" He may simply point. If so, **prompt** by saying, "Do you want the big car or the broken car?" Continue to play with all of the cars, providing opportunities to use attribute words. *This is a good activity to stimulate other action words. These do not have to be only logical actions (e.g. push, ride, get), but illogical actions like shake, drop, kiss.*

E30

Treatment Objective: The child will use possessor-possession.

Goal: The child will increase spontaneous use of word combinations. (EG5)

Communicative Intent (pragmatics)
    Commenting
        On object
        On action

Semantic-Syntactic Relations
    Possessor–possession
    Action–object
    Entity-locative

Morphemes
    Possessive 's

Activity: Mommy's and Mine

Expected age: 18–21 months

Materials/Toys: duplicates of items belonging to parent and child (e.g., shoes for each, cup for each)

Engage the child in play with the items. As he takes one of the items, use a two-word combination to describe to whom it belongs (e.g., "Mommy's shoe," "Willie's cup"). Wait to see if the child will use this combination. If not, **prompt** by holding up one of the items and asking, "Is this Willie's shoe?" or, you might use the wrong possessor (e.g., asking "Is this Mommy's shoe?" when it is the child's shoe) to see if the child will correct you. You can also **prompt** by saying the two-word phrase, "Willie's shoe." (It is not necessary for the child to use the possessive 's.') Note: A child this age may indicate possession without using the **-s** (e.g., Mommy shoe).

This is a good activity for using comparatives such as "Too small" or "Too big" and locatives such as "Hat on" or "Socks off" and for modeling early pronouns (e.g., my, mine, yours). The verb "Pull" can be stimulated as you pull socks off. Children think it's funny to put their socks (or a parent's sock) on over their shoes. This makes it even more fun to pull them off. You can also stimulate other unexpected actions with the objects, such as "Throw socks," "Drop cup," or "Shake shoes."

E31

Treatment Objective: The child will use agent-action.

Goal: The child will increase spontaneous use of word combinations. (EG5)

Communicative Intent (pragmatics)
   Commenting
      On action

Semantic-Syntactic Relations
   Agent-action

Morphemes
   Present Progressive -*ing*

Sentence Structure
   Declarative

Activity: What Can Teddy Do?   **Expected age:** 18–21 months

Materials/Toys: child's favorite toys (e.g., stuffed toy or doll, ball, car)

Sit on the floor with the child and a favorite toy. Tell the child that "It's (name of toy)'s turn to do some things." Tell him you'll make the toy do something and then the child can tell what he is doing. Have the toy perform actions, such as kissing the child, running, walking, hugging, dancing, falling, sitting down, jumping, standing, crying, and riding. While the toy is performing the action, ask, "What is (name of toy) doing?" The expected response is "(name of toy) + verb" (child does not need to use the -ing). If the child just uses the verb, **prompt** by modeling the two-word phrase. You can make the use of the agent more natural by having two toys. Only have one of the toys perform the action. Then if the child uses just the verb, you can say "Is (name of toy) verb + ing or is (name of second toy) verb + ing?"

E32

Treatment Objective: The child will use action-object.

Goal: The child will increase spontaneous use of word combinations. (EG5)

Communicative Intent (pragmatics)
   Commenting
      On object

Semantic-Syntactic Relations
   Action-object
      Non-existence or disappearance

Sentence Structure
   Declarative
      Action + object

Activity: Paper, Paper Everywhere   **Expected age:** 18–21 months

Materials/Toys: any paper the child can tear up, trash can

Sit on the floor with the child with the trash can nearby. Take a piece of the paper and model how to tear the paper. Give the child a piece so he can tear it up as you model the phrase "Tear paper." Hold up your torn piece of paper and say, "See paper." Wad up the paper after you have torn it and throw it in the trash can as you model, "Throw paper." Children enjoy doing things that seem silly or unexpected, so use other action words, such as "Pull paper," "Kick paper," or "Kiss paper." *When the activity is finished, stimulate the phrase "All gone" or "All done."*

E33

Treatment Objective: The child will use agent-object.

Goal: The child will increase spontaneous use of word combinations. (EG5)

Communicative Intent (pragmatics)
   Commenting
      On object
      On action

Semantic-Syntactic Relations
   Agent-object

Activity: Playhouse

Expected age: 18–21 months

Materials/Toys: dollhouse with people and furniture

Play with the house and people. Have a person perform an action with an object and instead of modeling action-object (e.g., "Push chair"), use agent-object (e.g., "Daddy chair" or "Boy door") to describe the actions. Then perform the actions again and wait to see if the child will use this form. If not, **prompt** by modeling the phrase. You can also do this activity with family members, real furniture, and a variety of objects the child is familiar with.

E34

Treatment Objective: The child will use vocalizations and gestures to request toys or food.

Goal: The child will increase spontaneous use of single words. (EG4)

Communicative Intent (pragmatics)
   Requesting
      Object

Communicative Function
   Recurrence
   Negation
      Non-existence or disappearance

Activity: Want More?

Expected age: 18–21 months

Materials/Toys: small food items that appeal to child

> Note: Check with the caregiver before you give the child any food to find out about food allergies and dietary preferences.

Place the child in his high chair or equivalent with a clean surface in front of him. Put two food items on the tray or table and draw his attention to them by saying, "Look! Yummy! Yummy!" Take one piece and eat it. Allow the child to get the other piece. Stimulate the name of the child's favorite food. **Prompt** if the child fails to take the food by handing it to him or bringing it toward his mouth. Once the child has eaten the first piece, show him the container that the food came from. Tell the child, "I want more" and help yourself to another piece. If the child reaches toward the container, ask, "More?" If the child makes any attempt to say "More," sign "more," or make another vocalization indicating that he wants more, give him another piece. Attempt to disengage visually (i.e., don't look at the child) while holding the container of food out of his reach in an attempt to get the child to vocalize/verbalize. When he does so successfully, acknowledge his effort and say, "I liked the way you used your words to tell me you wanted more." If the child fails to vocalize, **prompt** by simply taking a piece of food and placing it where the child can see it easily but where it is out of reach. Get his attention and ask, "More?" If he then points to the food, give it to him. If in successive trials he makes any vocalization, acknowledge that he "told" you what he wanted. *When the snacks are gone, you can stimulate "All gone."*

E35

Treatment Objective: The child will name a few pictures.

Goals: The child will increase spontaneous use of single words. (EG4)
(Note: If the child is using phrases to name the pictures, then EG5 is more appropriate.)

    Communicative Intent (pragmatics)   Communicative Function
      Commenting   Naming
        On object
        On action

The child will increase spontaneous use of word combinations. (EG5)

    Communicative Intent (pragmatics)   Semantic-Syntactic Relations   Morphemes
                                         Demonstrative-entity

Activity: What's That?   **Expected age:** 18–21 months

Materials/Toys: book with realistic pictures (ideally photographs) that are familiar to the child (e.g., spoon, cup, bib, shoe, sock, banana, dog, baby, car, diaper, cracker, cookie, ball, pacifier)

Hold the child on your lap. He will probably spend more time participating in the activity if he is on your lap rather than sitting by you or on the floor across from you where it is easy to jump up and do something else. *Stimulate the word "read" when you get out the book.* When the child sees the pictures, wait to see if he spontaneously labels them. If not, **prompt** with the following technique. Look at the book with the child and use carrier phrases, such as "I see _____" or "Here's a _____," filling in the word each time. Then point to the items to see if the child generates his own response. You can also **prompt** by asking, "What's that?" and tapping the picture. You may have to repeat this activity a few times before the child spontaneously labels the pictures.

E36

Treatment Objective: The child will use entity-locative.

Goal: The child will increase spontaneous use of word combinations. (EG5)

    Communicative Intent (pragmatics)   Semantic-Syntactic Relations
      Commenting   Entity-locative
        On object

    Morphemes
      in
      on

Activity: Dollhouse Play   **Expected age:** 21–24 months

Materials/Toys: dollhouse with people and furniture

Play with the house and people. Put different people in different locations (e.g., on the bed, on the floor, on the stairs, under the bed, in the yard, in the kitchen). Model entity-locative (e.g., "Boy bed," "Boy inside," "Dog outside," "Dog floor," "Boy stairs," "Mommy bed," "Daddy kitchen"). Then put the person in another location and wait to see if the child will use this entity-locative form. If not, **prompt** by modeling the phrase. You can also do this activity with family members, real furniture, and a variety of objects the child is familiar with.

E37

Treatment Objective: The child will use action-locative.

Goal: The child will increase spontaneous use of word combinations. (EG5)

Communicative Intent (pragmatics)
  Commenting
    On action

Semantic-Syntactic Relations
  Action-locative

Morphemes
  in
  on

Activity: Where Can We Hide?

Expected age: 21–24 months

Materials/Toys: large cardboard box, some toys

Play with the toys and the box. Perform actions with the toys relative to the box and use two-word phrases to describe (e.g., "Put in," "Throw in," "Put under"). If the box is big enough, let the child play with the box and follow your directions (e.g., "Get in," "Crawl under," "Jump in," "Go under, Get up"). Wait to see if the child will use this action-locative form to describe the location of the toy (e.g., "Ball in," "Put on"). If not, **prompt** by modeling the phrase.

E38a

Treatment Objective: The child will use his own name to refer to himself.

Goal: The child will increase spontaneous use of single words. (EG4)

Communicative Intent (pragmatics)
  Answering
  Calling attention

Communicative Function
  Existence

Activity: Who Am I?

Expected age: 21–24 months

Materials/Toys: none

(Note: This is a good activity to include other family members. If there aren't others around, use dolls or stuffed animals that have names.)

Sit down with the child and anyone else you are able to include in the activity. Sing the song on the next page to the tune of "Frère Jacques."

I see (child's name).
I see (child's name).
Yes I do!
Yes I do!
I see (child's name).
I see (child's name).
Yes I do!
Yes I do!

As you say the child's name (or that of someone else participating), be sure to physically pat him so it is easy for the child to associate what the name refers to. Sing the song several times through to allow the child to become familiar with it and then join in. Don't expect the child to sing the whole song. **Prompt** by singing the first two words "I see." Then pause for the child to fill in his name.

This is a good activity to stimulate the pronouns "you" and "me." If other family members are present, it's a good opportunity to stimulate use of their names too.

(Note: This is a great activity for the beginning and end of every session. It's a good way to bring the child's focus to you and your activities and something for him to anticipate as part of his routine during the time he spends with you.)

E38b

Treatment Objective: The child will use his own name to refer to himself.

Goal: The child will increase spontaneous use of single words. (EG4)

Communicative Intent (pragmatics)
 Answering
 Calling attention

Communicative Function
 Existence

Activity: Who Is That?   **Expected age:** 21–24 months

Materials/Toys: large mirror

(Note: This is a good activity to include other family members. If there aren't others around, use dolls or stuffed animals that have names.)

Sit on the floor with the child in front of a mirror. Touch your image in the mirror and say, "That's (your name)." Touch the child's image and say, "Who is that? That's ____ (child's name)." Pause to see if the child will take a turn and do the same thing. If not, **prompt** by touching the child's image in the mirror and asking, "Who is that?" If the child still doesn't respond, further **prompt** by saying, "Is that ____? Can you say ____?" *You can also stimulate "me" and "you."*

E39

Treatment Objective: The child will use early pronouns occasionally.

Goals: The child will increase spontaneous use of single words. (EG4)
(Note: If the child is using short sentences, such as "I want one" or "Give me one," then EG5 is more appropriate.)

Communicative Intent (pragmatics)	Communicative Function
Answering	Possession
Requesting	*Action on object*
Action	*Locative action*
Commenting	
On object	

The child will increase spontaneous use of word combinations. (EG5)

Semantic-Syntactic Relations	Morphemes	Sentence Structure
Agent-action	*on*	Declarative
Denial		Subject + verb + object

Activity: Give It To Me!   **Expected age**: 21–24 months

Materials/Toys: any form of toy that child can build with (e.g., blocks, Legos)

This activity works best if you include a family member. Tell them "We're going to build." Then ask, "Who wants a block?" Ask the family member to say "Me!" Repeatedly ask the question, encouraging the child to say "Me." You can combine your question with a gesture for "me" by putting your hand against your chest and saying "me" at the same time. **Prompt** by saying, "Tell me 'me.' " If the child does not attempt to say "me," he may copy the gesture for "me" and then on subsequent trials at a later date, may achieve the verbalization. *You can also stimulate phrases like "Gimme block," "That block," "Put it there," and "Make a tower." The word "on" can be used in phrases (e.g., "on floor," "on top," "on leg").*

If the child needs extra help with pronouns, here are some books you might read:
    Are You My Mother? by P. D. Eastman
    Brown Bear, Brown Bear, What Do You See? by Bill Martin Jr & Eric Carle
    Here Are My Hands by Bill Martin Jr & John Auchambault
    Look There's My Hat by Maureen Roffey
    My House by Noelle Carter

E40a

Treatment Objective: The child will imitate two numbers or unrelated words on request.

Goal: The child will increase imitation of words. (EG2)

Communicative Intent (pragmatics)	Communicative Function
Commenting	Naming
On object	

Activity: Let's Be a Parrot   **Expected age**: 24–27 months

Materials/Toys: hand puppet of any type of animal or a puppet made out of an old sock

Place the puppet on your hand and introduce him to the child. (Be aware that some children can be afraid of puppets.) Tell the child that the puppet's name is Polly. Explain that Polly likes to play a game where she says two words and someone repeats what she says.

Say the child's name in a silly voice and then say, "Polly wants me to copy her. She said 'bed, shoe' so I have to say it too." Repeat what Polly said. Then go around the room labeling things that are familiar to the child or have the familiar objects gathered in front of you. Remember to name things that are not related (e.g., Don't say, "shoe, sock"). Point to or hold up the objects and have the puppet name them. Copy what the puppet says. Tell the child that Polly wants him to copy to. **Prompt** by repeating the words again, and telling the child, "You say it."

As is, this activity introduces many nouns. In order to introduce verbs, you can perform two actions and have the puppet tell what you did (e.g., "run, walk"). You can also have the child perform the actions with you and then have the puppet say what you did. Have the child copy the words the puppet said.

(Note: Having a family member participate in this activity may encourage the child to participate.)

E40b

Treatment Objective: The child will imitate two numbers or unrelated words on request.

Goal: The child will increase imitation of words. (EG2)

Communicative Intent (pragmatics)　　Communicative Function
　Commenting　　　　　　　　　　　　　Naming
　　On object

Activity: How Many?　　　　**Expected age:** 24–27 months

Materials/Toys: any toy or object with lots of pieces (e.g., puzzle, dry macaroni, child's socks)

Put several objects on the table with some in one pile and some in a separate pile (e.g., four socks: one on one side of the table and the other three in a separate pile). Point to the piles and say the number of items in each pile (e.g., "one . . . three"). Ask the child to repeat as you point again (the object is not to teach number concepts or to have the child count, but simply to have the child repeat the numbers you say). **Prompt** by holding up the number of fingers for the numbers you are saying.

E41

Treatment Objective: The child will sing phrases of songs.

Goal: The child will increase spontaneous use of word combinations. (EG5)

Communicative Intent (pragmatics)　　Semantic-Syntactic Relations
　Repeating/practicing

Morphemes　　　　　　　　　　　　　　Sentence Structure

Activity: Sing Along　　　　**Expected age:** 24–27 months

Materials/Toys: none

This activity is one that probably needs to be repeated each session and is great for a home program. Have the child sit comfortably on your lap or on the caregiver's lap where the child can easily see you. Slowly sing a song such as "Itsy Bitsy Spider." Use the actions if at all possible. (If you can get the caregiver to join in, all the better.) Sing the song a couple of times through. The child may spontaneously join in (especially with the actions). If the child does not spontaneously begin to sing part of the song with you, **prompt** by pausing to see if the child will fill in the end of a phrase.

Note: In a song such as "Old MacDonald," you can allow the child to choose the animals you will use. You can do this by pausing after "And on this farm he had a _____." If the child is unable to label an animal, show him some pictures of farm animals or try stuffed animals/plastic animals (as long as the toys don't distract him from singing the song).

E42

Treatment Objective: The child will name objects in photographs.

Goals: The child will increase spontaneous use of single words. (EG4)
(Note: If the child is using phrases to name objects, then EG5 is more appropriate.)

Communicative Intent (pragmatics)	Communicative Function
Commenting On object Answering	Naming

The child will increase spontaneous use of word combinations. (EG5)

Semantic-Syntactic Relations
  Demonstrative-entity

Activity: Name Game   **Expected age**: 24–27 months

Materials/Toys: book with realistic photographs of familiar things for child (Dorling Kindersley books are excellent) or photographs in newspaper circulars of things that are familiar to the child

Have the child sit comfortably on your lap or by you. Show him the picture and name it. Use a carrier phrase such as "I see (name of item)" or "I found (name of item)." Then tell him, "Your turn." If the child simply points to the picture, label it so he can hear your production. You may need to repeat the activity several times before child is able to spontaneously label.

E43

Treatment Objective: The child will use action words.

Goals: The child will increase spontaneous use of single words. (EG4)
(Note: If the child is using phrases, such as "Push the ball" or "Kick the ball," then EG5 is more appropriate.)

Communicative Intent (pragmatics)	Communicative Function
Requesting Action	Action on object

The child will increase spontaneous use of word combinations. (EG5)

Semantic-Syntactic Relations	Sentence Structure
Action-object	Declarative

Activity: Roll It! Throw It! Bounce It!   **Expected age**: 24–27 months

Materials/Toys: ball

Sit far enough away from the child so he can easily propel a ball toward you in whatever fashion works best for him. Spend a couple of minutes passing the ball back and forth as you describe what you are doing (e.g., "I'm going to bounce the ball," "I'm going to roll the ball"). Then stop the activity and say to the child, "Shall I roll the ball or bounce the ball?" Hopefully this will elicit the desired response of an action word. Other action words are acceptable responses (e.g., push, give, kick, hide). **Prompt** by asking the child to "Say '_____.'"

If the child needs extra help with action words, here are some books you might read:

Babies by Gyo Fujikwa	*I Used to Be the Baby* by Robin Ballard
Carl's Birthday by Alexandra Day	*Jesse Bear, What Will You Wear?* by Nancy White Carlstrom
Cat's Play by Lisa Campbell Ernst	*Jessica* by Kevin Henkes
Chester's Way by Kevin Henkes	*Only You* by Rosemary Wells
D. W.'s Guide to Preschool by Marc Brown	*There is a Big, Beautiful World Out There* by Nancy Carlson
I Love You Because You Are You by Liza Baker	*What Mommies Do Best* by Laura Numeroff

If the child is having difficulty with this activity, you may need to first use easier books that feature only one action per page. **Prompt** by pointing to the picture and labeling the action. You could also physically **prompt** by helping the child point to the target action. When the child has mastered this task, then move on to books that feature more than one action per page. Some easier books you might consider are:

Max Drives Away by Rosemary Wells
Sam Loves Kisses by Yves Got
Show Me! by Tom Tracey
Wibbly Pig Likes Bananas by Mick Inkpen

E44

Treatment Objective: The child will name one color.

Goals: The child will increase spontaneous use of single words. (EG4)
(Note: If the child is using a phrase, such as "That's blue" to answer, then EG5 is more appropriate.)

Communicative Intent (pragmatics)   Communicative Function
  Answering   Attribution

The child will increase spontaneous use of word combinations. (EG5)

Semantic-Syntactic Relations   Morphemes
  Demonstrative-entity   Contractible copula

Sentence Structure
  Declarative
    Subject + Copula + Complement

Activity: Pick a Color, Any Color   **Expected age:** 27–30 months

Materials/Toys: large blocks (e.g., Duplo)

Play with the blocks, being sure to label the color that is the target of the session. Do not label the other colors (e.g., if the target color is red, name red as you pick it up but don't name green or blue or yellow). When you come across one that is not the target color, simply say, "Not _____" and put it aside. After modeling this several times, hold up a block of the target color and ask, "What color?" **Prompt** by modeling the word you want the child to say. This is also a good opportunity to stimulate the use of "That" in "That one" or "That one is _____."

You may want to see if there is a particular color that the child shows a preference toward. There may be a color that is significant for the child (e.g., his cup, his coat, his favorite color Popsicle), so ask the caregiver before you begin the activity.

Remember that children start naming just one or two colors, so if they are introduced to too many during a therapy session it may be confusing. Stay with one color until the child definitely knows this color before choosing another color to have the child name. This does not preclude the caregiver labeling all colors during daily activities.

=== E45 ===

Treatment Objective: The child will consistently refer to himself by pronouns.

Goals: The child will increase spontaneous use of single words. (EG4)
(Note: If the child is using a phrase containing a pronoun, such as "I do" or "I want one," then EG5 is more appropriate.)

Communicative Intent (pragmatics)   Communicative Function
   Answering   Possession

The child will increase spontaneous use of word combinations. (EG5)
Semantic-Syntactic Relations   Sentence Structure
   Action-object   Declarative
   Agent-object   Agent + action
                                         Subject + verb + object

Activity: Give It to Me   **Expected age**: 27–30 months

Materials/Toys: any toy that child can build with (e.g., blocks, Legos)

This activity works best if you include a family member. Tell them, "We're going to build." Then ask, "Who wants a block?" Ask the other participant to say "Me!" each time you ask. Encourage the child to say "Me." You can combine the word "me" with a gesture, such as putting your hand against your chest and saying "Me" at the same time. If the child fails to attempt to say "Me," he may initially copy the gesture. On subsequent trials at a later date, he may achieve the verbalization. Try to get the child to use the whole phrase "Give it to me."

=== E46 ===

Treatment Objective: The child will use two sentence types.

Goal: The child will increase spontaneous use of word combinations. (EG5)

Communicative Intent (pragmatics) 　Requesting 　　Information 　Commenting 　　On action	Semantic-Syntactic Relations 　Agent-action
Morphemes 　Present Progressive *-ing* 　Contractible auxiliary	Sentence Structure 　Declarative 　　Subject + auxiliary + verb + object

Activity: Barney Says **Expected age**: 27–30 months

Materials/Toys: Barney or another familiar character or stuffed toy that is interesting to the child

Tell the child that you are going to play a game with Barney (or whatever character you choose). Start by modeling some different simple noun + verb sentences with Barney (e.g., "Barney is sleeping," "Barney is jumping," "Barney is eating"). If the child makes an attempt to imitate, restate the phrase. **Prompt** the child by modeling what Barney is doing.

Then hide Barney behind you or behind a piece of furniture so the child can't see him. Tell the child that he has to ask what Barney is doing and then you'll show him (e.g., "What's Barney doing?").

(Note: Within the context of this simple activity, there are a variety of simple sentence types that can be modeled [e.g., declarative, negative, interrogative].)

E47

Treatment Objective: The child will respond to greetings consistently.

Goal: The child will increase spontaneous use of single words. (EG4)

Communicative Intent (pragmatics) 　Greeting	Communicative Function 　Social interaction

Activity: Greetings Everyone! **Expected age**: 27–30 months

Materials/Toys: variety of stuffed toys or figures

Place the toys or figures on the floor in front of you. Tell the child, "Our friends are going to say 'Hi!' " Pick up the first toy and move it around. Have it say, "Hi! (child's name)" (e.g., "Barney said, 'Hi Lucy!' "). Then go on to other toys, "Superman says, 'Hi Lucy!,' " "Teddy says, 'Hi Lucy!,' " and so on.

Now tell the child, "It's our turn to say 'Hi!' " Pick up one toy and say, "Hi Barney." Pause to see if the child will repeat. Then say, "Hi Superman!" Again pause to see if the child will repeat. If the child fails to imitate, **prompt** by picking up the toy and in a voice meant to be the toy's voice, have the toy tell the child "Hi!" Wait for a response. If the child doesn't say anything, say, "Superman can't hear you." It may be necessary to model numerous times or repeat activity at another time. You can also **prompt** by telling the child to "Say, 'Hi' to _____."

As you put the toys away, stimulate the use of "Bye" as you say "Bye" to each toy.

E48

Treatment Objective: The child will use past tense.

Goal: The child will increase spontaneous use of word combinations. (EG5)

Communicative Intent (pragmatics)
   Commenting
     On action

Semantic-Syntactic Relations
   Agent-action

Morphemes
   Regular past tense -ed

Sentence Structure
   Declarative
     Agent + action

Activity: Do What I Do

Expected age: 27–30 months

Materials/Toys: none

Tell the child "Let's play 'Follow the Leader.'" Start by being the leader and tell the child to do what you do. Do things like waving, jumping, and knocking. Try to do things that have regular –ed past tense endings (as opposed to "blowing" where the past tense is "blew"). Go through the sequence a couple of times and tell the child what he did (e.g., waved, jumped, knocked). Then go through the sequence again and wait for the child to say what he did after you demonstrate the actions. Another way to elicit the target is while you are performing the actions, tell the child, "Look. I'm jumping." Then stop and say, "What did I do? I _____." If the child simply says "jump," say "That's right. I jumped."

If the child needs extra help with past tense, here are two books you might read:
   It's the Bear by Jez Alborough
   The Ball Bounced by Nancy Tafuri

E49

Treatment Objective: The child will request actions or objects.

Goal: The child will increase spontaneous use of word combinations. (EG5)

Communicative Intent (pragmatics)
   Requesting
     Object

Semantic-Syntactic Relations
   Action-object

Morphemes
   Articles

Sentence Structure
   Declarative
     Subject + verb + object

Activity: I Want It

Expected age: 27–30 months

Materials/Toys: several toys/objects that are familiar to the child, drawstring bag or brown paper bag

Spend some time with the child looking at the items, describing them and labeling them. Then put them in the bag where the child can't see them. Say, "I want the duck." Put your hand in and pull out the duck. Repeat the sequence a few times so it is familiar to the child, putting the object back into the bag each time.

Then say to the child, "Hmm, I wonder what's in here." Attempt to elicit a response (e.g., "duck, "ball"). If the child has trouble remembering specific items, **prompt** with "Do you want the duck or the ball?" When the child names the item, rummage until you find the item and say, "Yes! You told me what you wanted." You could also **prompt** by modeling the phrase and asking the child, "Tell me 'I want the ball.' " Have the child use "Gimme + ____" or "Give me + ____." You can extend the activity to include family members/caregivers by saying, "I wonder what (family member's name) wants." Encourage the child to ask the family member what she wants and then to use a phrase to request the item to give it to the family member.

(Note: If the child is having problems remembering several items in the bag, reduce it to two or three [e.g., favorite blanket and Barney] to make it easier.)

E50

Treatment Objective: The child will name five pictures.

Goals: The child will increase spontaneous use of single words. (EG4)
(Note: If the child is using phrases to name the pictures, such as "That's a ____," then EG5 is more appropriate.)

Communicative Intent (pragmatics)
   Commenting
     On object
   Answering

Communicative Function
   Naming

The child will increase spontaneous use of word combinations. (EG5)

Semantic-Syntactic Relations
   Demonstrative-entity

Morphemes
   Articles

Sentence Structure
   Declarative

Activity: Name That Picture   **Expected age**: 27–30 months

Materials/Toys: picture book with photographs that are familiar to the child or newspaper circulars

Sit somewhere comfortable with the child (couch, chair, floor) so you have his attention. If he is sitting on your lap, place your arms loosely around him. This may reduce the likelihood that he will get distracted.

Start at the beginning of the book and simply label the pictures. You can use a carrier phrase (e.g., "I see ____," "It's a ____") or simply label the items. If the child repeats or spontaneously labels items, you may be able to elicit five words. If the child repeats what you say, but doesn't label anything spontaneously, **prompt** by pointing to items and saying, "I see ____."

E51

Treatment Objective: The child will use negation.

Goal: The child will increase spontaneous use of word combinations. (EG5)

Communicative Intent (pragmatics)	Semantic-Syntactic Relations
Commenting	Denial
On object	
Morphemes	Sentence Structure
in	Negative

Activity: Where Does It Go? **Expected age:** 27–30 months

Materials/Toys: wooden puzzle with no more than four or five pieces (preferably with knobs)

Sit down on the floor or at a table where the child is comfortably positioned. Start by doing the puzzle yourself. As you put it together, stimulate language by saying, "The _____ goes here" or "Put it here." Then purposely try to put a piece in the wrong hole as you model use of negation (e.g., "That's not right," "Not there," "Not in here," "That doesn't fit," "It won't fit," "Not here").

Then have the child try. Clap and cheer every time he gets a piece in the right spot. If the child is not verbalizing actions using negatives, interrupt his activity and purposely put a piece in the wrong spot. Pause to see if the child will use negation to describe your action. If not, **prompt** by asking, "Does it go here?" Model the negation in a phrase, such as "Won't go here" or "Not here." Then put the piece in the correct place, say "Yes!" and clap.

(Note: Some children may put a piece in the wrong spot by themselves after they have put it in the right spot a few times just to see your reaction. If so, this is a great time to model "Not there" or "Not in that hole" if the puzzle piece is in the wrong place.)

If the child needs extra help with negation, here are some books you might read:
  But Not the Hippopotamus by Sandra Boynton
  Do You Want to Be My Friend? by Eric Carle
  Have You Seen My Cat? by Eric Carle

(Note: Many books can be adapted for work on negation. Books with opposites, for example, can be used by saying "not + the attribute [e.g., "hot" and "not hot" vs. "hot" and "cold"]").

E52

Treatment Objective: The child will answer questions with "yes" or "no."

Goal: The child will increase spontaneous use of single words. (EG4)

Communicative Intent (pragmatics)	Communicative Function
Answering	Negation
	Denial
	Existence

Activity: Where's Teddy? **Expected age:** 30–33 months

Materials/Toys: small stuffed animal that the child is interested in but not so interested that he won't let you hide it

Show the child the stuffed animal and say, "This is Teddy. Teddy likes to play hide-and-seek. Teddy's going to hide." When the child isn't watching, move the stuffed animal to a less obvious spot (e.g., behind the couch, under the coffee table). Then say, "Where's Teddy?" With lots of expression say, "Teddy! Teddy! Where are you?" Ask the child a series of questions that require *yes/no* answers such, as "Is Teddy in my hand?" or "Is Teddy in your lap?" Each time, wait for the child to respond "No!" If the child doesn't respond, **prompt** by modeling "No, Teddy's not there." Then give the appropriate location and ask, "Is Teddy behind the couch?" Wait for the child to say "Yes." If he doesn't, **prompt** by saying in a "Teddy bear" voice, "Yes! Yes! I'm behind the couch!" Teddy can also answer "I'm here." On the next round, hide the stuffed animal in a slightly more difficult spot (e.g. under a cushion) and use several rounds of "No, not there" before you help the child find the stuffed animal and say "Yes!"

If the child needs extra help answering *yes/no* questions, here are some books you might read:
Are You My Mother? by P. D. Eastman
Double Trouble by Rose Greydanus
Pretend You're a Cat by Jean Marzollo & Jerry Pinkney
Where's Spot? by Eric Hill

E53

Treatment Objective: The child will imitate a series of three numbers or unrelated words.

Goal: The child will increase imitation of words. (EG2)

Communicative Intent (pragmatics)
  Commenting
    On action

Communicative Function
  Naming

Activity: 1-2-3
Materials/Toys: none

Expected age: 30–33 months

Tell the child you are going to play a jumping game. Stand together and hold his hand. Tell him that you are going to "count" and then make a BIG jump. Swing his arm as you count "One! Two! Three!" and then jump forward. You can do similar activity on the playground as you go down the slide or you hold the child on a swing. When you get to "three," give the child a big push. Repeat the activity and ask the child to count after you do. Swing your arms, count to three, and jump. Then ask the child to imitate. **Prompt** by saying the numbers with the child when it is his turn.

E54

Treatment Objective: The child will use plurals.

Goals: The child will increase spontaneous use of single words. (EG4)
(Note: If the child is using plurals in phrases, such as "I want bubbles" or "Make more bubbles," then EG5 is more appropriate.)

Communicative Intent (pragmatics)
  Requesting
    Object

Communicative Function
  Commenting

The child will increase spontaneous use of word combinations. (EG5)

Semantic-Syntactic Relations
   Agent-object
   Attribute-entity
	Morphemes
	   Regular plurals -s
	   Present progressive –ing
	   Articles

Sentence Structure
   Declarative
      Subject + verb + object	

Activity: One Bubble or Two?   **Expected age**: 30–33 months

Materials/Toys: bubble soap

Sit on the floor with the child. Tell the child you are going to play bubbles and that sometimes you're going to make one bubble and that other times you're going to make bubble "friends." Start by blowing a single bubble and then telling the child that this bubble wants some "friends." *Use phrases to stimulate language such as "I'm blowing" or "That's a big bubble."* Then blow more and use the word "bubbles" multiple times, stressing the plural marker. Pause and ask the child, "What should I blow?" **Prompt** by asking, "Do you want one bubble or lots of bubbles?" If the child says "bubble" and you blow one and the child seems upset or tells you "No," use the opportunity to say, "Oh, you wanted more. You wanted lots of bubbles."

(Note: If the child has a phonological disorder, he may not be able to produce final /s/. If that is the case, you will not be able to work on this goal until the child has a final sibilant to mark plurality.)

E55

Treatment Objective: The child will use prepositions.

Goal: The child will increase spontaneous use of word combinations. (EG5)

Communicative Intent (pragmatics)
   Requesting
   Action
   Answering
	Semantic-Syntactic Relations
	   Action-locative

Morphemes
   on
   in
	Sentence Structure
	   Declarative
	      Subject + verb + object

(Note: Other prepositions appropriate at this age are "inside" and "under.")

Activity: Hats Off!   **Expected age**: 30–33 months

Materials: a variety of hats

Sit on the floor with the child and tell him you're going to try on some hats. As you put on each hat, be sure to label what you are doing (e.g., "This hat is *on* my head"). Use "off" as you take off the hat or accidentally let it fall off. Then pick up a different hat and ask the child, "What should I do with this?" in an attempt to elicit "on" in a phrase such as "Put on" or "Put it on." Similarly ask the child what you should do while you are wearing a hat. If the child doesn't immediately come up with the desired target, **prompt** by giving him the choice of "off" or "on." You can extend the activity by putting the hats "on" and "off" other people or stuffed toys.

You can also put the hats in funny places to teach prepositions (e.g., put a hat under a chair or in a box).

If the child needs extra help with prepositions, here are some books you might read:
Each Peach Pear Plum by Allan & Janet Ahlberg
Everything Has a Place by Patricia Lillie
Inside, Outside, Upside Down by Stan & Jan Berenstain
One Gorilla by Atusko Morozumi
Snake In, Snake Out by Linda Banchek

E56

Treatment Objective: The child will state his gender. (Note: This objective is best met using people that are familiar to the child as points of reference.)

Goals: The child will increase spontaneous use of single words. (EG4)
(Note: If child is using phrases or sentences to answer, such as "I'm a boy," then EG5 is more appropriate.)

| Communicative Intent (pragmatics) | Communicative Function |
| Answering | Attribution |

The child will increase spontaneous use of word combinations. (EG5)

| Semantic-Syntactic Relations | Morphemes |
| Attribute-entity | Contractible copula |

Sentence Structure
Declarative
Subject + copula + compliment

Activity: He's a Boy and She's a Girl   **Expected age:** 30–33 months

Materials/Toys: family photo album or picture book with people

Look at the photo album with the child seated by you or on your lap. Point to the people and label them as "boy" or "girl." **Prompt** by asking the child to say these with you as you look at the pictures. You can also point to a picture and ask the child, "Is that a boy/girl?" and wait for a response. Then ask, "Are you a boy or a girl?" The child should answer "I am a ____" or "I'm a ____." They may use a single word answer (e.g., "boy" or "girl").

E57

Treatment Objective: The child will state his first and last name.

Goal: The child will increase spontaneous use of single words. (EG4)

| Communicative Intent (pragmatics) | Communicative Function |
| Answering | Naming |

Activity: What's Your Name?   **Expected age:** 30–33 months

Materials: none

Tell the child your name, saying your first and last name. Then tell the child his name. Encourage the child to get a sense of there being two parts in his name by jumping forward for his first name and then jumping again for his last name. If there are other people present, do the same activity for their names. You can also give the dolls or characters first and last names. Then ask the child, "What's your name?" **Prompt** by saying, "You're ____ ____. Can you tell me your whole name?"

(Note: This is the sort of activity that can be done briefly at the same time during each session for it to become routine.)

=== E58 ===

Treatment Objective: The child will use verb forms.

Goal: The child will increase spontaneous use of word combinations. (EG5)

Communicative Intent (pragmatics)
  Commenting
    On action

Semantic-Syntactic Relations
  Agent-action

Morphemes
  Regular past tense *-ed*

Sentence Structure
  Declarative
    Agent + action

Activity: Let's Jump, Crawl, and Walk   **Expected age**: 33–36 months

Materials: none

Tell the child you're going to play some "move-around" games. Start by crawling around the floor (not appropriate in some homes, but you'll have to be the judge of that). As you crawl, tell the child repeatedly "We're crawling, crawling, crawling!" Then shout "Stop!" and say "We crawled." Continue by using present progressive *-ing* as you do the activity and *-ed* when you stop. After you have completed the activity a few times, ask the child, "What did you do?" or "What are you doing?" to elicit the appropriate tense. Try other actions with regular past tense like walk, hug, dance, jump, cry, kick, drop, and push. **Prompt** the appropriate verb tense by modeling the response you'd like the child to use.

If the child needs extra help with *-ing*, here are two books you might read:
  Alligators All Around by Maurice Sendak
  Chicken Soup with Rice by Maurice Sendak

=== E59a ===

Treatment Objective: The child will ask "What," "Who," and "Where" questions.

Goal: The child will increase spontaneous use of word combinations. (EG5)

Communicative Intent (pragmatics)
  Requesting
    Information

Sentence Structure
  Interrogative

Activity: What Do You Want?   **Expected age**: 33–36 months

Materials/Toys: puppet, a variety of toys, a bag to hold the toys

Put the toys in the bag and put the bag in front of the child. Tell the child the puppet isn't sure what he wants to play with. The child's job is to ask the puppet, "What do you want?" (or a variation of this "what" question, such as "What you want?" or "What you want to play with?"). Encourage the child to put his hand in the bag and then ask the puppet, "What do you want?" The puppet should "answer" with the name of one of the objects in the bag. Have the child get that item from the bag and the child and puppet can play for a while. If the child does not ask the question, **prompt** by modeling the question. You can also **prompt** by switching roles and letting the child hold the puppet while you control the bag of toys.

E59b

Treatment Objective: The child will ask "What," "Who," and "Where" questions.

Goal: The child will increase spontaneous use of word combinations. (EG5)

Communicative Intent (pragmatics)	Morphemes
Requesting Information	Contractible copula

Sentence Structure
  Interrogative
    Inversion appears with copula in what/where + copula + subject

Activity: Who's There? **Expected age:** 33–36 months

Materials/Toys: toy dollhouse with door that opens or a cardboard box with door cut into it, toy people that will fit through the door

Tell the child that he gets to "live" in the house and some friends are going to come and visit. When he hears the doorbell ring (or knock on the door), he should ask, "Who is it?" or "Who's out there?" Have different little people approach and knock on the door or ring the bell. Wait for the child to ask "Who is it?" When he does, the little person should say, "It's _____. May I come in?" If the child does not ask the question, **prompt** by modeling the question. You can also **prompt** by switching roles and letting the child control the people coming to visit while you live in the house.

E59c

Treatment Objective: The child will ask "What," "Who," and "Where" questions.

Goal: The child will increase spontaneous use of word combinations. (EG5)

Communicative Intent (pragmatics)	Morphemes
Requesting Information	Contractible copula

Sentence Structure
  Interrogative
    Inversion appears with copula in what/where + copula + subject

Activity: Hide and Seek **Expected age:** 33–36 months

Materials/Toys: any toy that can be hidden (e.g. stuffed animal, toy characters) or real people can play the game

Activities Book
The Early Intervention Kit

Tell the child you are going to play "Hide and Seek" with a stuffed animal or toy. Have the child close his eyes while you hide the toy. Tell the child that he has to ask where the toy is (e.g., "Where's the _____?"). When he asks, give him a hint, such as "Look near the couch." If the child doesn't see the toy, he should ask again, "Where's the _____?" Give another clue, such as "Look behind the couch." If the child does not ask the question, **prompt** by modeling the question. You can also **prompt** by switching roles and letting the child hide the toy while you look for it.

E60a

Treatment Objective: The child will count to three.

Goal: The child will increase spontaneous use of single words. (EG4)

Communicative Intent (pragmatics) Communicative Function
   Commenting   Recurrence
      On object

Activity: Count On It 1   **Expected age:** 33–36 months

Materials/Toys: ball

Sit on the floor across from the child. Tell him you are going to roll the ball, but first you have to say the "Magic words." Say, "One, two, three!" and then roll the ball. Have the child roll it back to you. The child may spontaneously say "One, two, three!" If he doesn't, **prompt** by saying, "Don't forget the magic words: one, two three!" An additional **prompt** would be holding up one finger at a time as you count or you could clap your hands each time you say a number to add a more physical component to the activity.

E60b

Treatment Objective: The child will count to three.

Goal: The child will increase spontaneous use of single words. (EG4)

Communicative Intent (pragmatics) Communicative Function
   Commenting   Recurrence
      On object

Activity: Count On It 2   **Expected age:** 33–36 months

Materials/Toys: big blocks that are easy to stack or any stacking toy

Sit by the child on the floor. Put one block (or piece of the stacking toy) in front of you and say, "one." Grab another block, place it on the first, and say, "two." Grab another block and say, "three." Do this a couple of times and then say, "Let's do it together." Wait to see if the child will count to three. **Prompt** by holding up fingers for 1, 2, and 3 or even saying each number for the child to repeat. Instead of building a taller tower, start again and build a three-block tower.

E60c

Treatment Objective: The child will count to three.

Goal: The child will increase spontaneous use of single words. (EG4)

Communicative Intent (pragmatics)　　Communicative Function
　Commenting　　　　　　　　　　　　　Recurrence
　　On action

Activity: Count On It 3　　　　　　**Expected age:** 33–36 months
(Note: Only perform this activity if the child can stand and walk up the stairs with assistance.)

Materials/Toys: stairs

Hold the child's hand as you walk up the stairs. As you go up the first step, say, "one." Go up another step and say, "two." Go up another step and say, "three." Then start counting at "one" again. Say to the child, "Help me count." **Prompt** by holding up fingers for 1, 2, and 3 or saying each number for the child to repeat.

E60d

Treatment Objective: The child will count to three.

Goal: The child will increase spontaneous use of single words. (EG4)

Communicative Intent (pragmatics)　　Communicative Function
　Commenting　　　　　　　　　　　　　Recurrence
　　On object

Activity: Count On It 4　　　　　　**Expected age:** 33–36 months
Materials/Toys: slide (inside or outside)

Encourage the child to climb to the top of the slide. Gently hold the child in place while you say, "One, two, three–go!" Release the child as you say "Go!" Use your fingers to demonstrate the numbers, holding up 1, 2, and then 3 fingers. Let the child go down the slide a couple of times. Then gently restrain him from sliding down and say, "Help me count." He may try to use his fingers too. **Prompt** by holding up fingers for 1, 2, and 3 or even saying each number for the child to repeat.

E61

Treatment Objective:	The child will recite a few nursery rhymes.
Goal:	The child will increase spontaneous use of word combinations. (EG5)

Communicative Intent (pragmatics) Repeating/practicing	Semantic-Syntactic Relations
Morphemes	Sentence Structure

Activity:	Baa, Baa Black Sheep	**Expected age**:	33–36 months
Materials/Toys:	none (book of nursery rhymes is optional)		

Choose one or two nursery rhymes the child really seems to enjoy. Say/read them frequently to the child. At first, the child will be able to repeat only an occasional phrase. However, the more often the child hears the nursery rhyme, the more parts of it he will be able to repeat.

Goals and Treatment Objectives for Sound Production Development (Chapter 10)

Long-term goal

The child will speak intelligibly as compared to developmental age peers.

Short-term goals

SG1   The child will imitate target consonants in isolation.

SG2   The child will imitate target consonants in words.

SG3   The child will produce target consonants in words.

SG4   The child will imitate target vowels in isolation.

SG5   The child will imitate target vowels in words.

SG6   The child will produce target vowels in words.

SG7   The child will produce target consonants in connected speech.

SG8   The child will produce target vowels in connected speech.

SG9   The child will demonstrate mastery of phonological patterns.

There are nine goals for sound production, ranging from imitation of the sound in isolation to use of the sounds in connected speech. As written, most activities are geared toward imitation or production at the word level (and hence, those goals are referenced on each treatment activity: Goals 2 and 3 for consonants and Goals 5 and 6 for vowels).

Any of these activities could be adapted for production of the sound in isolation by modeling a sound from the target word (e.g., modeling just the /p/ instead of the word "pop"). Therefore, the goal for isolation consonants (Goal 1) is indicated in parentheses in the chart on the next page, but won't be listed on the actual activity. However, the goal for isolation vowels (Goal 4) is referenced on each appropriate treatment activity.

In addition, any of these activities (vowels or consonants) could be adapted for producing the target in connected speech by increasing the length of utterance in which the target word is modeled and then expected. Therefore, Goals 7 and 8 are also indicated in parentheses and won't appear on the actual treatment activity. The phonologically-focused activities have only Goal 9 listed. For most of these, there are no specific activities written, but rather a reference given to other activities that can be used to stimulate use of that pattern.

Sound Production Ages of Acquisition/Treatment Objectives

Expected age of development	Short-term goal (SG)	Treatment Objectives	Activities to help achieve treatment objectives
24–27 months	(1), 2, 3, (7)	Uses these consonants in the indicated position of words: Initial /t/ Initial /n/ Initial /k/ Initial /g/ Initial /p/ Initial /m/ Initial /h/ Final /n/ Final /p/ Final /m/	S1a, b S2a, b S3a, b S4a, b S5a, b S6a, b S7a, b S8a, b S9a, b S10a, b
	4, 5, 6, (8)	Produces these vowels: ɔ u æ ɑɪ ɛ ɪ e oʊ (o) i ɔɪ	S11a, b S12a, b S13a, b S14a, b S15a, b S16a, b S17a, b S18a, b S19a, b S20a, b
	9	Consistently uses prevocalic consonants	S21
27–30 months	(1), 2, 3, (7)	Uses these consonants in the indicated position of words: Initial /d/ Initial /f/ Initial /dʒ/ Final /s/ Final /d/ Final /k/ Final /f/ Final /ŋ/	S22a, b, c, d S23a, b, c S24a, b, c, d S25a, b S26a, b S27a, b S28a, b S29a, b
	9	Produces consonants in final position of VC or CVC words	S30
	9	Consistently uses voiceless consonants in the prevocalic position	S31
	9	Stops using diminutives	S32

continued on next page

Expected age of development	Short-term goal (SG)	Treatment Objectives	Activities to help achieve treatment objectives
30–33 months	(1), 2, 3, (7)	Uses these consonants in the indicated position of words: Initial /w/ Final /t/ Final /r/ Final /b/	S33a, b S34a, b, c S35a, b, c S36a, b, c
33–36 months	(1), 2, 3, (7)	Uses these consonants in the indicated position of words: Initial /s/ Final /l/ Final /g/	S37a, b S38a, b S39a, b
	9	Includes all syllables (even weak) when using multisyllabic words	S40

S1a

Treatment Objective: The child will produce initial /t/ in words.

Goals: The child will imitate target consonants in words. (SG2)
The child will produce target consonants in words. (SG3)

Activity: Counting 1, 2   **Expected age:** 24–27 months

Materials/Toys: any toys or objects in multiples of two (e.g., two cars, two balls, two spoons, two cups), a bag

Pull two similar objects out of the bag and hold them up. As you lift each one up, say, "one" and then "two." Tell the child to count and then she can have the items. Hold and wiggle one of the objects. If the child does not begin counting, **prompt** by putting each object down and holding up one finger and then two fingers. You can further **prompt** by modeling the counting for the child.

S1b

Treatment Objective: The child will produce initial /t/ in words.

Goals: The child will imitate target consonants in words. (SG2)
The child will produce target consonants in words. (SG3)

Activity: Wiggle Your Toes   **Expected age:** 24–27 months

Materials/Toys: none

Take off the child's shoes and socks and tell her you need to count her toes. As you touch each toe, instead of counting, say, "Toe, toe, toe . . ." Then ask the child to help you. Touch one of the child's toes and wait for her to say "Toe."

S2a

Treatment Objective: The child will produce initial /n/ in words.

Goals: The child will imitate target consonants in words. (SG2)
The child will produce target consonants in words. (SG3)

Activity: No, No, No   **Expected age:** 24–27 months

Materials/Toys: puppet or a sock

Tell the child the puppet wants to do some silly things. It's the child's job to tell the puppet "No." Have the puppet ask, "Can I drive the car?" Model "No, no, no." You can even wiggle your finger at the puppet as you say this.

S2b

Treatment Objective: The child will produce initial /n/ in words.

Goals: The child will imitate target consonants in words. (SG2)
The child will produce target consonants in words. (SG3)

Activity: Right Now! **Expected age:** 24–27 months

Materials/Toys: puppet, sock puppet, stuffed animal, or any toy that can pretend to talk; variety of objects/toys the puppet can interact with (e.g., book, car, pillow)

Tell the child the puppet is being very slow today and she has to help him get things done "right now." Have the puppet say, "I'm going to read a book," but the puppet should not move toward the book. Model "Now" or "Right now" and have the puppet hurry to the book. After the puppet has looked at the book, have the puppet say, "I'm going to push the car" and then not move toward the car. If the child forgets to tell the puppet "Now" or "Right now," model it.

S3a

Treatment Objective: The child will produce initial /k/ in words.

Goals: The child will imitate target consonants in words. (SG2)
The child will produce target consonants in words. (SG3)

Activity: Keys! **Expected age:** 24–27 months

Materials/Toys: toy keys on a ring or assortment of real keys on a ring

Tell the child that the keys want to play hide and seek, but the keys will only come back when you call them. Show the child the keys and practice saying "key" as you look at each key on the ring. Then have the child close her eyes as you hide the keys (behind your back or under a cloth is fine). Then have the child open her eyes. Ask, "Where are those keys? We'd better call them." Model by calling, "Keys, keys . . . where are you?" When the child calls for the keys, get the keys from their hiding place.

S3b

Treatment Objective: The child will produce initial /k/ in words.

Goals: The child will imitate target consonants in words. (SG2)
The child will produce target consonants in words. (SG3)

Activity: Okay **Expected age:** 24–27 months

Materials/Toys: none

Tell the child that you are going to play a game. Explain that if the child wants you to do a motor movement (e.g., jump), she must answer your question with the magic word "kay" (short for "Okay"). For example, ask, "Do you want me to jump?" Model the "kay" response. If the child says "kay" (or even "Okay" with the /k/ in the more difficult medial position), then you have to jump. Continue with other motor movements.

S4a

Treatment Objective: The child will produce initial /g/ in words.

Goals: The child will imitate target consonants in words. (SG2)
The child will produce target consonants in words. (SG3)

Activity: Go, Go, Go   **Expected age:** 24–27 months

Materials/Toys: any toy that can be pushed (e.g., a toy car)

Tell the child that the cars are going to have a race. The child gets to be the starter for the race. The cars won't go until the child tells the cars to "GO!" Line up two cars and tell the child you're ready for the race. If the child doesn't immediately say "Go," model this word for her and encourage her to imitate.

S4b

Treatment Objective: The child will produce initial /g/ in words.

Goals: The child will imitate target consonants in words. (SG2)
The child will produce target consonants in words. (SG3)

Activity: All Gone   **Expected age:** 24–7 months

Materials/Toys: any stuffed animal or puppet, pretend or play food

Tell the child the puppet is very hungry today. Place the play food in front of the puppet and have the puppet gobble it all up. Model the response for the child by saying, "Gone" or "All gone." Give the puppet to the child and encourage her to imitate you.

S5a

Treatment Objective: The child will produce initial /p/ in words.

Goals: The child will imitate target consonants in words. (SG2)
The child will produce target consonants in words. (SG3)

Activity: Pull It!   **Expected age:** 24–27 months

Materials/Toys: any toy that can be pulled or a towel, diaper, or other cloth material

If using the pull toy, model the word *pull* as you pull the toy. Then give the child a turn pulling the toy. You might offer some resistance to this pulling action by holding back on the toy as the child attempts to pull. This may increase her motivation to say the word *pull*. If using the towel/material, have the child hold one end and you hold the other. Model the word *pull* as you pull on the towel.

S5b

Treatment Objective: The child will produce initial /p/ in words.

Goals: The child will imitate target consonants in words. (SG2)
The child will produce target consonants in words. (SG3)

Activity: Pop the Bubbles **Expected age:** 24–27 months

Materials/Toys: bubbles

Blow bubbles for the child. When the child pops a bubble with her finger, say, "Pop." Encourage the child to say "Pop" in order to get another turn.

S6a

Treatment Objective: The child will produce initial /m/ in words.

Goals: The child will imitate target consonants in words. (SG2)
The child will produce target consonants in words. (SG3)

Activity: That's Mine **Expected age:** 24–27 months

Materials/Toys: any of the child's favorite toys

Most young children do not enjoy sharing toys, especially their favorite toys. *Mine* also seems to be an early word for many. Emphasize the initial /m/ in the word *mine* as you hold the child's toy to your chest. Ask the child, "Is this really mine?" Encourage the child to say "Mine!"

S6b

Treatment Objective: The child will produce initial /m/ in words.

Goals: The child will imitate target consonants in words. (SG2)
The child will produce target consonants in words. (SG3)

Activity: More, Please **Expected age:** 24–27 months

Materials/Toys: any toy that has multiple small parts (e.g., puzzle, blocks) or food during mealtime or snack time

Hold all of the pieces in your lap or on your side of the table and ask the child if she wants some of the pieces. Give the child just one piece. Then say, "Do you want more?" Encourage the child to say "More" as you complete the puzzle, build a block tower, or give her food.

S7a

Treatment Objective: The child will produce initial /h/ in words.

Goals: The child will imitate target consonants in words. (SG2)
The child will produce target consonants in words. (SG3)

Activity:	Hop Hop	**Expected age**: 24–27 months
Materials/Toys:	none	

Hold the child's hand and hop. Each time you hop, say, "Hop." Encourage the child to say "Hop!"

S7b

Treatment Objective:	The child will produce initial /h/ in words.
Goals:	The child will imitate target consonants in words. (SG2) The child will produce target consonants in words. (SG3)

Activity:	Right Here	**Expected age**: 24–27 months
Materials/Toys:	a placemat or blanket, several small toys, bag for the toys	

Put a placemat or small blanket in front of the child. Tell the child that you have some toys in your bag that you want to put on the blanket, but you need her help. Take a toy out of the bag and, pointing to the blanket, say, "Should I put it here?" and then, touching a spot farther away from the child, say, "or should I put it over there?" The child is likely to respond by saying "Here" so the toy will be closer to her. If not, model the response for the child.

S8a

Treatment Objective:	The child will produce final /n/ in words.
Goals:	The child will imitate target consonants in words. (SG2) The child will produce target consonants in words. (SG3)

Activity:	That's Mine	**Expected age**: 24–27 months
Materials/Toys:	small toys or objects, a puppet, bag for the toys	

Tell the child you have lots of small toys in your bag and you're going to give some to the child to play with and some to the puppet. Take a toy out of the bag and have the puppet quickly exclaim, "That's mine" or "Mine" (if the child can't produce a two-word phrase). Then take another object out of the bag and wait for the child to use the word *mine*. Model the response for the child as needed.

S8b

Treatment Objective:	The child will produce final /n/ in words.
Goals:	The child will imitate target consonants in words. (SG2) The child will produce target consonants in words. (SG3)

Activity:	Run, Run	**Expected age**: 24–27 months
Materials/Toys:	doll	

Tell the child the doll has been sleeping all day and now the doll wants to get out and play. Make the doll say, "I want to run. Can you tell me to run?" If the child says "Run," make the doll run fast. If the child doesn't say "Run," model the word for the child.

S9a

Treatment Objective: The child will produce final /p/ in words.

Goals: The child will imitate target consonants in words. (SG2)
The child will produce target consonants in words. (SG3)

Activity: Hop Like a Bunny   **Expected age**: 24–27 months

Materials/Toys: none

Tell the child you are going to be bunny rabbits. Show her how to hop around the house or outside. As you hop, say "Hop" while emphasizing the final /p/. Encourage the child to imitate.

S9b

Treatment Objective: The child will produce final /p/ in words.

Goals: The child will imitate target consonants in words. (SG2)
The child will produce target consonants in words. (SG3)

Activity: Blow Bubbles   **Expected age**: 24–27 months

Materials/Toys: bubbles

While you blow bubbles, model popping bubbles with your finger. Say "Pop" each time you pop a bubble, emphasizing the final /p/. Encourage the child to imitate.

S10a

Treatment Objective: The child will produce final /m/ in words.

Goals: The child will imitate target consonants in words. (SG2)
The child will produce target consonants in words. (SG3)

Activity: Yum, Yum   **Expected age**: 24–27 months

Materials/Toys: puppet or doll, food (pretend, play, or real)

Give the puppet (or doll) a bite of the food and have the puppet say, "Yummm." Then let the child put the puppet on her hand and present another bite of food to the puppet. Wait to see if the child uses the word *yum*. If not, model the word for the child.

S10b

Treatment Objective: The child will produce final /m/ in words.

Goals: The child will imitate target consonants in words. (SG2)
The child will produce target consonants in words. (SG3)

Activity: Bam! **Expected age:** 24–27 months

Materials/Toys: toy workbench (where the pieces are hit in place with a hammer) or a wooden spoon and a plastic bowl

Hit one of the pieces with the hammer. With each stroke of the hammer, say "Bam!" Then give the hammer to the child and encourage her to say "Bam" each time she hits the toy.

> Note: There are two activities written for each vowel (labeled a and b). The first one (a) is designed to elicit production of that vowel in isolation. This may be needed for a child with a motor-planning problem (i.e., suspected developmental verbal dyspraxia). If the child is already producing the vowel in isolation, select the other activity in which the vowel is used in a word (b). For the (a) activities, Goal 4 is indicated. For the (b) activities, Goals 5 and 6 are listed. Use Goal 5 if the child is imitating and Goal 6 if the child is producing the word without a model. If the child is using the vowel in connected speech, use Goal 8. Because this is not the typical level of production for work on vowels, Goal 8 is not listed for the activity but could be added if appropriate for the child.

S11a

Treatment Objective: The child will produce /ɔ/.

Goal: The child will imitate target vowels in isolation. (SG4)

Activity: Awww . . . What a Cute Baby **Expected age:** 24–27 months

Materials/Toys: baby doll

Show the child the baby doll and say, "Isn't she cute?" Hug the baby doll and say "Awww." Give the child a turn to hug the doll and encourage her to say "Awww" as she hugs the doll..

S11b

Treatment Objective: The child will produce /ɔ/.

Goals: The child will imitate target vowels in words. (SG5)
The child will produce target vowels in words. (SG6)

Activity: Kiss the Dog's Paw **Expected age:** 24–27 months

Materials/Toys: stuffed dog

Show the child the stuffed dog and say, "This doggie has four feet. His feet are called paws. I think I'll give him a kiss on his paw." Then kiss one of the paws and say, "Paw." Kiss another paw and say, "Paw." Continue with each of the four paws. Then give the dog to the child and encourage her to say "Paw" each time she kisses the dog's paw.

S12a

Treatment Objective: The child will produce /u/.

Goal: The child will imitate target vowels in isolation. (SG4)

Activity: Oooo . . . Icky   **Expected age:** 24–27 months

Materials/Toys: bubbles or other sticky material

Stick your finger in the bottle of bubbles. When you pull your finger out, say, "Oooo . . . that's icky." Let the child take a turn. Cue her to say "Oooo" as needed.

S12b

Treatment Objective: The child will produce /u/.

Goals: The child will imitate target vowels in words. (SG5)
The child will produce target vowels in words. (SG6)

Activity: Boo!   **Expected age:** 24–27 months

Materials/Toys: a puppet or stuffed animal

Tell the child that the puppet likes to hide so he can scare you. Put the puppet behind your back. Wait a few seconds, then bring the puppet out and have him say "Booooo." Say "Boooo" back to the puppet. Encourage the child to imitate.

S13a

Treatment Objective: The child will produce /æ/.

Goal: The child will imitate target vowels in isolation. (SG4)

Activity: A Wild Ride   **Expected age:** 24–27 months

Materials/Toys: small toy person or animal, a car or other toy with wheels the toy person can ride in

Tell the child that the toy person or animal is going for a ride in the car. Tell the child that the toy person likes to go fast, but he's a little afraid. When he goes fast, he says, "Aaeee." Demonstrate for the child as you push the toy person in the car fast and say "Aaeeee" in a "toy voice." Then give the child a turn.

S13b

Treatment Objective: The child will produce /æ/.

Goals: The child will imitate target vowels in words. (SG5)
The child will produce target vowels in words. (SG6)

Activity:	That One	**Expected age**: 24–27 months
Materials/Toys:	a variety of toys	

Sit next to the child. Put two toys in front of you slightly out of the child's reach. Ask the child, "Do you want that one or that one?" as you point to each of the toys. The child is to say "That" or "That one" to get the toy. **Prompt** by modeling "That one" if the child doesn't respond.

S14a

Treatment Objective:	The child will produce /ɑɪ/.	
Goal:	The child will imitate target vowels in isolation. (SG4)	
Activity:	Find the Eye	**Expected age**: 24–27 months
Materials/Toys:	puppets and stuffed animals with obvious eyes, a bag for the puppets/animals	

Tell the child you have a lot of animals with you today and you need to count their eyes. (Note: The goal is not to actually count the eyes, but to repeat the word *eye* over and over.) Pull an animal out of the bag, touch each eye, and say "Eye." Hand that animal to the child and ask her to do the same. Repeat with the other animals.

S14b

Treatment Objective:	The child will produce /ɑɪ/.	
Goals:	The child will imitate target vowels in words. (SG5) The child will produce target vowels in words. (SG6)	
Activity:	That's Mine	**Expected age**: 24–27 months
Materials/Toys:	a group of toys or objects that belong to the child, a puppet, bag for the toys	

Put all of the toys/objects in a bag. Put the puppet on one hand, pull an object out of the bag with the other hand, and ask, "Whose _____ is this?" If the child doesn't say "That's mine" or "Mine," have the puppet shout, "That's mine!"

S15a

Treatment Objective:	The child will produce /ɛ/.	
Goal:	The child will imitate target vowels in isolation. (SG4)	
Activity:	Motor Boat	**Expected age**: 24–27 months
Materials/Toys:	toy boat or any object that floats, a piece of blue paper or cloth (pretend water) (Note: You can use real water if you don't mind getting a little wet!)	

Put the boat or object on the "water" and tell the child the boat is having trouble going. You'll need to help the boat go by making a motor sound ("eh eh eh eh eh eh"). Take turns making the sound and pushing the boat.

S15b

Treatment Objective: The child will produce /ɛ/.

Goals: The child will imitate target vowels in words. (SG5)
The child will produce target vowels in words. (SG6)

Activity: Go to Bed   **Expected age:** 24–27 months

Materials/Toys: any toy animal or person, a toy bed or little blanket for pretend bed
(Note: You can also use a real bed and bigger stuffed animal.)

Tell the child that it's nighttime, and the toy (e.g., horse) has to go to bed. Have the toy say, "I'm so tired. Where should I go?" Wait to see if the child tells the toy what to do. If not, **prompt** by having the toy act confused and say, "I'm so tired, but what should I do?" If the child still doesn't respond, **prompt** by modeling for the child, "Go to bed."

S16a

Treatment Objective: The child will produce /ɪ/.

Goal: The child will imitate target vowels in isolation. (SG4)

Activity: Baby Animal Sounds   **Expected age:** 24–27 months

Materials/Toys: any stuffed animal or toy animal that the child won't know what sound it makes (e.g., a turtle, a hippo)

Tell the child, "Look, this is a baby turtle. He can't talk yet. The only sound he can make is 'ih ih ih ih.' Can you help him make his sound?" Encourage the child to take a turn saying the sound. You might hold the turtle while you make the sound and give the turtle to the child contingent upon her imitating the sound.

S16b

Treatment Objective: The child will produce /ɪ/.

Goals: The child will imitate target vowels in words. (SG5)
The child will produce target vowels in words. (SG6)

Activity: I Did It!   **Expected age:** 24–27 months

Materials/Toys: puppet or stuffed animal

Challenge the child and the puppet or stuffed animal by saying, "Can you do what I do?" Then say, "I can jump." Jump and say, "I did it." Have the puppet jump and proudly say, "I did it." Then encourage the child to jump. If the child doesn't, **prompt** by having the puppet jump again and say, "I did it." You can also let the child hold the puppet and make the puppet perform the action and answer if the child doesn't like to imitate.

=== S17a ===

Treatment Objective: The child will produce /e/.

Goal: The child will imitate target vowels in isolation. (SG4)

Activity: Hey!   **Expected age:** 24–27 months

Materials/Toys: any puppet with hands or mouth (so it can pick things up) or sock puppet, small toys or objects

Explain to the child that the puppet likes to sneak up when you're not looking to get or "steal" things. Tell the child that if she sees the puppet getting a toy, she can "holler" at him. Then talk with the child to distract her. While you're talking to the child, have the puppet sneak up and grab a toy. Catch the puppet, wiggle your finger at him, and say /e/ in a prolonged fashion and with exaggerated intonation. Encourage the child to imitate.

=== S17b ===

Treatment Objective: The child will produce /e/.

Goals: The child will imitate target vowels in words. (SG5)
The child will produce target vowels in words. (SG6)

Activity: Yay!   **Expected age:** 24–27 months

Materials/Toys: stuffed animal or doll

Explain to the child the stuffed animal (or doll) has been practicing _____ (name any activity such as walking, hopping, clapping, or running) and can perform the action really well. Tell the child that when the stuffed animal does the action, she can cheer so the stuffed animal knows what a good job he did. Then have the stuffed animal perform an action. Clap and say, "Yay" for the stuffed animal. Encourage the child to imitate.

=== S18a ===

Treatment Objective: The child will produce /oʊ/ (o).

Goal: The child will imitate target vowels in isolation. (SG4)

Activity: What a Surprise!   **Expected age:** 24–27 months

Materials/Toys: a blanket or towel, small toys, box or bag for the toys

Have the toys in a box or bag so the child can't see them. Show the child the blanket (towel) and tell her it is a magic blanket. When you say the magic words, there will be a toy hiding under the blanket. Spread the blanket on the floor. Have the child close her eyes so you can put a toy under the blanket. When the child opens her eyes, say the magic word "Abracadabra" or "Prestidigitation" or any other magical word you choose and remove the blanket with a flourish. When the object is revealed, say "Oh" with exaggerated inflection. Encourage the child to imitate.

=== S18b ===

Treatment Objective: The child will produce /oʊ/ (o).

Goals: The child will imitate target vowels in words. (SG5)
The child will produce target vowels in words. (SG6)

Activity: Oh, No!   **Expected age:** 24–27 months

Materials/Toys: puppet or doll, something the puppet or doll can walk along the edge of (e.g., table, couch)

Introduce the puppet (doll) to the child. Then tell the puppet, "I need you to be careful today. Don't walk along the edge of the table (or couch or bed) because you might fall." Then engage the child in another brief activity. While engaged in that activity, make the puppet walk along the edge of the table and fall off. Exclaim "Oh, no!" Encourage the child to imitate. Pick up the puppet and hug it to make sure it's all right. Continue with your other activity for a few minutes, then repeat the falling activity with the puppet.

=== S19a ===

Treatment Objective: The child will produce /i/.

Goal: The child will imitate target vowels in isolation. (SG4)

Activity: Whee!   **Expected age:** 24–27 months

Materials/Toys: doll or puppet (optional)

Do this activity with the child if she enjoys being held and moved. Otherwise, substitute a doll or puppet. Hold the child firmly under her arms. Lift her up in the air as you say, "Eeeee" (as in "whee"). Encourage the child to imitate.

=== S19b ===

Treatment Objective: The child will produce /i/.

Goals: The child will imitate target vowels in words. (SG5)
The child will produce target vowels in words. (SG6)

Activity: Who Wants to Do It?   **Expected age:** 24–27 months

Materials/Toys: puzzle in a tray
(Note: If the child is a reluctant talker, using a puppet or doll to model the target word will help.)

Take the pieces out of the puzzle tray. Give the child the empty puzzle tray. Hold up one piece and ask, "Who wants to put this piece in?" The child should respond "Me."

(Note: If the child uses a more sophisticated response, such as "I want to," or "I do," then the child probably doesn't need to be working on production of the /i/ vowel.)

════════════════════════ **S20a** ════════════════════════

Treatment Objective: The child will produce /ɔɪ/.

Goal: The child will imitate target vowels in isolation. (SG4)

Activity: Siren Sounds **Expected age:** 24–27 months

Materials/Toys: toy fire truck or police car

Push the fire truck or toy police car. Approximate the sound of a siren by saying, "Oh eee, Oh eeee." (When the two sounds are said quickly together, the diphthong is produced.) Encourage the child to imitate.

════════════════════════ **S20b** ════════════════════════

Treatment Objective: The child will produce /ɔɪ/.

Goals: The child will imitate target vowels in words. (SG5)
The child will produce target vowels in words. (SG6)

Activity: Give It to the Boy **Expected age:** 24–27 months

Materials/Toys: a boy and girl doll, blocks or puzzle pieces

Put the boy and girl dolls on the floor or table and tell the child you're going to pass out the blocks (or puzzle pieces). Have the child tell you whether the boy or the girl gets the next block. Hold up a block and say "Girl or boy?" If the child favors the girl and you aren't getting any responses with the /ɔɪ/, tell the child that the boy is sad and really needs a block.

════════════════════════ **S21** ════════════════════════

Treatment Objective: The child will consistently use prevocalic consonants.

Goal: The child will demonstrate mastery of phonological patterns. (SG9)

To help the child master use of this phonological pattern (prevocalic consonants), use any of the activities listed below.

See activities: 1a, b   7a, b   **Expected age:** 24–27 months
                 2a, b   22a, b, c, d
                 3a, b   23a, b, c
                 4a, b   24a, b, c, d
                 5a, b   33a, b
                 6a, b   37a, b

════════════════════════ **S22a** ════════════════════════

Treatment Objective: The child will produce initial /d/ in words.

Goals: The child will imitate target consonants in words. (SG2)
The child will produce target consonants in words. (SG3)

Activity: Going Down the Stairs   **Expected age**: 27–30 months

Materials/Toys: stairs (optional)

Walk down the stairs with the child. On each step down, model the word *down* and encourage the child to imitate. If the child can't say the whole word, accept an approximation such as "Dow" or "Du." If there are no stairs available, stand up and hold the child. Say, "Down" as you put the child down.

S22b

Treatment Objective: The child will produce initial /d/ in words.

Goals: The child will imitate target consonants in words. (SG2)
The child will produce target consonants in words. (SG3)

Activity: Playing with Family Dolls   **Expected age**: 27–30 months

Materials/Toys: doll set with parents, a boy, and a girl

Name each doll family member: Mom, Dad, Danielle (girl), Dave (boy). Play with the dolls, using phrase length appropriate to the child to stimulate language. Use the names "Dad," "Danielle," and "Dave" frequently as the adult male doll and the child dolls perform actions. Ask the child to repeat "Dad," "Danielle," or "Dave" each time you say the word. If the child is using phrases, stimulate phrases, such as "Dad did it" or "Danielle did it" by having a doll perform an action and then asking the child, "Who did that?" Help the child reply as needed.

S22c

Treatment Objective: The child will produce initial /d/ in words.

Goals: The child will imitate target consonants in words. (SG2)
The child will produce target consonants in words. (SG3)

Activity: Dots   **Expected age**: 27–30 months

Materials/Toys: paper, crayons

Place the paper on the table. Use crayons to make dots on the paper. Each time you make a dot, say "Dot." (Note: Because "dot" ends with an alveolar sound, it may be easier to say than some other /d/ words.)

S22d

Treatment Objective: The child will produce initial /d/ in words.

Goals: The child will imitate target consonants in words. (SG2)
The child will produce target consonants in words. (SG3)

Activity: Don't Do That   **Expected age**: 27–30 months

Materials/Toys: puppet or stuffed animal

Tell the child that the puppet is going to do some things we know he shouldn't do. Have the puppet perform a silly or inappropriate action (e.g., eating paper, kissing the floor). Encourage the child to tell the puppet, "Don't do that."

S23a

Treatment Objective: The child will produce initial /f/ in words.

Goals: The child will imitate target consonants in words. (SG2)
The child will produce target consonants in words. (SG3)

Activity: Fan **Expected age:** 27–30 months

Materials/Toys: handheld battery-operated fan or a piece of paper folded into a fan

Say the word *fan*. Exaggerate the airflow of the /f/. As you are doing so, turn on the handheld fan or wave the paper fan. Tell the child that you will turn on the fan each time she says the word *fan* with a good /f/.

S23b

Treatment Objective: The child will produce initial /f/ in words.

Goals: The child will imitate target consonants in words. (SG2)
The child will produce target consonants in words. (SG3)

Activity: Funny Face **Expected age:** 27–30 months

Materials/Toys: none

Tell the child you are going to make funny faces whenever she tells you to. To get you to make a funny face, the child needs to say, "Funny face" with a good /f/.

S23c

Treatment Objective: The child will produce initial /f/ in words.

Goals: The child will imitate target consonants in words. (SG2)
The child will produce target consonants in words. (SG3)

Activity: Food **Expected age:** 27–30 months

Materials/Toys: toy food, puppet with a mouth that opens

Tell the child the puppet is very hungry and wants to eat. Put the toy food in front of the child as you hold the puppet. Tell the child you will open the puppet's mouth for a bite of food each time the child says, "Food" with a good /f/.

═══ S24a ═══

Treatment Objective: The child will produce initial /dʒ/ in words.

Goals: The child will imitate target consonants in words. (SG2)
The child will produce target consonants in words. (SG3)

Activity: Jumping Jack **Expected age**: 27–30 months

Materials/Toys: boy doll

Introduce the doll to the child and tell her the doll's name is Jack. To get Jack to jump, the child needs to say, "Jump Jack." Model "Jump Jack" as needed.

═══ S24b ═══

Treatment Objective: The child will produce initial /dʒ/ in words.

Goals: The child will imitate target consonants in words. (SG2)
The child will produce target consonants in words. (SG3)

Activity: Jumping **Expected age**: 27–30 months

Materials/Toys: none

Hold the child's hand and jump. Use the word *jump* each time you jump. Encourage the child to imitate the word. Stop jumping. Wait to see if the child will say, "Jump" to get you to start again.

═══ S24c ═══

Treatment Objective: The child will produce initial /dʒ/ in words.

Goals: The child will imitate target consonants in words. (SG2)
The child will produce target consonants in words. (SG3)

Activity: In the Jar **Expected age**: 27–30 months

Materials/Toys: jar with lid, small things to fit in the jar

Put the small objects in the jar and put the lid on tight. Shake the jar and ask the child if she'd like to see one of the items in the jar. When she indicates that she would, ask, "Where is it?" Model "Jar" or "In the jar" as needed. When the child says the word *jar*, let her choose an item from the jar.

═══ S24d ═══

Treatment Objective: The child will produce initial /dʒ/ in words.

Goals: The child will imitate target consonants in words. (SG2)
The child will produce target consonants in words. (SG3)

Activity: Jelly **Expected age**: 27–30 months

Materials/Toys: puppet with a mouth that opens, picture of jelly or small jar of jelly

Tell the child the puppet is hungry and wants some jelly. Hold up the picture of jelly or the jar of jelly, and have the puppet say "Jelly." Give the picture to the puppet. Take the jelly from the puppet and give the puppet to the child. Encourage the child to ask the puppet, "Do you want more jelly?" Model the response as needed.

━━━━━━━━━━━━━━━━━━━━━━━ S25a ━━━━━━━━━━━━━━━━━━━━━━━

Treatment Objective: The child will produce final /s/ in words.

Goals: The child will imitate target consonants in words. (SG2)
The child will produce target consonants in words. (SG3)

Activity: Let's Tell a Story **Expected age**: 27–30 months

Materials/Toys: none

Select four or five words containing /s/ and think of a short story. (An example is provided below.) Say, "I am going to tell you a story. Then you can tell me the story and I will help you."

Begin the story. Remember to emphasize the target sound by stretching out the sound or making the sound louder.

"Guess who lives in the house down the street? A white goose with a red dress lives in the house down the street. The goose wears a red dress to school every day. Now do you know who lives in the house down the street? A goose with a red dress!"

Repeat the story several times as needed. Then say to the child, "Now it's your turn. I will start the story and you can help me with it."

Allow time for the child to fill in each blank. If she fails to do so after 6-8 seconds, help her. If the child is able to tell the whole story without you starting the sentence, allow the child to tell the story. If the child fails to say the target correctly, stop her only to provide the correct model and then allow her to continue the story.

"Guess who lives in the _____ down the street? A white _____ with a red _____ lives in the _____ down the street. The _____ wears a red _____ to school every day. Now do you know who lives in the _____ down the street? A _____ with a red _____!"

━━━━━━━━━━━━━━━━━━━━━━━ S25b ━━━━━━━━━━━━━━━━━━━━━━━

Treatment Objective: The child will produce final /s/ in words.

Goals: The child will imitate target consonants in words. (SG2)
The child will produce target consonants in words. (SG3)

Activity: Hit or Miss **Expected age**: 27–30 months

Materials/Toys: wadded piece of paper, receptacle (e.g., trash can)

Wad up some pieces of paper and tell the child you're going to shoot baskets. If the wad of paper goes in, say "Hit." If it lands on the floor, say "Miss." Take turns shooting.

S26a

Treatment Objective: The child will produce final /d/ in words.

Goals: The child will imitate target consonants in words. (SG2)
The child will produce target consonants in words. (SG3)

Activity: Head, Head, Head   **Expected age:** 27–30 months

Materials/Toys: dolls or stuffed animals

Sit the dolls/animals in a semi-circle in front of you and the child. Tell the child you're going to play a game. You'll touch each doll on the head, and the last one touched gets to stand on her head. Touch each doll and say, "Head, head, head." When you get to the last doll, say, "Head." Have the doll react in an excited way and say, "I get to stand on my head, head, head" as you turn the doll over. Then ask the child to make the doll stand on her head as she says "head."

S26b

Treatment Objective: The child will produce final /d/ in words.

Goals: The child will imitate target consonants in words. (SG2)
The child will produce target consonants in words. (SG3)

Activity: Bad!   **Expected age:** 27–30 months

Materials/Toys: stuffed animal, a treat to eat or a picture of a treat

Tell the child you have a treat that you and the child are going to eat. The stuffed animal is not supposed to have any. Have the stuffed animal creep up to the treat and take a "bite." Shake your finger at the stuffed animal and say, "Bad, bad. That's our treat." Ask the child to tell the animal, "Bad, bad." Repeat the activity and wait for the child to say "Bad." Model as needed.

S27a

Treatment Objective: The child will produce final /k/ in words.

Goals: The child will imitate target consonants in words. (SG2)
The child will produce target consonants in words. (SG3)

Activity: Walk, Walk   **Expected age:** 27–30 months

Materials/Toys: none

Hold the child's hand and tell her you are going for a walk. Explain that you can only take a step each time she says "Walk." Model the word *walk* and take a giant step. Wait for the child to say "Walk" before you take another step.

=== S27b ===

Treatment Objective: The child will produce final /k/ in words.

Goals: The child will imitate target consonants in words. (SG2)
The child will produce target consonants in words. (SG3)

Activity: Bark! **Expected age:** 27–30 months

Materials/Toys: stuffed dog or toy dog

Tell the child that the dog is a special dog that can only "speak" when we tell him to. Tell the dog "Bark!" and then make the dog bark. Ask the child to take a turn telling the dog, "Bark!"

=== S28a ===

Treatment Objective: The child will produce final /f/ in words.

Goals: The child will imitate target consonants in words. (SG2)
The child will produce target consonants in words. (SG3)

Activity: Laugh or Cry **Expected age:** 27–30 months

Materials/Toys: doll or puppet

Tell the child that the doll is a special doll that can laugh or cry when we tell her to. Tell the doll "Laugh!" and then make the doll laugh. Then tell the doll "cry" and make the doll cry. Ask the child, "Do you want the doll to laugh or cry?" Encourage the child to give the doll a direction, and then make the doll respond appropriately. If the child always has the doll cry, ask the child to "make the doll happy."

=== S28b ===

Treatment Objective: The child will produce final /f/ in words.

Goals: The child will imitate target consonants in words. (SG2)
The child will produce target consonants in words. (SG3)

Activity: Off the Table **Expected age:** 27–30 months

Materials/Toys: pair of dice, book

Sit at a table with the child. Tell her that you are going to roll the dice (or one die) off the book you have placed on the table and practice saying the word *off*. Say, "We'll play a game. I will roll the dice off the book and onto the table and see what number I get. If I roll a six, then I will say the word *off* six times. If I roll a two, I only have to say the word *off* two times. Then it will be your turn. Are you ready?"

Roll the dice and say the word *off* the number of times shown on the dice. Then have the child take a turn.

S29a

Treatment Objective: The child will produce final /ŋ/ in words.

Goals: The child will imitate target consonants in words. (SG2)
The child will produce target consonants in words. (SG3)

Activity: Ring, Ring   **Expected age:** 27–30 months

Materials/Toys: two toy phones or real phones

Place a phone in front of you and the child. Tell the child that you can't answer the phone until you hear it ring. Then say, "Ring, ring, ring." Wait for the child to answer her phone. Have a brief conversation and then hang up. Tell the child it is her turn to call you. She has to say "Ring, ring, ring." Model the response as needed.

S29b

Treatment Objective: The child will produce final /ŋ/ in words.

Goals: The child will imitate target consonants in words. (SG2)
The child will produce target consonants in words. (SG3)

Activity: Ding Dong   **Expected age:** 27–30 months

Materials/Toys: dollhouse, two toy people or a real door bell

Put one of the toy people inside the house. Have the toy person say, "I hope I hear my doorbell go 'ding dong.' That means someone has come to visit." Give the child the other toy person and have him come to visit you. Encourage the child to make her toy person go up to the door and say, "Ding dong." Don't respond right away, or say, "I think I heard the doorbell, but I'm not sure." Encourage the child to say "Ding dong" again.

S30

Treatment Objective: The child will produce consonants in final position of VC or CVC words.

Goal: The child will demonstrate mastery of phonological patterns. (SG9)

To help the child master the use of this phonological pattern (use of final consonants), use any of the activities listed below.

See activities: 8a, b   29a, b   **Expected age:** 27–30 months
9a, b   34a, b, c
10a, b   35a, b, c
25a, b   36a, b, c
26a, b   38a, b
27a, b   39a, b
28a, b

S31

Treatment Objective: The child will consistently use voiceless consonants in the prevocalic position.

Goal: The child will demonstrate mastery of phonological patterns. (SG9)

To help the child master the use of this phonological pattern (prevocalic voiceless consonants), use any of the activities listed below.

See activities:
- 1a, b
- 3a, b
- 5a, b
- 7a, b
- 23a, b, c
- 37a, b

Expected age: 27–30 months

S32

Treatment Objective: The child will stop using diminutives.

Goal: The child will demonstrate mastery of phonological patterns. (SG9)

Activity: Name the Animals   **Expected age**: 27–30 months

Materials/Toys: stuffed horse, dog, pig, and any other animals the child produces with a diminutive; pictures of the animals; or real animals in the environment

Engage the child in play with the stuffed animals (or look at the pictures). If she uses a diminutive to name the animal (e.g., horsie, doggie, piggy), model the correct non-diminutive form of the word. Encourage the child to imitate. (Note: You will only address diminutives as they occur so this objective may be easier to address during other activities.)

S33a

Treatment Objective: The child will produce initial /w/ in words.

Goals: The child will imitate target consonants in words. (SG2)
The child will produce target consonants in words. (SG3)

Activity: Wait a Minute!   **Expected age**: 30–33 months

Materials/Toys: any favorite toy or activity of the child's, a doll or stuffed animal

Show the child the toy or activity you are going to play with. Explain that the doll or stuffed animal is not very polite because she likes to take a turn without asking. Tell the child that when the doll does that, you will have to tell her "Wait." Begin playing with the toy. Have the doll interrupt and ask for a turn. Tell the doll, "Wait." Encourage the child to imitate.

=== S33b ===

Treatment Objective: The child will produce initial /w/ in words.

Goals: The child will imitate target consonants in words. (SG2)
The child will produce target consonants in words. (SG3)

Activity: In the Wagon   **Expected age:** 30–33 months

Materials/Toys: toy or real wagon, objects that can be placed in the wagon

Give the wagon to the child. Tell her that you need to fill up the wagon so you can take the objects for a ride. Hold up an object and ask the child, "Where should we put this?" If the child does not respond with "Wagon," model the word and encourage the child to imitate.

=== S34a ===

Treatment Objective: The child will produce final /t/ in words.

Goals: The child will imitate target consonants in words. (SG2)
The child will produce target consonants in words. (SG3)

Activity: Come Out!   **Expected age:** 30–33 months

Materials/Toys: stuffed animal, box (or something that can be the animal's home)

Tell the child that the animal wants to hide in his "house," but you want him to come out and play. Explain that the animal will come out if someone calls him. Put the stuffed animal in his "house" and ask the child to call him. The animal will come out when the child calls "Come out."

=== S34b ===

Treatment Objective: The child will produce final /t/ in words.

Goals: The child will imitate target consonants in words. (SG2)
The child will produce target consonants in words. (SG3)

Activity: Toot, Toot   **Expected age:** 30–33 months

Materials/Toys: two empty paper towel rolls

Have a parade. Tell the child the band has to play in the parade. Give the child a paper towel roll. March with the child as you say, "Toot, toot" into your paper towel roll. Encourage the child to imitate.

=== S34c ===

Treatment Objective: The child will produce final /t/ in words.

Goals: The child will imitate target consonants in words. (SG2)
The child will produce target consonants in words. (SG3)

Activity:	Don't	**Expected age**: 30–33 months	
Materials/Toys:	stuffed animal or puppet, a few crayons, drawing paper		

Tell the child that the animal wants to eat the crayons, but you don't want him to because you want draw. Explain that the child's job is to tell the animal "Don't." Put paper in front of you and the child. Have the animal try to "eat" a crayon as you begin to draw. If the child says "Don't" with a good /t/, have the animal give the crayon to the child.

― S35a ―

Treatment Objective: The child will produce final /r/ in words.

Goals: The child will imitate target consonants in words. (SG2)
The child will produce target consonants in words. (SG3)

Activity: Car, Come Here   **Expected age**: 30–33 months

Materials/Toys: several toy cars

Sit on the floor with the child. Line up all of the cars in front of you. Tell the child that you will roll the cars to her one at a time when she says the magic words, "Car, come here."

― S35b ―

Treatment Objective: The child will produce final /r/ in words.

Goals: The child will imitate target consonants in words. (SG2)
The child will produce target consonants in words. (SG3)

Activity: Over Here   **Expected age**: 30–33 months

Materials/Toys: doll or stuffed animal

Tell the child she can move around the room and the doll will come wherever she is as long as she tells the doll where she is. When the child moves to another location, the child is to call to the doll, "Over here." Then move the doll to that place in the room.

Then tell the child that she is going to play a game with the doll. The doll is going to "hide" her eyes while the child moves somewhere in the room. When the doll "uncovers" her eyes, have the doll say, "Where are you?" (This allows you to model more correct productions of /r/.) Then have the child call to the doll, "Over here." Move the doll to the child. You can use the phrase "There you are!" to further model correct productions.

― S35c ―

Treatment Objective: The child will produce final /r/ in words.

Goals: The child will imitate target consonants in words. (SG2)
The child will produce target consonants in words. (SG3)

Activity: On the Paper **Expected age**: 30–33 months

Materials/Toys: some toys, a sheet of paper

Put the toys on the floor in front of you. Put a sheet of paper on the floor in front of the child. Tell the child she can have the toys, but they have to stay on the paper. Pick up a toy and say, "Uh-oh, where does the _____ need to go?" When the child says "On the paper," place the toy on the paper.

S36a

Treatment Objective: The child will produce final /b/ in words.

Goals: The child will imitate target consonants in words. (SG2)
The child will produce target consonants in words. (SG3)

Activity: Rub, Rub, Rub **Expected age**: 30–33 months

Materials/Toys: any toy that you can pretend is dirty, sponge or rag

Tell the child that the toy is dirty so you need to clean it. Give the child the toy and ask her, "What are you going to do with the sponge?" Encourage the child to say "Rub." When she says "Rub" with a good /b/, give her the sponge. After she rubs the toy once or twice, take the sponge away. Encourage her to say "Rub" again to get the sponge.

S36b

Treatment Objective: The child will produce final /b/ in words.

Goals: The child will imitate target consonants in words. (SG2)
The child will produce target consonants in words. (SG3)

Activity: Tub **Expected age**: 30–33 months

Materials/Toys: baby bathtub, baby doll, things needed to give the doll a bath

Tell the child you are going to give the doll a bath, but first you have to put all the things in the tub. Put the tub in front of the child. Hold up one of the items and ask the child, "Where are we going to put the _____?" Encourage the child to answer "Tub" with a good /b/ to get the item.

S36c

Treatment Objective: The child will produce final /b/ in words.

Goals: The child will imitate target consonants in words. (SG2)
The child will produce target consonants in words. (SG3)

Activity: Bob **Expected age**: 30–33 months

Materials/Toys: toy male doll or stuffed animal you can name Bob

Tell the child that the doll's name is Bob and he likes to hide. He will come out only when someone calls his name. Have the child cover her eyes while you hide Bob. Then ask the child to call "Bob" using a good /b/ sound.

37a

Treatment Objective: The child will produce initial /s/ in words.

Goals: The child will imitate target consonants in words. (SG2)
The child will produce target consonants in words. (SG3)

Activity: Silly Sally **Expected age**: 33–36 months

Materials/Toys: *Silly Sally* by Audrey Wood

Read *Silly Sally* slowly while emphasizing the initial /s/ sounds. As the child learns the story, encourage her to "read" to you. If the child is not producing the /s/ sound, say it with her while she reads.

S37b

Treatment Objective: The child will produce initial /s/ in words.

Goals: The child will imitate target consonants in words. (SG2)
The child will produce target consonants in words. (SG3)

Activity: Sad Sue **Expected age**: 33–36 months

Materials/Toys: any puppet or female doll, a game that requires turn-taking (e.g., board game, puzzle)

Show the puppet to the child and introduce her as "Sue." Tell the child that Sue is sad so she needs to cheer Sue up. To cheer Sue up you're going to let her play a game with you. Put the game on the floor and keep all the pieces. Ask the child, "Who should we give this piece to? Encourage the child to say "Sad Sue" each time the doll gets a piece. When Sue begins to get pieces of the puzzle (game), ask questions such as "Who has the yellow piece?" to give the child other opportunities to answer "Sad Sue."

S38a

Treatment Objective: The child will produce final /l/ in words.

Goals: The child will imitate target consonants in words. (SG2)
The child will produce target consonants in words. (SG3)

Activity: Roll Ball **Expected age**: 33–36 months

Materials/Toys: ball

(Note: Most children do not have difficulty producing final /l/. In the final position of words, /l/ is vocalic. Some children may omit this final "vowel.")

Sit on the floor with the child several feet away from you. Roll the ball to the child and say, "Roll ball." Encourage the child to imitate.

===== S38b =====

Treatment Objective: The child will produce final /l/ in words.

Goals: The child will imitate target consonants in words. (SG2)
The child will produce target consonants in words. (SG3)

Activity: I'm Full   **Expected age**: 33–36 months

Materials/Toys: puppet, doll, or stuffed animal with a mouth that opens; play food

Have the puppet pretend to gobble up all the food and then announce "I'm full." Give the puppet to the child so she can take a turn.

===== S39a =====

Treatment Objective: The child will produce final /g/ in words.

Goals: The child will imitate target consonants in words. (SG2)
The child will produce target consonants in words. (SG3)

Activity: In the Bag   **Expected age**: 33–36 months

Materials/Toys: two bags that differ slightly (e.g., size, color), one small toy that can hide in either

Show the child the toy you are going to hide. Then show the child the bags. Have the child close her eyes as you hide the toy in one of the bags. Have the child open her eyes and guess where the toy is. The child should use the word *bag* or a phrase, such as "In that bag" or "Red bag" as appropriate.

===== S39b =====

Treatment Objective: The child will produce final /g/ in words.

Goals: The child will imitate target consonants in words. (SG2)
The child will produce target consonants in words. (SG3)

Activity: Give a Hug or Kiss   **Expected age**: 33–36 months

Materials/Toys: doll, stuffed animal, or puppet

Tell the child that the doll (or stuffed animal or puppet) loves to get hugs and kisses. Tell the child you will give the doll a hug or a kiss when she tells you what to do. Encourage the child to use the word *hug*.

S40

Treatment Objective: The child will include all syllables (including weak) when using multisyllabic words.

Goal: The child will produce target vowels in connected speech. (SG9)

Activity: Home Life **Expected age:** 33–36 months

This activity will need to be completed when the child uses a multisyllabic word and omits the weak syllable in everyday conversation. For example, the child may say, "Nana" for "Banana" or "Ghetti" for "Spaghetti." Model the word with all of the syllables included. You can slightly exaggerate the weak syllable by lengthening it. You may also want to clap as you say each syllable.

Parent Handouts

by Jennifer Perry Blevins

This section provides informational handouts for parents and caregivers. Be sure to go over the information in these handouts with the parents before giving them out. The handouts provide families with general information regarding speech and language development as well as information about communication disorders found in the birth-to-three population. Descriptions of intervention strategies to facilitate communication development can be found on pages 159–161.

The remainder of the chapter provides activities for parents to do at home to work on intervention objectives that have been set by the team. These activities are intended to complement the intervention strategies found in this book.

In this section, you will find:

- a speech and language developmental milestones chart (pages 152–154)

- information explaining pre-linguistic/play skills, expressive language, receptive language, and developmental language delay (page 155)

- information explaining apraxia, articulation disorder, phonological disorder, and fluency disorder (pages 156–158)

- strategies to facilitate communication (pages 159–161)

- a list of daily activities to target speech, language, and pre-linguistic/play skills that parents can use to implement communication objectives (page 162)

- a blank form that can be copied for parents and filled out to give specific guidance about what to work on and how to do it (page 163). (Note: Use the activities in the *Activities Book* along with other ideas you might have to complete this form for the parents.)

- sample daily activity (bath time) appropriate for all age groups (birth to three) that includes suggested techniques for pre-linguistic/play skills, receptive language, expressive language, and sound production (pages 164–185). (Note: You can add additional information on the "Other" line as needed. These pages can serve as a model for you as you fill out the blank form on page 163 for the parents.) For other activities, see page 162.

- a list of resource materials (e.g., books, videotapes, Web Sites) that parents may find helpful (pages 186–187)

Please note that this chapter is not all-inclusive. As with any client, you will have to individualize the activities and strategies for parents in order to meet the needs of a specific child.

Speech and Language Developmental Milestones

This list is not intended to be all-inclusive of a child's speech and language skills. The absence of one or more skills doesn't necessarily constitute a speech or language delay. If your child has not been evaluated by a speech-language pathologist, one should be consulted if you are concerned about your child's speech and language development.

Expected Age of Development	Pre-linguistic Skills (play and cognitive skills)	Receptive Language (what your child understands)	Expressive Language (what your child says)	Sound Production
0–3 months	• Child makes eye contact with adult • Alerts to sounds • Watches a speaker's mouth	• Quiets to a familiar voice • Moves in response to voice • Discriminates between angry and friendly voices	• Has a hunger cry • Vocalizes to show pleasure	• Makes sounds in the back of the throat
3–6 months	• Maintains eye contact with speakers • Turns head to other's voice • Imitates facial expressions with adults • Reaches for and hits objects	• Begins to recognize own name • Responds to "no" • Smiles in response to speech	• Takes turns vocalizing	• Makes "raspberries"
6–9 months	• Imitates gestures of adult • Responds to noises that are not visible and searches for hidden objects • Attends to pictures • Begins to play games with adults	• Responds to "no" most of the time • Moves toward or looks for family members when named • Responds to "Come here" (only if your child is mobile [able to roll, scoot, or crawl])	• Vocalizes in response to objects that move • Shouts or vocalizes to gain attention	A variety of sounds will be produced as the child adds new words. Information regarding sound production is listed for ages when 75% of children correctly produce the specific sound.
9–12 months	• Plays "Peek-a-boo" • Waves *hi* and *bye* • Holds toy out to show others	• Responds to some verbal requests such as giving objects and gesturing when asked "Want up?" • Identifies two body parts on self • Participates in speech routine games like "So Big"	• Says "Mama" or "Dada" • Says 1–2 words spontaneously	(See comment at 6–9 months.)

Adapted from D. L. Hedrick, E. J. Prather, & A. R. Tobin (1975, 1984) *Sequenced Inventory of Communication Development*; L. Rossetti (1990). *The Rossetti Infant-Toddler Language Scale*; and I. L. Zimmerman, V. G. Steiner, & R. E. Pond (2002) *Preschool Language Scale*.

Speech and Language Developmental Milestones, continued

Expected Age of Development	Pre-linguistic Skills (play and cognitive skills)	Receptive Language (what your child understands)	Expressive Language (what your child says)	Sound Production
12–15 months	• Initiates turn-taking routines (e.g., sharing something to eat, beeping each other's noses) • Hugs dolls, stuffed animals, people • Hands toys to adults	• Follows one-step commands during play (e.g., "Put it on" with blocks, "Push it down" with toy with button) • Responds to "Give me" • Identifies three body parts on self or doll • Understands some prepositions such as *up* and *down*	• Shakes head *yes* or *no* • Says 8–10 words spontaneously • Tries to sing along with familiar songs • Imitates new words • Imitates three animal sounds	(See comment at 6–9 months.)
15–18 months	• Plays ball with an adult • Imitates housework activities • Identifies self in mirror • Requests assistance from an adult (e.g., with wind-up toy or other toy that cannot operate on own; child gives to adult to help)	• Identifies six body parts or clothing items on a doll • Chooses two familiar objects when asked (e.g., gets items as you name them, such as bottle, ball, or shoes) • Identifies objects by categories (e.g., able to put blocks with other blocks, balls with other balls, and animals with other animals)	• Says 15 meaningful words • Asks for "more" • Asks "What's that?" • Names 5–7 objects when asked	• Uses consonants *t, d, n, h* in isolation
18–21 months	• Pretends to play musical instruments • Pretends to dance • Uses two toys together in pretend play	• Identifies four body parts and clothing items on self • If mobile, follows directions to "Sit down" and "Come here" • Understands the meaning of action words • Identifies pictures named	• Imitates two- and three-word phrases • Requests toys or food with vocalizations and gestures • Names some pictures	(See comment at 6–9 months.)
21–24 months	• If mobile, pushes a stroller or shopping cart • Stacks and assembles toys and objects, such as nesting blocks • Matches sounds to pictures of animals	• Puts away toys on request • Follows two-step related commands (e.g., "Get the diaper and bring it to me" or "Pick up the cup and take a drink.")	• Says two-word phrases frequently • Uses 50 different words • Says three-word phrases occasionally • Says own name to refer to self	(See comment at 6–9 months.)

Speech and Language Developmental Milestones, continued

Expected Age of Development	Pre-linguistic Skills (play and cognitive skills)	Receptive Language (what your child understands)	Expressive Language (what your child says)	Sound Production
24–27 months	• Pretends to write • Pretends to talk on the phone • Slaps hand in response to "Gimme five"	• Points to four action words in pictures • Understands size concepts (*big* and *little*) • Understands the concept of *one* (e.g., "Give me one block" or "Get one cup.")	• Imitates two numbers or unrelated words • Uses three-word phrases frequently • Uses action words (e.g., *sit, eat, cry, sleep, kick, throw, roll*)	• Uses *t, n, k, g, p, m, h* at the beginning of words or syllables • Uses *n, p, m* at the end of words or syllables • Correctly produces vowel sounds
27–30 months	• Matches shapes and colors	• Responds to simple questions (e.g., "Where's Mommy?" when in the same room; "What do you drink?" when playing with baby and dishes) • Understands two prepositions/location phrases, such as *on, in, by, under*	• Names one color • Refers to self by pronouns consistently (*I, me, my*) • Uses two sentence types (declarative sentences like "Dog eat" or "Give me cookie" and asks questions like "Mommy go?" or "Bye bye?") • Uses past tense (regular or irregular forms like *jumped, stopped, ate, sat*) • Uses negation (*no, not, don't*)	• Uses *d, f, y* at the beginning of words or syllables • Uses *s, d, k, f, ng* at the end of words or syllables
30–33 months	• Sorts shapes (e.g., puts circles with other circles, squares with other squares) • Stacks rings in correct order	• Follows two-step unrelated commands (e.g., "Give the dog a bone and bring me the book.") • Understands the concept *all* • Answers *yes/no* questions correctly	• Answers questions with "yes" and "no" • Uses plurals • Uses prepositions • States gender • Says first and last names	• Uses *w* at the beginning of words or syllables • Uses *t, r, b* at the end of words or syllables
33–36 months	• Plays house • Sorts colors (e.g., puts red block with other red item, blue block with other blue item)	• Follows three-step unrelated commands (e.g., "Get your ball, Give baby a drink," and "Push the car.") • Answers *wh-* questions • Identifies parts of objects	• Uses verb form *-ing* • Asks *wh-* questions, including *what, who,* and *where* • Talks in sentences 3–5 words in length • Counts to 3 • Recites some nursery rhymes	• Uses *s* at the beginning of words or syllables • Uses *l* and *g* at the end of words or syllables • Says all syllables in a multisyllabic word

Areas of Language Development

Pre-linguistic/Play Skills

Pre-linguistic and play skills refer to how your child attends to and interacts with objects and people. These skills are important to facilitate your child's language development as well as his or her cognitive skills. Some areas that may be targeted during therapy to improve your child's play include:

- engaging in appropriate play
- taking turns with others
- demonstrating cause and effect (e.g., pushing a button to cause a door on a toy to open)
- performing pretend play
- showing problem-solving skills (e.g., placing nesting blocks inside of each other in the correct order)

Expressive Language

Expressive language refers to what your child says (or communicates through an alternative means). Components of language that may be assessed or targeted during therapy as expressive language include:

- semantics (word meanings or vocabulary, such as labels for objects, action words, and pronouns)
- morphology (units of meaning, such as plurals, verb endings, and possessives)
- syntax (sentence structure, which is word order, and use of different types of sentences)

Obviously, as children are first beginning to talk, they are not expected to use sentences. However, by the time a child is three years old, it is expected that he or she should be talking in sentences. In addition to the words and word combinations your child says is a component of language known as *pragmatics*. Pragmatics is how your child uses language (e.g., for requesting objects, actions, and information; answering questions; refusing; teasing; clarifying; continuing topics of conversation).

Receptive Language

Receptive language is what your child understands. Some skills that demonstrate what your child understands include:

- responding to verbalizations
- identifying body parts
- pointing to pictures named in books
- following directions
- showing understanding of size and color concepts
- answering questions

A younger child is expected to understand less, but by three years of age, a child should be following three-step directions and answering *wh-* questions (e.g., *who, what, where*).

Developmental Language Delay

A developmental language delay may occur if your child's language skills are not developing at a similar rate as same-age peers. This delay may be in your child's expressive language, receptive language, or both. As seen in the *Speech and Language Developmental Milestones* chart on pages 152–154, skills generally develop in age ranges (e.g., 9 to 12 months) rather than precisely at 10 months of age.

Speech Problems that Affect How Your Child's Speech Sounds

Apraxia

Apraxia of speech is a motor planning disorder which may result in difficulty planning, programming, and implementing the movements needed to produce sounds for speech. It is also called *developmental apraxia of speech* or *developmental verbal apraxia*.

In this disorder, you frequently see frustration when speech attempts are not successful. Errors may be inconsistent so that words may be produced differently from one attempt to another, such as saying "baby" correctly one time and then saying "gagy" on another attempt. Vowels may also be incorrectly produced. For children with apraxia of speech, therapy may include repetitive activities to focus on improving the ability to sequence particular sounds of speech. Therapy may also include gestures in which body movements are associated with sounds to facilitate productions. Because of the frustration a child may have over the difficulty of being understood, children with apraxia of speech are frequently given systems such as sign language and/or pictures to improve their ability to communicate. These systems are intended to be temporary to minimize frustration and to maximize communication rather than to permanently replace verbal speech.

Articulation Disorder

Articulation refers to sound production skills. In an articulation disorder, the errors are generally in the consonant sounds that your child says. When listening to these sounds, please note that the sounds do not necessarily correspond to the letters that are used to spell a word. The four types of articulation errors are:

Substitution—This is when your child says one sound in place of another. For example, if you hear your child say "tup" for "cup," he/she is substituting a *t* for a *k* sound.

Omission—This is when your child leaves out a sound in a word. For example, if you hear your child say "no" for "nose," he/she is deleting the final *z* sound.

Distortion—This is when a sound is produced in an imprecise manner. For example, your child makes an *s* sound with his tongue between his/her teeth.

Addition—An addition is when your child adds a sound to a word that is not normally pronounced. For example, your child says "balue" for "blue."

Though your child may have several of the errors described above, it is possible that your child's speech may be within normal limits for his or her age. There is a range of ages for typical development for each sound in English. Many errors that you may hear are developmentally appropriate until your child reaches an older age. In general, a child's speech should be 50% intelligible to unfamiliar listeners at two years of age. At three years of age this percentage should be 70%; and by four years of age, your child's speech should be about 90% intelligible to an unfamiliar listener.

Phonological Disorder

Phonology refers to the rules that are used for producing speech. These rules govern how sounds are combined in English. When a phonological disorder exists, your child's speech is probably very unintelligible and has errors in various rules. Fortunately, children with phonological disorders are following another set of rules and this makes it easier to remediate than if the child were randomly choosing ways to pronounce the words. Therapy for this type of speech disorder is generally completed in a cycle. A pattern is targeted in therapy for a designated number of sessions. Then a new pattern is targeted for a set number of sessions. Once all patterns have been addressed, the cycle is repeated. Your child's speech is not expected to be 100% intelligible, but by age three, the following error processes should not be seen.

> **Prevocalic Consonant Deletion**—This is when the consonant sound immediately preceding a vowel is deleted. For example, your child might say "og" for "dog" or "jump ope" for "jump rope." Prevocalic consonant deletion should disappear by 24 months of age.
>
> **Postvocalic Consonant Deletion**—Postvocalic consonant deletion is omitting a consonant sound that follows a vowel. Examples include saying "ha" for "hat" and "mokey" for "monkey." Postvocalic consonant deletion should disappear by 28 months of age.
>
> **Syllable Reduction**—This is when your child says fewer syllables than the word has. For example, your child might say "bay" for "baby," "tephone" for "telephone," or "el" for "elephant." Deleting syllables from words is a process that typically disappears between 29 and 36 months of age.

Additionally, there may be other patterns that are targeted to stimulate your child's speech. Two such error processes are *stridency deletion* and *velars*.

> **Stridency Deletion**—Stridents are sounds that are produced with an intense noise. There are eight strident sounds in English: *s, z, f, v, sh, ch, j,* and *zh* (as in "beige"). Stridency deletion is when these sounds are not produced in your child's speech. Your child may substitute another sound for the target sound or omit it completely. Of the strident sounds, only *f* and *s* are expected to develop prior to age three. Seventy-five percent of children are able to say *f* at the beginning and at the end of words by 28 months of age. The majority of children are able to say *s* at the end of words or syllables between 27 and 30 months and are able to say *s* at the beginning of words or syllables between 33 and 36 months of age. By 44 months of age, children should be producing *sh* and *ch*. The sounds *v, z, zh,* and *j* may not be correctly produced until 48 months or later.
>
> **Velars**—Velar sounds are *k* and *g*. Typical sound substitutions include *t* and *d*. These substitutions should disappear sometime between 30 and 36 months of age.

Fluency Disorder/Stuttering

Disfluent speech is when your child repeats whole words (e.g., *My . . . my turn.* or *Bailey is . . . is sleeping*), parts of words (e.g., *do-dog*), and/or phrases (e.g., *I want . . . I want to go*). To a degree, all speakers are disfluent at times. People may repeat words, revise what they are saying, and use interjections, such as *uh, um,* and *er*. All of these are considered disfluencies. Other types of disfluencies include prolongations of sound (e.g., *My name is Saaaaaaally.*) and tense pauses (e.g., *Rerun is a . . .* [tongue pushed up to top of mouth but no sound being made] *. . . dog*).

When children are acquiring language, particularly when they have rapid growth in their use of language, they may experience periods when they are more disfluent. The degree of disfluency may fluctuate with more fluent days and less fluent days. While language development may influence the degree of fluency, other factors that may impact fluency include motor learning, other developmental growth, and environmental influences (e.g., others' speaking rates and

Speech Problems that Affect How Your Child's Speech Sounds, continued

frequency of being interrupted). Normal disfluency or developmental stuttering is frequently seen in children ranging in age from 18 months to 6 years. Table 13-1 differentiates types of disfluencies/stuttering.

Characteristic	Normal Disfluency	Borderline Stuttering	Beginning Stuttering
Typical Age Range	• 1½ to 6 years, though some normal disfluency continues in mature speech	• 1½ to 6 years	• 2 to 8 years
Number of Disfluencies	• 10 or less disfluencies per 100 words	• 11 or more disfluencies per 100 words	• More important than the number of disfluencies is the type of disfluencies.
Types of Disfluencies	• Interjections (e.g., "uh," "um"), revisions, and word repetitions. After children turn three, a decrease is generally seen in the number of part-word repetitions.	• More repetitions and prolongations. Fewer revisions or incomplete phrases. Typically relaxed when disfluent.	• Rapid and irregular repetitions. Child may have muscle tension, rise in pitch, fixed mouth postures, and escape behaviors (e.g., eye blinks, head nods, ums). Frequently child inserts a schwa vowel ("uh") at the end of repeated syllable (e.g., "puh-puh-play").
Number of Repetitions	• Typically one, sometimes two	• Frequently more than two repetitions	• Varied, may see prolongations, filler such as "uh" or "um," and escape behaviors (e.g., blink eyes, nod head)
Awareness of Stuttering	• Generally child has no reactions to disfluencies	• Child rarely reacts to disfluencies though may occasionally show surprise or mild frustration	• Child aware of disfluencies and may express frustration

Table 13-1 Information compiled from Guitar, B. (1998). *Stuttering: An integrated approach to its nature and treatment* (2nd ed.). Baltimore: Lippincott, Williams & Wilkins.

At times when your child's speech is more disfluent, it may be beneficial to change the way that you speak to him or her. Using slow, easy speech is a way to model unhurried speech for your child. This may be beneficial because it is possible that your child feels that he or she can never achieve the rate at which you speak. The rate of slow, easy speech is saying about two words per second.

Strategies to Facilitate Communication

A *strategy* is a technique that can be used to help your child achieve a goal. Your child's clinician will provide specific examples of how these strategies can be used in day-to-day activities to help your child with his specific treatment objectives. This handout gives a general description of these techniques. You may incorporate more than one strategy at a time. For example, you may put an item *out of reach* which causes your child to point to what he wants. Then to try to get your child to say the name of the object, you may *model* the name of the item or give your child a *choice* between two things.

Expansion—Add words to what your child says. If your child says "dog," you can say "Dog eat" or "The dog is eating." Expansion encourages your child to combine words.

Forgetfulness—After your child is used to a routine, purposely forget something that is part of the routine. For example, get milk out of the refrigerator and then hand your child the cup without pouring any milk into it.

Giving Choices—When your child uses non-specific pointing to indicate that he wants something (like pointing in the general direction of the refrigerator), give your child a choice between two items and try to get your child to use a word to let you know what he wants. For example, if your child points to the refrigerator, say, "Do you want milk or juice?"

Guided Learning—This strategy may not result in any speech production as it is basically for children who are not yet talking. It involves arranging the environment so that something challenging will attract your child's attention. Perhaps your child is beginning to play routine games by pushing a car back and forth. You might try routine games where your child has to push other things back and forth.

Imitation—One of the best ways to teach your child that imitation is fun (and helpful for learning lots of skills!) is to imitate something your child starts. Your child will particularly enjoy imitation if it is something silly. Watch for opportunities to imitate (e.g., your child puts a pan on his head and then sees you do it). You can also imitate your child's vocalizations (e.g., If your child says "eee," do it back; if your child makes raspberries, do it back).

Let Your Child Lead—When playing with your child, let him choose the activity. This strategy may not directly result in any speech production but by doing activities your child chooses, you can model speech that is of interest to him.

Modeling—Children learn from imitation. Encourage your child to use words to talk about what he is doing by modeling. Show or say what you want your child to do before you expect him to do it. For example, let your child hear you say the target sound or word or see you stack the rings on the pole before he attempts it.

Novelty—Introduce something new into the environment, something that doesn't usually go with a routine. For example, if you are playing with toy tools, put a baby's bottle in with them. See if your child notices the new or unexpected item. If your child does not appear to notice the new item, draw his attention to it by saying, "Oh, look at that" as you point to it and name it.

Strategies to Facilitate Communication, continued

Out of Reach—You might purposely put something you know your child will want out of reach or in a container your child cannot open. Putting the item out of reach creates a situation for your child to point to an item to indicate what he wants. You can then try to get your child to say/sign the name of the desired object or another word, such as "Gimme," "Want," or "Please" before you give it to him.

Parallel Talk—This is when you give a running commentary about your child's actions. Consider yourself the play-by-play announcer. Describe each thing your child does, using language at the level you want your child to talk or understand. For example, if your child is playing in his bath, describe what is happening: "Tyler is getting the soap. Oops, the soap is slippery. Tyler got it this time. Tyler is washing his foot. Tyler is pushing the boat."

Paraphrasing—If your child seems not to have understood what you have said, try putting it in other words. Your child may understand you better if you use simpler language. For example, say, "Sit down," instead of "You have to sit down and eat so we can go to see Grandma later."

Picture Stimuli—Pictures of objects and activities may be used to help children communicate. Use of pictures is intended to reduce your child's frustration and to improve your child's ability to indicate his wants and needs. He may do this by pointing to or handing you a picture in exchange for the desired object or activity. Your child may say the word at the same time as pointing to or handing you the picture or he may use the picture instead of saying the word. For most children, the use of pictures is temporary, but for some using pictures may be more permanent.

Piece-by-Piece—You can use this strategy when playing with toys or objects that have pieces. Don't give all of the pieces to your child at once. Hold some back to encourage communication.

Providing Prompts—The kind of prompt will change depending on the response. If you want your child to choose an object you name, the prompt might be moving the correct choice a little closer to him. If you want your child to use a sign, a prompt might be helping him shape his hands to make the sign. If you want your child to say a word or phrase, the prompt might be giving him two choices.

Supplementing Adult's Verbal Speech with Picture Stimuli—To help your child understand what you are saying, use pictures as you talk. For example, if you are asking your child if he wants a drink, you might say, "Drink" and show a picture of something to drink (e.g., glass of milk).

Questioning—Ask questions that are logical to the situation. Try not to ask *yes/no* questions if you want to elicit more of a response. *Yes/no* questions don't lend themselves to continuing a "conversation." If you want to elicit longer utterances from your child, try questions like "Where could the bear be?" or "How do I do this?" However, there may be times when you are specifically trying to improve your child's accuracy in responding to *yes/no* questions. If this is the case, you will want to ask simple *yes/no* questions (e.g., "Is this a ball?" or "Do you want milk?" rather than "Is this what Daddy plays with you?" and "Would you like me to give you something to drink?"). Once your child has mastered the simple questions, you can ask more difficult ones.

Strategies to Facilitate Communication, *continued*

Sabotage—This technique is to deliberately interfere with the successful completion of an activity. For example, hide a piece of the puzzle or take the batteries out of a toy. You may also give your child an item other than the one he wants. For instance, you may give your child a carrot when he wants a cookie. This creates a situation to encourage your child to use words/signs to communicate his wants and needs to you. After you have prevented your child from completing the activity, encourage him to use words/signs to indicate what he wants.

Self-talk—Self-talk is a running commentary about your actions. For example, while you are driving the car, you say things such as, "I'm going to stop," "I'm going to go," or "Mommy is putting on her seat belt."

Sign Language—Sign language is the use of a gestural system to communicate. Signs may be used with a child with a language delay or a speech disorder in order to reduce frustration and to give him a way to communicate his wants and needs. For some children, sign language may be used temporarily as a way to facilitate communication. Sign language often facilitates the development of verbal speech. For others, sign language may be used more permanently. If your child does not talk well yet, encourage him to use a sign/gesture with or instead of the word.

Supplementing Adult's Verbal Speech with Signs/Gestures—To help your child understand what you are saying, use gestures and/or pointing as you talk. For example, if you are asking your child if he wants a drink, you might say, "Do you want a drink?" as you use the sign for *drink* or say, "Do you want a drink of water?" and point to the sink.

Using Object with/instead of Word—If the goal is expressive language, but your child can't talk well yet, encourage your child to point to the object along with saying or instead of saying the word.

Using Touch Cue with the Sound—If the goal is better sound production, your child's clinician might use a physical cue to help your child remember how to say the sound. These cues are often called *touch cues* and involve touching the face near the mouth. (For more information, see pages 119–120 in the *Therapy Guide*.

Violating Expectations—After your child is used to a routine happening in a particular way, purposely do something that alters the predictable without warning (e.g., Put on your child's shoes and then get his socks to put on).

Wait and See—After starting a game or asking a question, wait and give your child time to respond.

Withholding an Object to Get the Desired Response—If you want to increase your child's expressive output (e.g., gestures, signs, picture system, words), don't give him what he wants until he gives you the desired response.

Daily Activities to Target Speech, Language, and Pre-linguistic/Play Skills

The best time to stimulate your child's speech and language development is during regular daily activities. Some activities can be used for any age, but other activities are only appropriate for certain age ranges. For example, bottle feeding is an ideal daily activity when working with an infant, but it is not appropriate for a two-year-old. Pretend play activities with toy people or tools are appropriate for older children but not infants. This list will give you some ideas of daily activities you can use to develop communication skills.

(Note to SLP: Work with the caregiver to choose an activity from the list. Then fill in the form on the next page. See pages 164–185 for a completed sample targeting bath time.)

bath time	grocery shopping	playing with toys
bedtime	nap time	• animals (stuffed, plastic)
bottle feeding	playground/swing set	• baby doll
brushing hair	playing with pets	• ball
brushing teeth	potty/toilet training	• blocks
changing diapers	preparing lunch	• bubbles
cleaning up toys	putting on makeup	• cars
cooking	reading books	• dishes
doing laundry	riding in a car	• fishing pole (plastic)
eating	riding toys (bikes, wagons)	• Mr. Potato Head
gardening	taking walks	• people
getting dressed	watching movies/television	• play food
		• puzzles
		• Slinky
		• tools (plastic)
		• train

Daily Activity to Work on Treatment Objectives

Child's Name _____   **Date** _____

Activity _____   **Skill Level** _____

Pre-linguistic/Play Skills

_____

_____

_____

Other: _____

Receptive Language

_____

_____

_____

Other: _____

Expressive Language

_____

_____

_____

Other: _____

Sound Production

_____

_____

_____

Other: _____

Sample Daily Activity to Work on Treatment Objectives

Child's Name _____   **Date** _____

Activity _Bath Time_____   **Skill Level** _0–3 months_____

> Note: Have all toys, washcloths, towels, and other objects ready before putting your child in the bathtub. Never leave your child unattended in the bathtub.

Pre-linguistic/Play Skills

Your child will make eye contact with an adult. Prior to washing each body part, look at your child and say something to him. If your child doesn't look at you and make eye contact when you are talking, get closer to his face and talk to him again.

Your child will watch a speaker's mouth. As you dry your child, place him on your lap and talk to him. Talk in simple phrases and vary the pitch of your voice. Get close to your child's face to try to get him to look at you as you are talking.

Other: _____

Receptive Language

Your child will quiet to a familiar voice. If your child becomes upset during bathing due to water getting in his eyes or some other event, talk to him. See if you notice a difference between quietly talking to your child to calm him as you wipe his eyes versus wiping his eyes without talking to him.

Other: _____

Expressive Language

_____
_____
_____

Other: _____

Sound Production

Your child will make sounds in the back of his throat. Talk to your child as you are bathing him. Say things like "cootchy cootchy coo" and other words that have *k*, *g*, and *h* sounds in them.

Other: _____

Sample Daily Activity to Work on Treatment Objectives

Child's Name _____   **Date** _____

Activity _Bath Time_____   **Skill Level** _3–6 months_____

> Note: Have all toys, washcloths, towels, and other objects ready before putting your child in the bathtub. Never leave your child unattended in the bathtub.

Pre-linguistic/Play Skills

**Your child will turn her head to another voice**. As you dry your child, have her sit sideways (facing left or right) on your lap. Talk to your child to try to get her to turn her head to your voice. If your child doesn't turn her head, turn her to face you as you keep talking to her. Then turn her either left or right and try again. You can also place your child so that she is facing away from the door and have someone else talk to her from the doorway to see if she will turn in the direction of the voice.

**Your child will reach for and hit objects**. Put objects, such as the washcloth, a rubber duck, or other toy near your child (e.g., in front of her, above her). Take your child's hand to reach for the object and to touch it. Give the object to your child and allow her to play with it. Then move the object a little further away to see if your child will reach for it again.

Other: _____

Receptive Language

**Your child will begin to recognize her own name**. Use your child's name as you are talking about what you are doing, such as "I'm washing (child's name) arms" or "We're making (child's name) a clean girl."

**Your child will smile in response to speech**. Model this behavior for your child. When your child makes a sound, smile at her. Change the pitch in your voice and smile while you are talking to try to get your child to imitate your smile.

Other: _____

Expressive Language

**Your child will take turns vocalizing**. Try to get your child to take turns with you by saying, "Ah, ah, ah" as you hit the water around her. Wait to splash again until your child makes a vocalization.

Other: _____

Sound Production

**Your child will make "raspberries."** As you dry your child, put her on your lap and get close to her face. Make raspberries and see if your child will imitate you.

Other: _____

Sample Daily Activity to Work on Treatment Objectives

Child's Name _____ **Date** _____

Activity _Bath Time_____ **Skill Level** _6–9 months_____

> Note: Have all toys, washcloths, towels, and other objects ready before putting your child in the bathtub. Never leave your child unattended in the bathtub.

Pre-linguistic/Play Skills

Your child will imitate an adult's gestures. Smack the water and say, "Splash, splash, splash." Then take your child's hand and smack the water. You can also clap when your child does something that you do and say, "Yeah." Use hand-over-hand assistance as needed to help your child clap if he doesn't do it on his own.

Your child will respond to noises that are not visible and will search for hidden objects. Have toys in the bathroom that make noise (e.g., rubber duck that squeaks). Make noise with the toy where your child cannot see it. Encourage your child to look for what is making the noise. Then, while your child is not looking, drop a small soft toy (can be the same toy as before or a new toy) into the water behind him to make a splash. See if your child will look to see what caused the splash. You can also get your child to search for hidden objects by showing him a toy and then putting it under the washcloth. Say, "Where is the _____?" and look under the washcloth. Try again with a different toy.

Other: _____

Receptive Language

Your child will respond to "Come here." After you have dried your child, put him on the floor, go to the doorway, and tell your child, "Come here." This may work better if there is someone who can do this with you so if your child doesn't respond, you can move him closer to the person talking.

Your child will move toward or look for family members when named. Have family members in the bathroom during bath time. Take turns saying, "Where's Mommy/Daddy/Grandma?" If your child doesn't look at the person named, point to that person and turn your child toward him or her.

Other: _____

continued on next page

Sample Daily Activity to Work on Treatment Objectives

6–9 months, continued

Expressive Language

Your child will imitate two-syllable combinations. As you are washing your child, say simple two-syllable combinations, such as "oo ah," "ee ow," and "oh ya." Pause between things you say to allow your child time to imitate you.

Your child will imitate duplicated syllables. Name things that you are using to bathe your child. Repeat the first sound of the things, such as "wa wa wa" for *water*, "duh duh duh" for *duck*, and "tah tah tah" for *towel*. Pause between things you say to allow your child to imitate you.

Other:

Sound Production

Other:

Sample Daily Activity to Work on Treatment Objectives

Child's Name _____   **Date** _____

Activity _Bath Time_____   **Skill Level** _9–12 months_____

> Note: Have all toys, washcloths, towels, and other objects ready before putting your child in the bathtub. Never leave your child unattended in the bathtub.

Pre-linguistic/Play Skills

Your child will play "Peek-a-boo." Hold the washcloth up between you and your child and play "peek-a-boo" with her.

Your child will wave "Hi" and "Bye." Have someone come to the doorway during bath time. When the person appears, wave "Hi" to that person as you say "Hi." Talk to the person for a moment. Then as he walks away, wave "Bye" to the person as you say "Bye."

Other: _____

Receptive Language

Your child will identify two body parts on herself. Talk about body parts as you wash and rinse them. Before you wash your child's feet, ears, hands, stomach, etc., say, "I'm going to wash your _____." Then say, "Show me your _____." Wait a few seconds before washing the body part you name to allow your child to show you the body part. If your child doesn't identify the body part when you ask her, touch the body part, name it, and then give her the direction to show you the body part again. If she still doesn't show you the body part, take her hand in yours and touch her hand to the correct body part as you name it again.

Your child will respond to some verbal requests, such as giving objects. When you hand your child a toy, say, "I give you the _____." When your child is holding a toy, say, "Give me the _____." If your child doesn't give you the toy, ask for it again and take her hand to place the object in your hand. Then give the toy back to your child and repeat, "I give you the _____." Again ask her to give you the toy. If she still doesn't hand you the toy, again take her hand to place the toy in your hand.

Your child will respond to "Want up?" Before picking up your child to dry her off, ask, "Want up?" Model putting your hands up in the air for your child. Give her a few seconds to imitate you, then raise your child's arms, and pick her up.

Other: _____

continued on next page

Sample Daily Activity to Work on Treatment Objectives

9–12 months, continued

Expressive Language

Your child will say "Mama" or "Dada." Point to your child and say her name. Then point to yourself and say "Mama" (or "Dada") You can also work on this by saying "Mama" (or "Dada") when your child reaches for you. Before saying anything else to your child, give her time to imitate "Mama" (or "Dada"). ***Your child will say one or two words spontaneously.*** Name things in your child's environment. Repeat the names to encourage your child to imitate you. Some suggested words that you could try to get your child to say during bath time are *soap, bath, duck, Mommy, Daddy,* and names of body parts.

Other: _____

Sound Production

_____

Other: _____

Sample Daily Activity to Work on Treatment Objectives

Child's Name _____ **Date** _____

Activity _Bath Time_ **Skill Level** _12–15 months_

> Note: Have all toys, washcloths, towels, and other objects ready before putting your child in the bathtub. Never leave your child unattended in the bathtub.

Pre-linguistic/Play Skills

Your child will initiate turn-taking routines. Touch your child's nose and say, "Beep." Take your child's hand, put it on your nose, and say, "Beep" again. Beep your child's nose one more time. Then wait for a few seconds to see if he will reach for your nose to start the game again. If your child doesn't reach for your nose, encourage him to do so. See if he will touch your nose. If he still doesn't touch your nose, guide his hand to your nose and say, "Beep."

Your child will hug dolls, stuffed animals, and people. You can use a tub toy, such as a doll or animal. Show it to your child and say, "I hug baby (bear, duck, etc.)," and then hug the toy. Give it to your child and tell him, "Hug baby (or other toy)." If your child doesn't do this, put the toy to your child's chest and put his arms around it to help him hug the toy. Once you have your child out of the tub, hug your child as you are drying him and say, "I hug you." Wait a few seconds and ask your child to hug you.

Other: _____

Receptive Language

Your child will follow one-step commands during play. Give your child a rubber duck or other toy that floats in the water. Say, "Push it." Wait to see if your child will follow your instruction. If he doesn't push the duck, take his hand, put it on the duck, and say, "Push it" as you help him push the duck.

Your child will understand some prepositions. Put a plastic container in the tub with your child. Also have a washcloth and some small toys (e.g., plastic eggs, fish). Take a toy, put it in the plastic container, and say, "In." Repeat with another toy and then tell your child to put the toy in. If he doesn't, put a toy in his hand and help him put the toy in the container. You can also work on "under" by putting a toy under the washcloth.

Other: _____

continued on next page

Sample Daily Activity to Work on Treatment Objectives

12–15 months, continued

Expressive Language

Your child will try to sing along with familiar songs. Sing songs, such as "Itsy Bitsy Spider" and "Pat-a-Cake." You can do this while your child is sitting in the tub or as you are drying your child. Include the hand motions while you are singing to encourage your child to sing with you.

Your child will imitate animal sounds. Put toy animals in the tub with your child. They can either be in a plastic container or on the bottom of the tub. Have your child reach in (down) and get an animal. As he grabs the animal and looks at it, make the sound that the animal makes. Encourage your child to imitate the sound.

Other:

Sound Production

Other:

Sample Daily Activity to Work on Treatment Objectives

Child's Name _____ **Date** _____

Activity _Bath Time_____ **Skill Level** _15–18 months_____

> Note: Have all toys, washcloths, towels, and other objects ready before putting your child in the bathtub. Never leave your child unattended in the bathtub.

Pre-linguistic/Play Skills

Your child will identify herself in the mirror. Hold your child in front of the mirror. Say, "Where's (child's name)?" Point to your child in the mirror after waiting a few seconds. Then ask the question again and wait for your child to reach for herself in the mirror. If she doesn't reach for herself, again ask, "Where's (child's name)?" and take her hand and put it on her reflection in the mirror. Then say, "There's (child's name)."

Your child will request assistance from an adult. Bring a clear, plastic container with a lid into the bathroom with you. The container should be one that your child cannot open. After your child has been playing with a toy during her bath, take the toy from her, put it in the container, and close the lid so your child cannot get the toy out. Put the plastic container into the tub with your child. See if your child will hand the container to you to get the toy out for her. If she doesn't, pick up the container and pretend to open it. Then give the container back to her. Again wait for her to give it to you to open it. If she doesn't give it to you, as she holds the container say, "I can open it for you." If she still doesn't hand you the container, help guide her hands to give you the container to open.

Other: _____

Receptive Language

Your child will choose familiar objects when asked. Put three familiar objects that float in front of your child (e.g., a bottle, a ball, a cup). Name one of the objects and see if your child will select it. If not, take her hand and touch the item named. Name each of the other objects, pausing between the two to give your child time to select the item named.

Your child will identify objects by categories. Take two or three sets of familiar objects into the tub (e.g., balls, dishes, blocks, animals, cars). Put plastic containers for each set in the tub with your child. Designate each container to hold one set of objects. Put at least two of each item in a container (e.g., two balls in one container, two dishes in another). Give your child one object and ask her where the other similar objects are. If she doesn't put the object with the others, guide her hand to the correct container. Repeat this with each set of objects.

Other: _____

continued on next page

Sample Daily Activity to Work on Treatment Objectives

15–18 months, continued

Expressive Language

Your child will ask, "What's that?" Take some items that are unfamiliar to your child into the bathroom with you (e.g., egg carton, measuring cup, fishing bobber). Hold up one of the items and, as you look at it, say, "What's that?" Wait to see if your child will imitate this phrase. If your child doesn't imitate the phrase, point to the item and tell her to say, "What's that?" When she does, name the item.

Your child will name five to seven objects when asked. Put some familiar toys into a plastic container or bucket. Play a game with your child to name the items. Have your child take a toy out of the container and name it. Have your child tell you what she has before taking another item. You can also put the toys under a towel or washcloth and have the child reach under to find the toys.

Other:

Sound Production

Your child will use consonants* t, d, n, *and* h *in isolation*. Exaggerate these sounds and say them repeatedly. Focus on one sound at a time. Get close to your child's face and say "t, t, t, t." Wait for a few seconds to see if your child will imitate you. If not, put your child's hand up to your mouth so she can feel the air when you make the sound again. Do this with each sound.

Other:

Sample Daily Activity to Work on Treatment Objectives

Child's Name _____   Date _____

Activity **Bath Time** _____   Skill Level **18–21 months** _____

> Note: Have all toys, washcloths, towels, and other objects ready before putting your child in the bathtub. Never leave your child unattended in the bathtub.

Pre-linguistic/Play Skills

Your child will use two toys together in pretend play. Use a boat and toy person. Demonstrate putting the person in the boat and then pushing the boat. Take the person out of the boat and give both toys to your child. Help him put the person in the boat if necessary.

Other: _____

Receptive Language

Your child will understand the meaning of action words. Play with a baby doll during bath time. Ask your child to complete actions with the doll, such as "Make baby sit," "Make baby swim," "Make baby drink," "Wipe baby's nose," "Wash baby's feet," "Rinse baby's hair," or "Dry baby's hands." Give your child one direction at a time and pause after giving each direction. If he doesn't complete the action given, repeat the direction, and demonstrate how to complete it. Give your child the direction again and give him assistance to complete the action.

Your child will follow directions to "Sit down" and "Come here."

Sit down — Put a towel on the floor. When you take your child out of the tub, stand him on the towel and tell him to sit down. If he doesn't follow the direction, gently help sit him down.

Come here — When you are ready for bath time, go to where your child is. Stand a few feet from him and say, "Come here." Sit on your knees so you are more at your child's level. Repeat the direction and motion for your child to come to you. If this doesn't get your child to move toward you, reach for his hand and pull him gently toward you as you repeat "Come here."

Other: _____

Expressive Language

Your child will imitate two- and three-word phrases. Talk in simple language to your child during bath time. Say things like "Dirty toes," "Wash feet," "Rinse hair," "Hot water," and "More soap" for two-word phrases. Some three-word phrases might be "Soap in water," "Little yellow duck," "Duck swims fast," and "Wash (child's name) hair."

continued on next page

Sample Daily Activity to Work on Treatment Objectives

18–21 months, continued

If your child says a single word like "duck," try to get him to say two words by adding a word to what he said. Say, "Little duck," "Yellow duck," "Duck quack," or "Duck swim." Wait for your child to imitate you. If he doesn't, say, "Duck . . . duck quack" to show him what you want him to do.

If your child says a two-word phrase like "Wash feet," say, "Wash my feet" to see if your child will imitate you. If he doesn't say the three-word phrase, say "Wash feet, Wash my feet" to show him what you want him to do.

Your child will request toys with vocalizations and gestures. Put toys your child plays with during bath time outside of the bathtub but within your child's sight. Put your child in the tub and do not put any toys, the soap, or a washcloth in the tub with your child. If your child doesn't point to the toys and other items, draw his attention to them but don't give them to him. Take your child's hand to point to one item and say its name. See if he will repeat the process for the next item. If not, help him again as you did with the first item. When your child "requests" an item, give it to him.

Other:

Sound Production

Other:

Sample Daily Activity to Work on Treatment Objectives

Child's Name _____   Date _____

Activity __Bath Time_____   Skill Level __21–24 months_____

> Note: Have all toys, washcloths, towels, and other objects ready before putting your child in the bathtub. Never leave your child unattended in the bathtub.

Pre-linguistic/Play Skills

Your child will stack and assemble toys and objects (e.g., ring stacker, nesting blocks). Put the ring stacker in the water in front of your child. Demonstrate putting the first two rings on the stacker. Give your child the third ring. Try to get her to stack it on top of the rings already on the stacker. If your child doesn't stack the ring by herself, guide her hand to do so. At this age, your child may not stack the rings in the correct order.
Other: _____

Receptive Language

Your child will put away toys on request. After you have finished bathing your child, have her help you put away toys (e.g., into a net that holds toys, into a plastic container). Demonstrate how to put away the toys as needed. You might want to sing a song to help motivate your child to clean up the toys (e.g., "Clean up, clean up. Everybody, everywhere. Clean up, clean up. Everybody do their share").
Your child will follow two-step related commands. This generally involves having your child doing two things with one object, such as "Get the duck and make him quack," "Pick up the soap and give it to me," or "Get the boat and push it." Do not use any gestures to prompt your child initially. If she doesn't complete the direction without a prompt, go ahead and prompt her with gestures by pointing to the object you are talking about. If that doesn't get her to complete the direction, take her hand and help her follow the steps.
Other: _____

Expressive Language

Your child will say two-word phrases frequently. When your child says a word, repeat what your child has said and add another word. For instance, if your child says "Feet," you say, "Dirty feet" or "Wash feet." If your child says "Water," say, "Water on" or "Hot water."
Your child will say her own name to refer to herself. Hold up your child in front of the mirror. Point to yourself in the mirror and say your name (what your child calls you). Then point to your child in the mirror and say her name. Try to get your child to do the same by taking her hand and touching her reflection.
Other: _____

continued on next page

Sample Daily Activity to Work on Treatment Objectives

Child's Name _____   **Date** _____

Activity _Bath Time_   **Skill Level** _24–27 months_

> Note: Have all toys, washcloths, towels, and other objects ready before putting your child in the bathtub. Never leave your child unattended in the bathtub.

Pre-linguistic/Play Skills

Your child will pretend to talk on the phone. You can use a plastic toy phone or pretend with a bar of soap. Make a ringing sound and then pick up the phone or soap and hold it to your ear. Pretend to talk to someone familiar to your child such as a grandparent, aunt, uncle, etc. Then say, "Oh, you want to talk to (child's name)." Give your child the phone or soap. Encourage him to talk into the phone.

Your child will slap your hand in response to "Gimme five." Give your child a direction that you know that he can do. Once he has completed the direction, clap and say, "Gimme five" and hold out your hand for him. If he doesn't slap your hand, take his hand and guide it to slap your hand as you repeat "Gimme five."

Other: _____

Receptive Language

Your child will understand size concepts. Describe objects that are _big_ and _little_, such as comparing your child's potty chair to the toilet, your child's hand to yours, a washcloth to a towel (preferably of the same color), or a little food container to a big bowl. As you point to each item, say either "Big" or "Little." Then present each pair of items to your child and ask, "Which one is big?" Wait until your child is consistently able to identify the big item of each pair before you ask him which one is little.

Your child will understand the concept of one. Present your child with several small toys, such as blocks, animals, or plastic eggs. Pick up one of the toys and say, "I want one." Wait a few seconds and then say, "Here's one for you" as you hand your child one. Pick up three or four of the toys and hold them in front of your child. Tell him to take _one_. If your child doesn't take any, take his hand and help him get one toy. If he takes more than one, say, "No, that's not one. Here's _one_." Take all but one toy out of your child's hand.

Other: _____

Expressive Language

Your child will use action words. Get toys, such as a toy person, a duck, and a frog. Take the person and stand it on the edge of the tub. Move it up and down and say, "Jump, jump, jump." Wait a few

continued on next page

Sample Daily Activity to Work on Treatment Objectives

24–27 months, continued

seconds to see if your child will say, "Jump." If he doesn't imitate you, take the person and say, "Jump" again as you make the person jump into the water. Repeat with the duck and the frog, and each time model "Jump, jump, jump" for your child. You can try this with other actions, such as *swim, sit,* and *sleep.*

Your child will say three-word phrases frequently. Try to use several three-word phrases while you are bathing your child (e.g., "I wash feet," "[child's name] sits down," "Turn water off," "Get me soap"). Encourage your child to use three-word phrases by adding a word to your child's two-word phrase. For example, if your child says "Yellow duck," you can say, "Little yellow duck" or "Yellow duck swims." If the child says "Yeah bubbles," say, "Yeah bubbles pop."

Other:

Sound Production

***Your child will use the consonants* t, n, k, g, p, m, *and* h *at the beginning of words or syllables*.** To improve your child's production of these sounds, exaggerate the initial sound as you say the targeted words. If your child incorrectly produces the beginning sound, repeat the word and say it correctly. The words listed below are words that can be incorporated into bath time. It is more beneficial for your child to work on these words when they are in meaningful contexts (e.g., *t* as in *towel* as you dry your child off, *k* as in *kiss* as you kiss your child when you pick him up out of the tub, *p* as in *pig* while he plays with a toy pig in the tub).

t — towel, toes, teeth, tummy	*n* — nose, no
k — comb, kiss, cold	*g* — go, give
p — potty, pig	*m* — me, Mommy, more
h — hot, horse, help	

***Your child will use the consonants* n, p, *and* m *at the end of words or syllables*.** To improve your child's production of these sounds, exaggerate the final sound as you say the targeted words. If your child incorrectly produces the ending sound, repeat the word and say it correctly. The words listed below are words that can be incorporated into bath time. It is more beneficial for your child to work on these words when they are in meaningful contexts (e.g., *n* as in *in* as you knock toys from the edge of the tub into the water, *p* as in *soap* as you put soap on the washcloth, *m* as in *Mom* as you point to yourself in the mirror).

n — in, on
p — soap, cup
m — Mom, thumb

Other:

Sample Daily Activity to Work on Treatment Objectives

Child's Name _____ **Date** _____

Activity _Bath Time_ **Skill Level** _27–30 months_

> Note: Have all toys, washcloths, towels, and other objects ready before putting your child in the bathtub. Never leave your child unattended in the bathtub.

Pre-linguistic/Play Skills

Your child will match colors. You'll need several blocks of different colors (have at least five of each color) and plastic containers that float in the tub. Place two blocks of one color in one container and two blocks of another color in another container. Point to the blocks in each container and name the colors (e.g., "Red, red . . . These are red," and "Blue, blue . . . These are blue"). Then take either a red block or a blue block and put it in the correct container. Give your child a red block to see if she will put the block in the container with the other red blocks. Do this again with the blue blocks. With the blocks that are left, give your child one block at a time and have her put them in the correct containers. (Note: When first working on this, it may be best to use only two colors of blocks [e.g., red and blue, yellow and green].)

Other: _____

Receptive Language

Your child will respond to simple questions. Ask your child questions about objects and events that she can see during bath time. For instance, you can ask, "What's that?" as you point to an object, "What does Mommy have?," "What is swimming?," and "What is Mommy doing?" If your child doesn't respond correctly, tell her the answer. Then ask the question again to see if she will repeat the answer to you.

***Your child will understand location phrases, such as* on, off, *and* under.**

on Turn a plastic container upside down and float it in front of your child. Place a few plastic toys that will float in the water next to the container. Pick up one at a time and say, "On" as you place them on top of the container. After doing this two or three times, give your child a toy and tell her to put it on the container. If she doesn't, take her hand and help her. Then give your child another toy and try to get her to put it on the container without helping her.

off Turn a plastic container upside down and float it in front of your child. Place a few plastic toys on top of the container. Pick up one at a time and say, "Off" as you drop them in the water. Do this with two or three toys and then encourage your child to move a toy off of the container. If she doesn't, take her hand and help her. Then try to get your child to move another toy off of the container until they all have been removed.

continued on next page

Sample Daily Activity to Work on Treatment Objectives

27–30 months, continued

under	Place a washcloth in front of your child. Take a toy and put it under the washcloth. As you do so, say, "Under" and leave the toy under the washcloth. Repeat this with two or three more toys. Tell your child to look under the washcloth. Wait a few seconds for her to respond. If she doesn't, take her hand and lift the washcloth. Say, "There they are! They are under the washcloth."

Other: _____

Expressive Language

Your child will name one color. You can work on this skill while you are working on matching colors as described above. Choose one container of blocks, point to each one, and name the color. Dump all but one of the blocks back into the tub. Pick up a block from the tub and put it in the container as you say its color. Have your child get the next block. Encourage her to say the color. If she doesn't say the color, say it for her.

Your child will refer to herself by pronouns consistently.

my	Look in the mirror, point to various body parts, and say, "My eyes," "My ears," "My hands," etc. Point to the same parts of your child and see if she will imitate what you said. If she doesn't imitate you, put an open hand on your chest as you say "My." Help her put her hand on her chest as you say the word "my" again.
me	Say "Give me" to get your child to hand you her toy. Hold the toy in front of her but where she cannot get it. When she reaches for the toy, say, "Give me." Wait to see if she will imitate you before you give her the toy. If she doesn't say anything, point to yourself as you say "Give me." Help her point to herself and say, "Me."
I	As you wash your child, say, "I wash feet," "I wash arms," etc. Give your child the washcloth and help her wash her feet. Repeat, "I wash feet" to see if your child will imitate you. If she doesn't, take the washcloth back and continue bathing your child, saying, "I wash." When your child reaches for the washcloth, hold it where your child cannot reach it and say, "I wash" or "I do." Wait until your child uses "I" before you give her the washcloth. If she doesn't say anything, help her point to herself to use the sign for *I/me*.

Other: _____

continued on next page

Sample Daily Activity to Work on Treatment Objectives

27–30 months, continued

Sound Production

Your child will use the consonants d, f, and y at the beginning of words or syllables. To improve your child's production of these sounds, exaggerate the initial sound as you say the targeted words. If your child incorrectly produces the beginning sound, repeat the word and say it correctly. The words listed below are words that can be incorporated into bath time. It is more beneficial for your child to work on these words when they are in meaningful contexts (e.g., *f* as in *foot* as you wash your child's foot, *y* as in *yuck* if your child gets bubbles in her mouth).

- *d* — duck, dog, dip, done, Daddy
- *f* — foot, feet, fun, fan
- *y* — yes, you, yuck

Your child will use the consonants s, d, k, f, and ng at the end of words or syllables. To improve your child's production of these sounds, exaggerate the final sound as you say the targeted words. If your child incorrectly produces the ending sound, repeat the word and say it correctly. The words listed below are words that can be incorporated into bath time. It is more beneficial for your child to work on these words when they are in meaningful contexts (e.g., *d* as in *bed* as you talk about going to bed after the bath, *ng* as in *sing* before you start to sing a song).

- *s* — kiss, horse, yes, toss
- *d* — bed, bad, mad, sad, Dad
- *k* — duck, yuck, back, pick
- *f* — laugh, off, puff
- *ng* — ring, sing, song, long, bang

Other:

Sample Daily Activity to Work on Treatment Objectives

Child's Name _____ **Date** _____

Activity _Bath Time_ **Skill Level** _30–33 months_

> Note: Have all toys, washcloths, towels, and other objects ready before putting your child in the bathtub. Never leave your child unattended in the bathtub.

Pre-linguistic/Play Skills

Your child will sort shapes. Use blocks that are circle, square, and triangle shapes. Have three of each shape floating in the tub. Tell your child to get the circle blocks. If he doesn't get any circle blocks, pick up a circle block to demonstrate. Tell him to get another circle. After he hands you the block, set it on the edge of the tub with the other circle. Repeat this until he has all of the circles. Then move on to the next shape. If your child doesn't give you the circles, pick up one block of each shape and show them to your child. Point to each one and name the shape as you point. Then ask your child to get the circle. If he doesn't, take his hand to choose the correct one. Repeat as needed until your child is able to choose the circle. Continue with the other shapes.

Your child will stack rings in the correct order. Use a ring stacker. Set it in the tub in front of your child with the rings on it in the correct order. Take the rings off, give your child the first ring (the largest one), and tell him to put it on the stacker. After he does this, ask him which one goes next. Wait a few seconds to see which one he chooses. If he doesn't choose the correct one, help him by taking his hand and placing it on the correct ring. Repeat this process until all of the rings have been put on the stacker.

Other: _____

Receptive Language

Your child will follow two-step unrelated commands. In one sentence, tell your child two things to do that do not involve doing two things with one object (e.g., "Pick up the washcloth and give me the duck" or "Push the boat and kiss the frog"). If your child doesn't complete the directions correctly, show him what you want him to do. Repeat the directions as you are doing them. To make this easier, give him the directions one step at a time. After he has done each step, give the directions again with both steps.

Your child will answer **yes/no** questions correctly. Ask _yes/no_ questions about things that your child knows (e.g., naming objects). Pick five toys and hold up each one as you ask a question. For example, if you have a cow, ask, "Is this a pig?" or "Does a cow say 'moo'?" If your child can use both _yes_ and _no_ appropriately to answer the questions, mix the questions to work on accuracy. If your child says only "no" or only "yes," work on questions that elicit the answer that your child doesn't say before you mix _yes_ and _no_ questions.

Other: _____

continued on next page

Sample Daily Activity to Work on Treatment Objectives

30–33 months, continued

Expressive Language

Your child will use plurals. Use blocks, cups, animals, or other toys your child likes to play with. Focus on one type of toy at a time. To try to get your child to use plurals, ask, "Do you want one block or a lot of block**s**?" (Exaggerate the plural **s**). If your child says the singular form (block), give him only one block. When your child reaches for another block, say "Oh, you wanted block**s**" (again exaggerate the **s**). Encourage your child to say the plural form of the word. Give him two or more blocks when he correctly says "Blocks."

Your child will use the prepositions **in** ***and*** **out**. Put a container in the tub with your child. Take a toy and move it back and forth from *in* the container to *out* of the container. As you are doing this, say, "In" and "Out." Then give your child a toy and move his arm so the toy he is holding goes from in the container to out of the container. Say "In" and "Out" as you move your child's arm. Encourage the child to do this on his own.

Other: _____

Sound Production

Your child will use the consonant **w** ***at the beginning of words or syllables***. To improve your child's production of this sound, exaggerate the initial sound as you say the targeted words. If your child incorrectly produces the beginning sound, repeat the word and say it correctly. The words listed below are words that can be incorporated into bath time. It is more beneficial for your child to work on these words when they are in meaningful contexts (e.g., *w* as in *water* as you pour water over your child's head to rinse the shampoo or *w* as in *wash* as you wash each body part).

   w — water, wash, wet, warm

Your child will use the consonants **t, r,** ***and*** **b** ***at the end of words or syllables***. To improve your child's production of these sounds, exaggerate the final sound as you say the targeted words. If your child incorrectly produces the ending sound, repeat the word and say it correctly. The words listed below are words that can be incorporated into bath time. It is more beneficial for your child to work on these words when they are in meaningful contexts (e.g., *t* as in *sit* as you sit your child down in the tub, *r* as in *wear* as you talk about what your child is going to wear after the bath).

   t — hot, wet, sit, foot, feet
   r — water, bear, mirror, wear
   b — tub, rub, knob

Other: _____

continued on next page

Sample Daily Activity to Work on Treatment Objectives

Child's Name _____ **Date** _____

Activity _Bath Time_   **Skill Level** _33–36 months_

> Note: Have all toys, washcloths, towels, and other objects ready before putting your child in the bathtub. Never leave your child unattended in the bathtub.

Pre-linguistic/Play Skills

Your child will sort colors. Have four or five objects of three different colors, such as red, yellow, and blue in front of your child. Ask her to get the red ones. If she doesn't get any red objects, pick up one of the red objects and set it on the edge of the tub. Then tell her to get another red object. After she hands you a red object, set it on the edge of the tub with the other red object. Repeat this until she has all of the red objects together. Move on to the next color. If she doesn't give you a red object, pick up a red object and one object of another color and show them to your child. Point to each one and name the color as you point. Then ask your child to get the red one. If she doesn't, take her hand to choose the correct one. Use two items again and do this until your child is able to choose the red one.

Other: _____

Receptive Language

Your child will answer wh- questions. Ask your child questions about things she can see as you ask her the questions. If she doesn't respond when you ask a question, prompt by using a gesture or by giving a choice between two things. Examples for each type of question are listed below.

What	"What is this?" "What was quacking (after you make a toy duck quack)?" "What does Mommy have (as you are holding a toy)?"
Who	Point to different people in the room, such as you, your spouse, your child, siblings, etc. and ask, "Who's this?" You can also ask things like "Who is in the tub?" and "Who has the soap?"
Where	Ask "Where is (child's name)?" "Where is Daddy?" "Where is the duck?" (Move it to different places, such as behind your child, in a bowl, under the washcloth, etc.)

Your child will identify parts of objects. Have two objects with similar parts (e.g., several plastic animals, a small plastic house and a toy car). For animals, show your child two animals, such as a pig and a horse. Say, "Show me the pig's tail" or "Show me the horse's ears." For the house and car, say, "Show me the door of the house" or "Show me the car's window." If your child doesn't respond, take her hand and put it on the part you named.

Other: _____

continued on next page

Sample Daily Activity to Work on Treatment Objectives

33–36 months, continued

Expressive Language

Your child will use verb forms, such as –ing. Demonstrate actions for your child and talk about them as you are doing them. Actions that you can talk about during bath time are washing, rinsing, drying, sitting, swimming (with a toy duck or fish), turning (water on and off), and pushing (with a boat). Exaggerate the *–ing* as you say it to further emphasize the meaning of the verb form.

Your child will count to three. Have blocks, animals, washcloths, or other objects in the tub. Set three of them on the edge of the bathtub and count them. Work on getting your child to count with you and then by herself.

Other: _____

Sound Production

Your child will use the consonant s at the beginning of words or syllables. To improve your child's production of this sound, exaggerate the initial sound as you say the targeted words. If your child incorrectly produces the beginning sound, repeat the word and say it correctly. The words listed below are words that can be incorporated into bath time. It is more beneficial for your child to work on these words when they are in meaningful contexts (e.g., *s* as in *suds* as you talk about the bubbles left in the tub).

   s — soap, suds, sit

Your child will use the consonants l and g at the end of words or syllables. To improve your child's production of these sounds, exaggerate the final sound as you say the targeted words. If your child incorrectly produces the ending sound, repeat the word and say it correctly. The words listed below are words that can be incorporated into bath time. It is more beneficial for your child to work on these words when they are in meaningful contexts (e.g., *l* as in *ball* as you push a ball back and forth in the water).

   l — ball, fall, bowl
   g — hug, big, frog

Other: _____

Resources for Parents of Infants and Toddlers

Books

> This list of books is adapted in part from Paul, R. (2001). *Language disorders from infancy through adolescence: Assessment & intervention*, (2nd ed.). St. Louis, MO: Mosby, Inc.

Autism & PDD Early Intervention (five-book set: *Time to Play, Time to Eat and Drink, Time to Sing, Time to Get Dressed*, and *Time to Be Healthy*)
P. Snair Koski 2001

Beyond Baby Talk
K. Apel & J. J. Masterson 2001

Building Blocks to Communication
M. Anzelmo & D. Bonanni 1997

The Carolina Curriculum for Infants and Toddlers with Special Needs (2nd ed.)
N. M. Johnson-Martin, K. G. Jens, S. M. Attermeier, & B. Hacker 1991

The Carolina Curriculum for Preschoolers with Special Needs
N. M. Johnson-Martin, S. M. Attermeier, & B. Hacker 1990

Developmental Play Group Guide
B. Browne, M. H. Jarrett, C. J. Hovey-Lewis, & M. B. Freund 1995

Early Communication Games: Routine Based Play for the First Two Years
D. G. Casey-Harvey 1995

The Early Intervention Dictionary: A Multidisciplinary Guide to Terminology (2nd ed.)
J. G. Coleman 1999

Every Day Matters: Activities for You and Your Child
American Guidance Service (AGS) 1992

It Takes Two to Talk: A Parents' Guide to Helping Children Communicate
A. Manolson 1992

Parent Articles for Early Intervention
M. Dunn-Klein 1990

A Parent's Guide to Down Syndrome, Toward a Brighter Future (Rev. Ed.)
S. M. Pueschel 2001

Since Owen: Parent-to-Parent Guide for Care of the Disabled Child
C. Callanan 1990

Special Children, Challenged Parents–The Struggles and Rewards of Raising a Child With a Disability (Rev. Ed.)
R. A. Naseef 2001

When Your Child Has a Disability: The Complete Sourcebook of Daily and Medical Care (Rev. Ed.)
M. L. Batshaw 2000

You Make the Difference in Helping Your Child Learn
A. Manolson, B. Ward, & N. Dodington 1998

Your Child at Play: Birth to One Year: Discovering the Senses and Learning About the World (2nd ed.)
M. Segal & W. Masi 1998

Your Child at Play: One to Two Years: Exploring Daily Living, Learning and Making Friends (2nd ed.)
M. Segal & W. Masi 1998

Your Child at Play: Two to Three Years: Growing Up, Language, and the Imagination (2nd ed.)
M. Segal & W. Masi 1998

Your Child Has a Disability: A Complete Sourcebook of Daily and Medical Care
M. Batshaw 1999

Videos

> This list of videos is adapted in part from Paul, R. (2001). *Language disorders from infancy through adolescence: Assessment & intervention*, (2nd ed.). St. Louis, MO: Mosby, Inc.

Family-Guided Activity-Based Intervention for Infants and Toddlers
Brookes Publishing Co. (1995)

continued on next page

Learning Language and Loving It–A Hanen Tape
The Hanen Centre 1993

Oh Say What They See
Educational Productions 1984

Successfully Educating Preschoolers with Special Needs: Ages 2 ½ to 5–A Guide for Parents, A Tool for Educators
G. Hanlon 2002

Successfully Parenting Your Baby with Special Needs–Early Intervention for Ages Birth to Three
G. Hanlon 2002

Together We Can Know the World (series of four videotapes: *Moving Forward with Music, Sharing Books, Creating Together,* and *Playing Games*)
The Hanen Centre

You Make the Difference in Helping Your Child Learn
A. Manolson, B. Ward, & N. Dodington 1995

Web Sites

American Cleft Palate-Craniofacial Association/
Cleft Palate Foundation
www.cleftline.org
Provides a glossary of terms and fact sheets that may be useful to parents of children with cleft lip and palate.

American Speech-Language-Hearing Association
www.asha.org
Includes developmental milestones, activities to facilitate communication, and information about the professions of speech-language pathology and audiology.

Apraxia Kids
www.apraxia-kids.org
Parents can find an apraxia listserv, newsletters, support groups, frequently-asked questions, and research articles on developmental apraxia of speech.

Autism Society of America
www.autism-society.org/site/PageServer
Includes information regarding autism, including characteristics of autism, how autism is diagnosed, treatment strategies, and other topics related to autism.

National Association for Down Syndrome
www.nads.org
Includes facts, resources, products, publications, and discussion boards regarding Down syndrome.

National Stuttering Association
www.nsastutter.org
Contains a section specifically for parents/family members of people who stutter. Also includes information regarding stuttering, stuttering treatment, suggestions for parents to help their child, and support resources for parents of children who stutter.

Net Connections for Communication Disorders and Sciences
www.mankato.msus.edu/dept/comdis/kuster2/welcome.html
Includes information regarding speech and language disorders, therapy materials, discussion forums, and links to commercial products and businesses related to communication disorders
(This web site is maintained by an SLP.)

United Cerebral Palsy National
www.ucp.org
Sections of this web site are devoted to education, housing, sports and leisure, employment, parenting and families, transportation, health and wellness, products and services, and travel. The parenting and families section provides information regarding introductory information, facts, and figures about cerebral palsy and about being a caregiver.

19-05-98765432